BETHLEHEM
IN PALÄSTINA

A Swiss explorer's study of the
town's history and people in
1845

Titus Tobler.

BETHLEHEM
IN PALÄSTINA

A Swiss explorer's study of the
town's history and people in
1845

Dr. Titus Tobler

Translated by Dr. Michelle Standley
Foreword by Dr. Khalil Shokeh & Maxim Sansour

BETHLEHEM IN PALÄSTINA

A Swiss explorer's study of the
town's history and people in
1845

First published in German in 1849 by St. Gallen and Bern: In
commission with Huber and Co.

Topographically and historically described based on examination
and sources

by

Dr. Titus Tobler,

practicing physician in Horn on Bodensee.

Published by: Planet Bethlehem
Email: msansour@gmail.com
© *Maxim Sansour 2023*
Translated from the original German by Dr. Michelle Standley

Design by Turbo Design
Printed in Bethlehem by Nour Printing Co.

Contents

9. Church of the Nativity, its Chapels and Monasteries

FOREWORD

In your hands is the first book ever written exclusively about our home city, the famous town of Bethlehem – the birthplace of Jesus Christ. Until now, this historic book, published in 1849 by the Swiss-German doctor, linguist and explorer Titus Tobler, had only existed in the German language, and in Gothic font for that matter. It is a dream come true for us to finally make it accessible in English and hopefully soon in other languages.

We knew that getting this book translated into English would reveal to us valuable information on life in Bethlehem in the mid-19th century and would add to what we already know of Tobler's extensive research on Palestine. The translation, however, delivered well beyond our expectations, as it turned out to be a meticulous historical study of Bethlehem's religious sites and a detailed socio-economic review of the town's population when Tobler was there. Instead of a mere glimpse of life in Bethlehem, we are gifted a full tour of the city's geography and churches, as well as a tapestry of stories depicting the thorny relationship between the town's different religious denominations. Even more impressively, the book delivers an extensive academic study of all available historical sources about Bethlehem from antiquity to Tobler's time and provides us with a valuable bibliography. Any researcher on Palestine, and on Bethlehem in particular, would want to examine this book, and its cited sources, and to compare the information and theories it holds with other historical research and assumptions.

Titus Tobler was a medical doctor who was born in the small town of Stein, Switzerland in 1806. He first visited Palestine in 1835-36 at the age of 29 in order to conduct medical research during a cholera pandemic. Soon after arriving, however, Tobler became fascinated not only with medical practices in Palestine, on which he wrote a lot, but also with the wider Palestine exploration scene. Progress in steamship travel and Ottoman reforms that allowed Europeans easier access to the region attracted many western explorers and historians from the USA, Britain, France, and most notably, Germany. The latter was a centre for geographical and biblical scholarship with a focus, among many researchers, on questioning the historicity of the Bible.

Tobler's research during his first Palestine trip garnered national praise and attention. This, coupled with increasing European rivalry in exploring the area, spurred the German scientific establishment to fund Tobler to conduct further research, which he undertook over the course of three subsequent trips to Palestine, in 1845-46, 1857 and 1865. His research focused mainly on Jerusalem, where he is credited with a few historical discoveries, and also included stays in Bethlehem and Nazareth. He published his research in 62 different publications during his lifetime, the most well-known being the *Bibliographia Geographica Palastinae* from 1867.

Tobler enjoyed significant renown during his lifetime as a leading authority on Palestinology and was affectionally referred to as the "Father of German exploration of Palestine". He was considered equal in stature to leading contemporary writers on the topic, such as the German historian Johann Nepomuk Sepp

(1816-1903) and the American historian Edward Robinson (1794-1863). Following his trips to Palestine, Tobler continued to work as a doctor while also developing a keen interest in the history of travelogues spanning the 3rd to the 5th centuries. He also used his fame as a platform to enter German politics as a member of parliament. He died in 1877.

While many of Tobler's books were well-known, *Bethlehem in Palästina* has largely been neglected by historians. This is particularly unfortunate given the very critical period in Bethlehem's history in which this book was written. Tobler was conducting research for this book from 1845 to 1848. This would have been just five years after the end of a short but influential period of Egyptian occupation of the town and just five years before the outbreak of the Crimean War in which Bethlehem had a starring role.

In 1831, the Egyptian army, under the command of Ibrahim Basha, invaded Palestine, including Bethlehem, and kicked out the Ottomans who had ruled the area since 1517. The local Bethlehemites initially welcomed the Egyptians, hoping that their presence would end centuries of oppressive Ottoman rule and taxation. They soon found out, however, that the Egyptians had no plans to be kinder to the locals. Instead, the new rulers demanded new taxes from them, imposed compulsory military service and required residents to hand over any weapons they might have in order to quell revolt. Bethlehemites found themselves having to sell their belongings to buy weapons from others just to satisfy the Egyptian soldiers coming to collect them and avoid being sent to prison in Egypt.

The Egyptian occupation ended abruptly in 1840 and the Ottomans returned. The Egyptians, however, left Palestine with some important lasting legacies. During their brief rule, they initiated some key political reforms that historians see as the nascent components of a nation-state with local involvement in governance – something that the Ottomans never bothered to do. They also opened Palestine up to western diplomatic missions and the British Consulate was the first to open in Jerusalem in 1839. As the Ottomans resumed their rule over Palestine, the changing dynamics in the area largely motivated them to undergo sweeping reforms in how they ruled others and to allow additional western consulates to open in Jerusalem, most of which were established during the years that Tobler was there.

Tobler would have seen these transformations first hand. His initial trip to Palestine in 1835-1836 was during Egyptian rule; and his second, in 1845-1846, was just a few years after the Egyptians left. Tobler's observations in the book reflect the impact of these dramatic events on Bethlehem. This is particularly noticeable in his accounts on taxation and the very high rate of inflation in the prices of basic goods, from which the locals suffered during and after the Egyptian period. Tobler also briefly describes the governance systems in town, which allowed local residents to take part in running the town's affairs. Additionally, he examines Bethlehem's predominantly Muslim neighbourhood, Al Fawaghreh, and notes how the Egyptians had forced the town's Christians to destroy it in 1834 because it was seen as the focal point for anti-Egyptian activity. During his stay, he observes that the previous Muslim inhabitants of the neighbourhood were slowly returning.

In 1853, just four years after the publication of this book, war broke out between Russia, who backed Greek Orthodox control of holy sites in Palestine, and France and its allies, who backed the Catholics. Tobler, of course, could not have predicted the Crimean War, but he provides us with very telling accounts of rising hostilities between the Roman Catholics and the Greek Orthodox at the Church of the Nativity. Particularly fascinating is his casual mention of the case of the mysterious disappearance of the star of the nativity – a silver star with Latin engraving that had marked the spot where Jesus Christ was born in the grotto of the Nativity Church for more than a century. Tobler describes how tensions had been particularly high in 1845, as the Catholics had accused the Greeks of removing the star because of the

Catholic insignia on it and ordered its immediate return. Tobler mentions that the French Consul in Jerusalem, representing Emperor Napoleon III of France, was incensed by this theft and had repeatedly, but unsuccessfully, demanded that the Ottoman authorities investigate this crime and ensure the star's return. As it happened, it is the theft of this star that many historians point to as the initial pretext for the eventual outbreak of the Crimean War, which resulted in the death of more than 750,000 people.

Bethlehem in Palästina also provides us with an important socio-economic review of Bethlehem's residents in the period between these historic events. This includes Tobler's estimates of the town's population, which he puts at no more than 3,300 individuals, and a detailed examination of mortality rates and death records, including those from cholera. He also describes the living conditions at the time, such as the levels of poverty, residents' access to water, their agricultural practices, access to education and their cultural customs, especially during weddings, funerals and religious festivals like Christmas. Tobler also writes about the main professions in town at the time, including baking, wine making, bee keeping, tattooing and, most importantly, the town's centuries-old focus on making and selling souvenirs from olive wood and mother of pearl. He describes the intimate involvement of the Italian Franciscans in the souvenir trade, which, he observes, meant that many Bethlehemites spoke Italian as a second language at the time and that it was taught to Catholic children in the schools he visited. His observations on the souvenir trade are particularly interesting as they cover a period just before many Bethlehemites successfully broke away from reliance on the Franciscans to sell Bethlehem souvenirs abroad by embarking on their own inspired global travels that created new networks to directly sell Bethlehem products worldwide, which eventually led to huge transformations in the town.

The book's most impressive sections, however, and probably the most valuable for researchers, are to be found in Tobler's meticulous survey of the Church of the Nativity, which he dedicates more than half the book to. Tobler clearly spent several days in the church to undertake his research, as he delivers an account with the measurements of every room, every column and every mosaic in it. For key items, such as the Grotto of the Nativity and the nativity crib, Tobler documents each item's mention in all historical literature available to him and tracks the changing accounts or assumptions about that item from Jesus Christ's birth until the mid-1800s. Tobler also engages in lengthy forensic investigations into the historical accuracy of centuries-long claims about the church, such as the location of the tomb of Saint Jerome, who translated the Bible into Latin at the church, the tomb of Saint Paula of Rome, a Roman aristocrat who funded Saint Jerome's work, and the location of the burial grounds of the infants whom Herod the Great is said to have had killed on the occasion of Christ's birth. Tobler also examines some claims that were popular during his time but no longer spoken about today, such as the location of a table near the Grotto of the Nativity on which the Virgin Mary is said to have eaten after Christ's birth, the location of Christ's circumcision and the location of a well into which Bethlehem's famous guiding star fell after it completed its mission.

Academics and observers at the time take special notice of Tobler's unique attention to detail in his account of the church. The German historian Johannes Nepomuk Sepp, for example, was also in Bethlehem in 1845 and encountered Tobler in the Grotto of the Nativity. He wrote about this fortunate coincidence as follows:

> *A welcome incident brought me to meet Dr. Titus Tobler. I still remember vividly the first meeting, after which we, without knowing each other, went to sleep for some hours after the celebration of the Nativity in the vault of the monastery in Bethlehem, beside a murderer running away from Egypt. I knelt before the altar of Christ's birth full of emotions I had never felt before, as a man to my left started measuring*

the steps with a measuring cord and a folding measure: one could think that he wanted to make sure that until his next visit the Holy Grotto would not be replaced: this was Tobler. I applauded with the fullest appreciation his extreme thoroughness; only a German can work as diligently as he. Never were greater scientific results achieved for smaller financial expense as by Tobler, who is suited to the task by his tough perseverance and effort.

It is important to also note that in addition to his research and writing, Tobler was an avid cartographer and produced several maps of Palestine, especially covering Jerusalem, which were very popular in Germany during his time. For this book, Tobler produced two maps of Bethlehem, a floor plan of the Church of the Nativity and three images depicting buildings and objects in the town. These were included in the original version of this book and are included here in the translation.

Having provided such a glowing review of the book and its author, it is important for us to point out that the book, as well researched as it is, has some significant flaws. Many readers might actually find these flaws more interesting than the book's main contents, especially in what they tell us about Tobler himself and the world in which he lived. The most noticeable flaw is Tobler's lack of impartiality. Despite continually reassuring his reader that he is neutral, he is in fact anything but. In reality, along with his careful study of the town, Tobler delivers his own running commentary that is filled with dislike for things that are not of Western-European origin. He has only a few good things to say about Muslim Bethlehemites – Mohammedans or Saracens, as he refers to them – and is even less impressed by the Greek Orthodox, whom he blames for much of the deterioration in the town's holy sites. Even Palestinian Catholics don't escape his scorn: Their appearance, in one Christmas mass, for example, disturbs his enjoyment of the music and the sublime choir at the Catholic Church of Saint Catherine.

The other notable flaw is that Tobler's research seems to have been undertaken with limited conversations with local residents. While Tobler, an accomplished linguist, was quite comfortable with conversing and referencing texts in German, Italian, Greek, Latin, French and English, he did not speak Arabic and only seldom refers to facts obtained directly from the locals. Instead, his research is largely based on his own observations, conversations with other Europeans in town and historic texts. Despite his fascination and stated admiration for the town, the actual residents of Bethlehem have no voice in his book and limited agency in the events around them. As a result, we learn very little about the perspectives of Bethlehemites themselves towards their Ottoman rulers, for example, and towards the various foreign institutions in town.

This critique of Tobler's work is, of course, not unique to Tobler at all, as the travelogues of many of his contemporaries have also been called into question in modern times for their bias, undeclared motivations and an inclination to depict Palestine as a primitive place waiting to be redeemed by Europeans. Tobler is actually noted by some historians to be slightly more positive than others on his observations of the locals and at least mentions that Bethlehemites were hardworking and that he had become fond of some of them and enjoyed their company. Still, *Bethlehem in Palästina* is unavoidably another piece of work to be examined in how it contributed to shaping European mindsets towards the Middle East in that period and subsequent European colonialist plans. For Palestine, these plans tragically culminated in the 1917 Balfour Declaration that promised a Jewish homeland in Palestine, the British Mandate over Palestine after WWI and eventually the creation of Israel through military force. The ongoing brutal Israeli military occupation of Palestinian towns has, to a great extent, decimated that same Bethlehem terrain that Tobler so carefully described in his book.

Finally, we must warn the reader that Tobler would have unlikely been a recipient of any literary awards for his writing style. His facts frequently flow like the notes of an excellent researcher in a hurry rather than a good storyteller. His rough writing style was noted by contemporary historians such as William Gage who wrote:

> Tobler is the first living authority, so far as the literature of Palestine is concerned; and no man has gone through more painstaking efforts than he, to extend the area of our knowledge respecting the Holy Land. It is all the more to be regretted that his brusqueness and occasional haste make his critical remarks less valuable than they would otherwise have been.

In the process of translating this book, we made the decision, with the book's translator, to deliver the most accurate translation of the original German text and to avoid any temptation to smooth out the language or create better linkages between sentences.

Dr. Khalil Shokeh & Maxim Sansour
Bethlehem, Palestine
2022

Researcher's Acknowledgments

Publishing this book has been a dream of mine for more than 22 years. I first became aware of its existence back in 1999 while I was writing my first book, "History of Bethlehem during the Ottoman Period (1517-1917)", which was published in 2000. While conducting research for that book, I got to examine the writings of western explorers and historians, such as Edward Robinson, Carl Ritter and many others, who travelled to Palestine in the mid-19th century and competed amongst each other to became the world's experts in Palestinology. In their writings, the name of Dr. Titus Tobler constantly came up as one the most comprehensive Palestine explorers of the time and I occasionally found his book "Bethlehem in Palästina" cited as an important source on living conditions in Bethlehem in the 1840s. I was very surprised to learn that there was a book out there, from that unique era, that was exclusively dedicated to my town, and I was determined to find it. No matter how hard I looked, however, the book remained mysteriously elusive. I found several of Tobler's other books on Palestine, in general, and on Jerusalem but this one on Bethlehem seemed to have vanished from all libraries. The closest I got to gleaming its contents was in the accounts of other writers from the 19th century who accessed it at the time and quoted passages from it.

In 2005, I was hopeful of making a break through with this quest when, on an academic trip to Istanbul, I was granted access to the library of the Organization of the Islamic Conference, which holds one of the world's most comprehensive collections on all books and documents covering the Ottoman Empire. There I found a treasure trove of Palestine travelogues, including many of Tobler's books but sadly again not *"Bethlehem in Palästina"*. Even the most diligent library on Ottoman related books didn't have it.

I finally miraculously found it four years later in the USA while visiting a library that specialized in collecting reprints of old books. The copy they had was in the original German – a language that I sadly do not read. With the internet becoming as comprehensive as it is I have since then found several digital copies of the original German but never one English. My fist attempt to have it translated was aimed only to extract the information in it for my own research so I gave it to a student in Germany who provided a rough translation of the book. That translation was enough to convince me that this was an essential and unique historic book that needed to be translated into English professionally, with all its footnotes, and to be published for all to access.

Having now accomplished this, I must thank a few people who made this dream come true. First, I am grateful to my friend and colleague, Maxim Sansour, who in 2019 agreed to partner with me on completing this mission. He worked hard to find us capable translators and a publisher and to follow up with them on all required work. Maxim and I are very grateful to the book's translator, Michelle Standley, for her hard work and attention to detail. Two translators whom we had previously engaged gave up soon after starting, but Michelle persevered with a difficult task.

We are also very grateful to Anna Horakova who undertook the tedious job of translating and arranging Tobler's more than 1,400 footnotes. Finally, we must thank Dr. Robert Schick for his very valuable advice and comments on this publication.

Dr. Khalil Shokeh
Bethlehem, Palestine
2022

TRANSLATOR'S NOTE

O little town of Bethlehem, how still we see thee lie!
Above thy deep and dreamless sleep, the silent stars go by,
Yet in thy dark streets shineth, the everlasting light.
The hopes and fears of all the years are met in thee tonight.

Nearly 8,000 miles and 2,000 years separated the birth of Christ in Bethlehem from my childhood in the desert suburbs of Southern California in the 1980s. But back then, whenever we sang the opening words, 'Oh little town of Bethlehem' there was no such geographic or temporal divide. I'd close my eyes and imagine I was there, in Bethlehem, on that holy night. I'd see a manger filled with straw and in it a baby. I'd see a fair-skinned, young woman with blue eyes and dark hair nearby, a blue shawl draped over her head and across her shoulders. I'd see a handsome, tall, bearded man in a robe with one arm around her. I'd see camels and donkeys and sheep. Then when we got to the part of the song when we'd sing about Bethlehem's 'dark streets' and 'the everlasting light' I'd see a bright star in an otherwise dark night. I'd see a village filled with thatch-roofed cottages, all dotted with freshly fallen snow.

Snow?! Well, why not? What did I know or even care about

the actual town where Jesus was said to have been born? The Bethlehem of my childhood imagination was a pastiche comprised of department-store Christmas villages, front-lawn nativity scenes, and Protestant religious iconography. The details or accuracy were less important than the sentiment of holiday cheer and sacredness. The real Bethlehem was a name only, a place nearly void of content: a star, a field inhabited by shepherds, and a manger filled with hay, and not much else besides. I knew nothing about its geography, climate, culture, or people in either the past or the present. I could not even locate it on a map.

How daunting then to find myself so many years later embarking on the translation of a historical work about that 'little town of Bethlehem', a place about which I knew so very little, written by a Swiss-German medical doctor of whom I had never heard. I was, in short: intimidated. But my excitement about the project outweighed my fears. I felt honoured to be able to contribute to the historical record and excited for the opportunity to dig in deep with a source text on a topic with which I am deeply familiar: travel and tourism. As part of my doctoral dissertation research, I had read a lot about their historical emergence and for several years, I had also taught a research seminar on the theory and history of tourism to undergraduate art, architecture, and engineering students. It was thus with an enthusiasm tempered by humility that I approached the task. The first thing I did was to buy a map of Palestine that I hung on the wall. I can now locate Bethlehem on it.

That issue settled, the next, most obvious, obstacle to surmount was the book's font, Fraktur, sometimes also referred to as 'Gothic'. The only extant copies of *Bethlehem in Palästina* are typeset in this somewhat florid script. This is hardly surprising considering that when Tobler's work appeared in 1849, Fraktur was the standard font for most German publications. Fraktur's origins lie further back, in the early sixteenth century, when at the behest of Kaiser Maximilian I, Johann Schönsperger created it for a book of prayers. Not long after, Hieronymous Andreae amended it further for the publication of painter Albrecht Dürer's theoretical treatises. It did not become common, however, until the late eighteenth century, when Johann Gottlob Immanuel Breitkopf modified and popularized it. Many publishing houses and newspapers in Germany continued to use it well into the twentieth century until 1941, when the National Socialists, who had initially declared it 'an authentic German type', denounced it as Jewish in origin and banned it outright. From then on, the Nazi regime allowed only typesets linked with Antiqua—the font family with which most modern German and English readers are familiar.

What makes Fraktur such a challenge to read? For one, it is a cursive or calligraphic hand font. Its name, from the Latin for 'fractura' or 'break', refers to the way its elongated letters have many 'breaks' and numerous angles. If you've grown up reading modern, Antiqua-based fonts, deciphering the swirls and flourishes of Fraktur can thus be a real challenge. Adding to the difficulties are some issues related to individual letters. In Fraktur there is no difference in appearance between the capital letters 'I' and 'J' and in addition to the German *Eszett* (ß), which is a sort of double 's', there are two forms of lower case 's': the 'long s' that looks somewhat like an 'l' and the 'short s' that looks more like a typical 's'. The good news is, with a little patience anyone who knows German can learn to read Fraktur. Nonetheless, it does slow down the translating process and opens up more potential for errors since you are forced to work at an additional remove. At various times, to help speed things up I sought assistance with the initial transcription of the Fraktur from my husband, Nick Sywak, and my colleague and friend, Anna Horakova. Without their assistance, I might still be translating *Bethlehem in Palästina*.

Like weeds in a garden, though, just as soon as I uprooted one issue, another quickly emerged: how to deal with Tobler's writing style? It's an issue with which every translator is confronted. How do you maintain the style and tone of the original while also trying to produce a work that reads and flows as if it had been written in the language into which you are translating? You never want a translation to read like a translation. With Tobler this issue proved particularly vexing.

Tobler's organizational strategies, syntax, and style are somewhat idiosyncratic. They deviate from other German and Anglo-American travel writing literature. In such classic texts, of which Tobler would surely have been aware, like Goethe's account of his Grand Tour of Italy (1786-1788) or Alexander von Humboldt's of his travels in the Americas (1799-1804) or Charles Darwin's of his journey in the Galapagos Islands (1838-1843), the authors all provide a clear narration. They proceed chronologically and organize the text according to their dates of travel. So too does the American Biblical scholar with whom Tobler is sometimes compared and upon whose work Tobler drew, Edward Robinson. Tobler, by contrast, does not share with the reader any details about his trip; when or how he arrived; whether he was traveling alone or with companions (apart from one section in which he mentions that he briefly hired a Jewish man to assist him). Nor does he offer evident organizational cues, like subheadings.

Tobler never says explicitly what guided his decision not to include details about his own travels. This contrasts with Robinson, for instance, who states at the outset of his study that it was only with reluctance that he chose to introduce any information about his personal journeys in Palestine. He worried it might detract from the scientific purpose of the text. Tobler presumably shared this concern. 'It is the force of truth', he notes in the introduction, 'that guides my pen'. He would arrive at this truth, as the subtitle of the work suggests ('a topographical and historical description based on observation and research') through a thorough examination of the written record — Tobler himself apparently had a personal library comprised of over 1,000 volumes — and first-hand observation. Tobler's aim foremost was to contribute to scholarship on the Holy Land and thus to create a work with an aura of objectivity and timelessness. Entertaining the reader was of lesser concern. In addition, he probably did not want to draw too much attention to himself and his own subject position. This would potentially have eroded the reader's trust that Tobler was providing an account freed from the constraints of a particular viewpoint or experience of the place.

Tobler's stress on impartiality finds expression in his style. It is, for the most part, rather flat, colourless even, as you would expect from a scientific text. When he does venture a metaphor now and again or wanders off on a highly subjective tangent, it can thus come off as awkward. It feels out of place and seems to contradict his professed aim of maintaining an objective perspective.

Potentially adding to the confusion is the way that Tobler moves between different methodological approaches. At times he seems to be operating as a historian (reviewing historical accounts like pilgrim's diaries), at others like a folklorist (recounting local myths or legends about a site), and still others as an anthropologist (recording rituals he observed). Such shifts were standard practice, however, among 19th-century travel writers. As the English literary scholar, Barbara Korte, has pointed out, even supposedly scientific works like Charles Darwin's *Zoology of the Voyage of H.M.S. Beagle* constituted a hybrid of influences. Darwin alternated between the Romantic tradition and a subjective perspective (offering poetic descriptions of the landscape, for instance) and the Enlightenment tradition and an objective one (recording minute details about the flora and fauna he found on the Galapagos Islands). In the way that he shifts between perspectives and methodologies, Tobler was thus very much in good company.

With this in mind, I did my utmost to let Tobler be Tobler. I thus resisted the ever-present temptation to clean up the text, to add introductory or concluding sentences or transitional phrases. I also sought to maintain the sometimes awkward shifts in perspective and pacing. The original sometimes reads like a scientific log and as such has a slow, deliberate pacing. In such sections you will find long lists and detailed descriptions. At other times it reads like a hastily-penned personal journal, and as such has an almost harried, frenetic pace, in which he seems to have rushed to record his emotional reactions to first-hand observations that upset or moved him.

On the level of sentence structure and grammar, Tobler's writing is generally uncomplicated. As is common with any German text, however, he ventures a page-long sentence now and again, comprised of subclause-after-subclause, joined by commas. In English, we call these run-on sentences and try to weed them out. Most Anglo-American writers also eschew the passive voice. In German, not only is it perfectly acceptable, but in academic writing it is often preferable. The passive voice lends an aura of authority and objectivity to the author's statements and observations. When it came to long sentences, in most cases, I chose to break them up. I wanted to help the reader better navigate the text and to make it feel less foreign in sensibility. With passive voice, however, I stuck more closely to the original. This was because I did not want to introduce historical agents or subjects where none existed in the original text. This is also because I wanted to impart the intended scientific tone of the original.

To develop a voice for the translation, I turned foremost to two works, John Philip Newman, *'From Dan to Beersheba;' or The Land of Promise as It Now Appears* (New York: Harper & Brothers, Publishers, 1864) and Edward Robinson, *Biblical Researches in Palestine, Mount Sinai and Arabia Petraea: A Journal of Travels in the Year 1838*, Vol. I (Boston: Crocker & Brewster, 1841). I sought to adopt their antiquated literary style to aid the reader in experiencing the text as a historical work, embedded in a particular era. I wanted to conjure for the contemporary reader associations with other works produced in the mid-to-late 19th century when travel writing reached its height in popularity in Europe and North America. I also looked to Newman and

Robinson for assistance in translating the names of historical sites and figures, and terms that referred to ethnic and religious groups, including terms no longer in use like 'Mohammedans'. My aim was to select terms that native English speakers at the time would have used.

O little town of Bethlehem! I spent the better part of a year dwelling in Tobler's vision of Bethlehem. I have stood on the roof of the Latin monastery and peered into the Shepherds' Field; tasted water from its many cisterns after a heavy downpour; have observed bees kept in barrels smeared with horse manure; learned how housewives produced flour at home by grinding it between two stones; watched women dance, cry, and scream at funerals; stood beneath the many chandeliers hanging in the Chapel of the Nativity; seen how light penetrates the Chapel of St. Jerome to illuminate an oil painting of the saint; found out about how the Milk Cave derived its name from miracles associated with the 'moon milk' made from consuming the ground stone of its rocks; and so much more. Filled with such vivid details, my image of Bethlehem now goes far beyond the one I had in childhood. I view Bethlehem as something other than the chorus of a popular American Christmas carol. While Tobler's account of Bethlehem is rooted in a particular time, place, and perspective, it has nonetheless broadened my own perspective and piqued my curiosity to know more. In this sense, I see the translation into English of Tobler's *Bethlehem in Palästina as* more than merely a contribution to the historical record. It's also an invitation to learn more about Bethlehem's rich past and present.

Dr. Michelle Standley
Berlin
2022

Sources:

Di Nepi, Serena and Arturo Marzano, eds. 'Introduction. Travels to the "Holy Land": Perceptions, Representations and Narratives', *Quest: Issues in Contemporary Jewish History*, Vol. 6 (December 2013): v-xv.

Furrer, Konrad. 'Titus Tobler; in *Allgemeine Deutsche Biographie*. Historical Commission of the Bavarian Academy of Sciences and Humanities, Vol. 38 (1894): 395-402.

Korte, Barbara. *English Travel Writing: From Pilgrimages to Postcolonial Explorations*. Translated by Catherine Matthias. New York: Palgrave, 2000.

Yannis Haralambous, 'Typesetting Old German: Fraktur, Schwabacher, Gotish and Initials', *Tugboat*. TeX Users Group, Proceedings of TeX90, Vol. 12, no. 1 (1991): pp. 129-38.

John Zilcosky, ed. *Writing Travel: The Poetics and Politics of the Modern Journey*. Toronto: University of Toronto Press, 2008.

Facing page and overleaf:
facsimile of the title page and opening page
of the foreword in the original edition, demonstrating
the Fraktur font described in the translator's note.

Bethlehem

in Palästina.

Topographisch und historisch nach Anschau und Quellen
geschildert

von

Dr. Titus Tobler,

praktischem Arzte in Horn am Bodensee.

Mit Karte und Tempelplan.

St. Gallen und Bern:

In Kommission bei Huber und Comp.

1849.

Vorwort.

Davids Vaterstadt, Jesus' Geburtsstätte, Hierony-
mus' Klosterstätte, der fränkische Bischofssitz, einer der
drei hervorragendsten Wallfahrtsorte der Christen, ein
Schauplatz von so hoher welthistorischer Bedeutung —
Bethlehem verdient doch wohl, daß es einmal ausführ-
licher oder umfassender geschildert werde. In unserem
Abendlande schrieb man über kleine, obskure Ortschaften,
über schattenreiche, im weiteren Kreise selten genannte
Klöster eine große Chronik zusammen, während der
Stadt Davids und unsers Religionsstifters in dieser
Beziehung weit weniger Aufmerksamkeit geschenkt wurde.
Der Abstand ist zu grell, die Vernachlässigung allzu
auffallend, als daß nicht ein Wanderer sich mit dem
Gedanken tragen sollte, längst Versäumtes nachzuholen
oder einem Bedürfnisse der Bücherei zu entsprechen.
Diese Aufgabe zu erreichen, trachte ich nun in gegen-
wärtiger Schrift. Wie weit sie mir gelang, darüber

PREFACE TO THE ORIGINAL EDITION

David's hometown, Jesus' birthplace, St. Jerome's monastery, the Frankish diocese, one of the three most preeminent places of pilgrimage from the Scriptures, a site of remarkable significance in world history. Bethlehem finally deserves to be described in more detail or more extensively. In our Western world, a grand chronicle was compiled about small, obscure villages, and shadow-bedecked monasteries of which no one had heard. The City of David and our religion's founder have been given far less thorough attention. The gap is so glaring, the neglect so conspicuous, that a mountain climber should not get it into his head that he will catch up along the ridge of the mountain or manage to somehow meet the library's needs. With this writing, I nonetheless now attempt to achieve just such a task. How far I have succeeded in getting it right is not up to

Facing page:
A reproduction of the first page of the original German-language edition, illustrating the Fraktur (Gothic) font used.

me; but I might possibly, and indeed shall, at the very least, lead the reader past the difficulties that I, myself, have encountered in pursuing this work. The pilgrims who visited Palestine have mostly chosen to stay in Jerusalem and usually made only a brief detour in Bethlehem. It is for this reason that their accounts of that city were more detailed and accurate, while those on the latter were, by comparison, quite wretched. Not long ago, accounts about Jerusalem appeared from Ball, Williams, Blackburn, Schulz, Krafft, and Fergusson, all of whom had little to say about Bethlehem. Certainly, impressions of the former may be stronger, but not to the extent that the existing respective descriptions of both cities might indicate.

Owing to the inaccurate and inadequate nature of extant reports about Bethlehem, and the need to include legends and historical truths connected to it, a monographic treatment of Bethlehem has numerous difficulties to surmount. I hesitate to call it unreliable, but anyone who is familiar with the literature would admit that the extant topographical description of Bethlehem is rather fragmented; to complete this tapestry, many new threads will have to be woven into the account. I will readily admit that the same could be said of this work, which is far from complete. It was perhaps more urgent to break new ground in the field of history so as to extend and better level the old one. My patient predecessor, the Capuchin Quaresmius, did not lack the space on paper where he could, on seventy folio pages, record his excellent research and opinions, nor did he lack the opportunity to draw on archival treasures; nor did his account want for impartiality. This made it possible to avoid pointless scholasticism, maintain a level of scholarship that is, on the whole, more balanced, and produce something of genuine substance. I have to acknowledge that some important sources have emerged since the middle of the last century. Nowadays one could not expect a Franciscan to produce an impartial account, the sort of which elucidates in equal measure the history of all parties involved, at least not about legends that tell of piety. He could not quite commit himself to consistently weaving with the thread of truth the fact that the historical records are often mutable and contradictory. Those historians who choose to maintain certain silences when they write are certainly not the worst offenders. They are still better off than those who hide genuine treasures, putting into circulation, false ones in their stead; I am not beholden to any guild or other such considerations; that allows me to speak where others have to remain silent, and to remain silent, where others have to speak. I have no vested interest and no professional standing that would require me to impede or destroy the truth.

Where the star shines forth, I reverently kneel on the ground, praise the Lord, and proclaim the truth. When one assumes such a, permit me to say, sacred office, it goes without saying that interdenominational feuds are of no consequence. I nevertheless worry that there will be those who want to launch a battle against an entire ecclesiastical institution, because the world does not cease to be populated with people who erect triumphal arches to passion, making it difficult to separate with more precision the wheat from the chaff, the essential from the insignificant. I would like to note that among the complex conditions required to produce this work is the force of something other than my own hand. When my pen strikes in a direction different from where I set out, it is akin to a stone that tumbles to the ground because it is being pulled by the force of gravity. It is the force of truth, extracted from my original discoveries, that guides my pen. As the original discoveries speak to me, so do I speak to the public. I want to visualize the past in the present, but not under the shroud of fantasies, not in a one-sided, skewed form, but impartially and accurately, free and lacking in timidity. In my zeal for the truth, I may have along the way sprinkled in some salt in this or that Babylonian whirl of confusion that emanates from the licentiousness of modern letters, or if an untruth managed to raise its head in triumph, or if I scattered into clouds the sand upon which a false prophet stood, it was not out of malice or ill will but out of the genuine desire to take what lie deep in my heart and therewith build a bridge that delivers it to as many as possible.

My original intention was to fit in a description of the city of Jerusalem and its surroundings, near and far; but the merit of the subject and its present conditions demanded a division, which, because Bethlehem has recently become more accessible to some, may also have its value. I cannot, however, avoid the unfortunate situation that some of the material relating to Bethlehem, like the description of the plough, the tools used in the making of rosaries, crosses, and images, the description of the traditional dress are described in more depth in previous sections; furthermore, if I included here an exhaustive list of all previously published literary sources on Jerusalem, then the main body of the work would be deprived of its component parts — if skipping some things remains unpleasant — if only the most essential were included, repetitions would have been unavoidable. One path had to be chosen; I chose the latter as the lesser evil. I have limited myself herewith to briefly noting the works that I found useful for the purposes of this present writing, which were written by:

Karl v. Raumer (*Palästina*, edition 1838, p.6 et seq.) and Edward Robinson (*Palaestina*, I, XVI et seq.) were not cited.

Ca. 1175. Fetall or Fretell. *De situ iherusalem.* Cod. manuscript. Vienna. hist. eccl., nr. 154, fol. 9 sqq.

1217. *Magister Thetmars Reise nach Palestine* in Malten's *Weltd.* (1844), p.184 et seq.

1320. *De loois terre sancte per me Fransiscum Pipinium*, Lat. handwriting from 1st library in Munich, Nr. 850. (1331 to 1341 Petrus von Suchen or Rudolph [the real name is Ludolph] von Suchen, written differently depending on the edition.)

Ca.1370. Rechtenstain. *Von der Stat zu Jerusalem.* Cod. Ms. Vienna. hist. prof., nr. 707, p. 94 et seq.

1384. Frescobaldi. *Viagg. in. .. Terra Santa.* Rome (1818).

1384. Sigoli. *Viagg. al Monte Sinai.* Milan (1841).

Ca. 1400. *Die Gelegenhayt. .. des Heyligen Land.* Cod. manuscript. Vienna. in Schwanderi repertory. nr. 4578.

1458. Pelchinger. *Von der Schuldung und Gestalt des h. Grabs.* Cod. manuscript. Vienna. hist. eccl., nr. 146.

1483. Fabri. *Evagatorium in Terra S.. .. Peregrinationem.* Stuttgart (1843). If I used the German edition of the Frankfurt collection of travel accounts, I wrote the name in German.

(1483. Breydenbach or Breitenbach, depending on the edition)

1491. Rapfman. Diß find die stet u. s. s. Cod. manuscript from the Catholic library in St. Gallen, nr. 610.

Ca. 1518. *Viaggio al Santo Sepoloro.* Venet (1605).

1542. Jod. A Meggen. *Peregrinatio Hierosol.* Diling (1580).

1565. Billinger. *Beschreibung der Hierusolomitanischen Reise.* Konstanz (1603).

(1575. Rauwolff or Rauchwolff, depending on the edition.)

1583. Lussy. *Reisebuch gen Jerusalem.* Freiburg (1590).

(1596. Bernadino Amico. By Robinson incorrectly listed as 1516.)

1612. Boucher. *Le Bouquet Sacré*, composé des Roses du Calvaire, des Lys de Bethlehem, de Jacintes d'Olivet. Lyon (1679).

1613. Amman. *Reise in das Gelobte Land.* 3rd Edition. Zurich (1678).

1614. Scheidt. *Reise-Beschreibung, Der Reiß. .. nach dem Gewesenen Gelobten Lande.* Helmstadt (1679).

Ca. 1620. 'H'Ayia Tñ. *A Very Remarkable Greek Description of the Country*; the use of which I owe to Mr. Dr. Schultz, former Prussian consul in Jerusalem.

1625. Steiner. *Heilige Wallfahrt in das S. Land.* Manuscript that is kept in Kaltbrunn, R. St. Gallen.

1658. Zwinner. *Blumen-Buch, deß Heiligen Lands.* Munich (1661).

1666. Bremond. *Viaggi Fatti. .. in Gervsalemme, Givdea ecc.* Rome (1679).

1673. Legrenzi. *Il Pellegrinagio nell' Asia.* Venice (1705).

1690. Caecia. *Brevis Relatio Locor. Sanctor.* Vienna (1693).

1699. *Relation Fidelle du Voyage de la Terre Sainte.* Paris (1754).

1719. Ladoire. *Voyage Fait à la Terre S.* Paris (1720).

1725. Neret. *Schreiben über Palästina* in Paulus' *Samml. von Reisen.* 4, p. 86 et seq.

1778. Binos. *Reise in das gelobte Land.* Bresl and Leipzig (1788).

1800. Wittman. *Reisen nach der Türkei u. f. f.* Weimar (1805).

1814. Light. *Travels in Egypt, Nubia, Holy Land.* London (1818).

1818. Borsum. *Reise nach. .. Palästina.* Berlin (1826).

1827. Failoni. *Viagg. in Siria.* Verona (1833).

1831. Wegelin. *Erinnerungen aus dem. .. Orient.* Zurich (1844).

1831. *Neueste Reise in Palästina.* Transl. from the Engl. Leipzig (1834).

1832 sq. D'Estourmel. *Journal d'un Voyage en Orient.* Paris (1844).

1834. Köser. *Reise nach Griechenland u. f. m.* Mergentheim (1836).

1840 (?). Hailbronner. *Morgenland und Abendland.* Stuttgart and Tübingen. 2nd edition (1845).

1842. Bartlett. *Walks about the City and Environs of Jerusalem.* 3rd edition. London (no year).

1843. Herschell. *Besuch in meinem Vaterland.* Basel (1846).

1843. Craigher. *Erinnerungen aus dem Orient,* Triest (1847).

1844. Reynaud. *Athènes à Baalbek.* Paris (1846).

1844. Sehlen. *Wallfahrt nach Bethlehem und Hebron,* Munster (1846).

1845. Marmier. *Du Rhin au Nil.. .Palestine.* Paris, (no year).

1847. Wolff, *Reise in das Gelobte Land,* Stuttgart (1849).

Other books, which are not included in Raumer's and Robinson's list, and which I did not use, I will describe in more detail in the course of this writing.

With the illustrations in the appendix, I hope to be of service to many readers. The special map of Bethlehem[i] is, to the best of my knowledge, the first of its kind, and admittedly requires a very generous assessment. As far as the ground plans of the Church of St. Mary are concerned, I have to confess that, regrettably, I did not take the measurements myself, and so the reduction in Parisian feet was not so easily done, especially since Quaresmius' plan, a copy of Bernardino Amico's, provides an incorrect scale, and Zwinner's contains a neat but inexact one. In making pictures of the Church of St. Mary, of a house and a crib, I was not necessarily driven to draw something interesting, but motivated to fill in a few gaps in an otherwise familiar image.

Part of my experiences in Bethlehem have already been passed along to the daily newspaper, *Das Ausland* (Junius 1849), which is published by Dr. Ed. Widenmann.

It now depends on the interest that the public may show in Bethlehem, whether my main work about Jerusalem and its immediate surroundings, which is now ready for publication and would be over 100 printed-pages-thick and on which the ground plan of the city appears so level as can be seen on the cover of this book, will sooner or later, in its entirety or in parts, be distributed by the press.

Born, near Rorschach, in the winter months of 1849

---

i   Antonio de Angelis' *Topographica Delineatio Civitatis Jerusalem* (Rome 1578), a topic which Breuning took up as 'Abriß oder Delineation der Stadt Jerusalem' (219), is mentioned only in passing: 79 Cisterna Davidis. 80 the city of Bethlehem. 81 Christ was born here. 82 Mary was hidden here. 84 the angels appeared to the shepherds here. 85 the Tower of Eder. 88 St. Paula und St. Eustachia prayed here and the little map for it has such a primitive, fanciful scale, and the placement such a crazy appearance that I would not deem the Franciscan de Angelis a true predecessor. Zuallart (Ital. edition. p. 201 et seq.), who drew on this to map David's Wells (K), Bethlehem (L), the House of Joseph (M), the village (N) and the Place of the Shepherds (0) in the whole area south of Jerusalem, does not come off much better.   If measurement is referred to in the text, then it is the Paris inch.

PART A

BETHLEHEM

CHAPTER I

Name, Location, Hills, Valleys, Climate

Bethlehem[i], Beit Lehem[ii], بيت لحم [iii] (house of meat[iv]), a little town in Palestine, in the Pashalik of Jerusalem, an easy two hours'

---

i For thousands of years, this name has been used without giving way to any other one. Le seul nom de Bethlehem a je ne sçay quoy de doux, qui flatte agreablement le coeur, et luy inspire de la devotion et de la tendresse. *Nau* 395. Different forms of the name can be found in Ireland (Palæst. Ex mon, v. ill.).

ii *Quaresm.* 2, 619. Bit-lehan. *Surius* 523. Beytleham. *Nau* 436. Baitlame. *Legrenzi* 1, 158. Bait-el-lahm. Bolney 2, 240. De Forbin in Joliffe 123. Berghaus's map. Beit Lahm. Robinson 3, 975.

iii *Edrisi* 345. *Jakut Ham.* and *Abulfeda* hist. Univers. C. 27, both in the geographic index in Bohad. vita Saladin. Scholz 206. Robinson 3, 873.

iv *Surius, Legrenzi*, Robinson 2, 380; 3, 975.

walk[i] south[ii] of the capital, on the left[iii] or east side of the road leading to Hebron, lies 2538' (Paris) above the Mediterranean Sea[iv] on two hills[v], a western and an eastern one, linked by a short saddle and bounded to the south by the Wâdi, or as the people there pronounce it, Wadi al-Rahib and Wadi al-Qawas.[vi] The western hill

---

i   This is how Tschudi (267), Belon (268), Maundrell (86), Korte (2 gute. 117), Hasselquist (166), Binos (201), Clarke (124), Mayer (330), Joliffe (not over 2), Schubert (3, 7) Robinson (2, 380) have found it as well. 35 stadiums (some 1 ½ hours). Justinus Martyr in Reland (645) agrees with the 4 miles (milia quarter) of the Bordeaux pilgrim (154). To the two hours correspond fully Eusebius's (onomast.) 6 Roman miles, Sulpitius Severus (in dialog on p. 4 S. Reland, 645), Arculfus (2, 7), Bernard (16), Saewulf (35), Phokas (22), Abulfeda (a. A. D.); Willibald counted 7 (according to the nun, 20); 4 according to Eugesippus (but 1 mile according to my calculations = ½ hour), (circa) mix Jakob de Vitry (59), (hardly) Baldenfel (120), Kapfman (9), (circa 4 miglia) Legrenzi (1, 175); some 5 miles according to Anshelm (1289), Fürer (64), Maundeville counted 2 miles (773), Rudolph v. Suchen counted 3 (842), 1 mile counted the anonymous writer in Allatius (8), Albrecht von Sachsen (2109), Rauchwolff counted 1 good German mile (643), Troilo counted 1 ½ German miles (388), Brocardus (c. 8) and Marinus Sanutus (3, 14, 11) calculated 2 leucæ, Benjamin von Tudela (47) calculated 2 parasangs (one p. = 30 stadiums or 1 hour 15 minutes), Medschir ed-Din (134) calculated ¼ parasang.

ii   Bethleem, civitas David … [in qua Dominus noster atque Salvator natus est].. Contra meridianam plagam (ab Aelia). *Euseb. et Hieron.* onomast. *Saewulf.* Brocardt 869 (c. 9). *Marin, Sanut.* l. c. and map. Tschudi 270. Ab Jherusalem spacio duarum leugarum versus Hebron, inter occasum et meridiem sita est. Gesta Francor. l. c. Regarding the distance and location, see the maps of Jakob Ziegler (S. little W.), Ireland (S.), Maas (S.), Berghaus (S. S. D.), Robinson (S. little W.). Cf. Raumer 307. Many untenable claims about the location in relation to Jerusalem can be found in Schubert 3, note 7.

iii   Inde (from Rahel's grave) milia duo a parte sinistra est Bethleem. Itiner. Burdig. Hieros. Juxta viam (after Hebron). *Euseb.* Et *Hier.* onomast. Left. Brocardt. *Marin. Sanut.*

iv   Rutzegger in the Price Book of the Orient, year 1839, 73.

v   Bethlehem is saddled between two hills and one of them is this very one. Prokesch 112. On a hill, divided in two parts, surrounded by chaos of less or more bare hills. Rutzegger a. a. D.

vi   In valle … quæ in meridiano latere sita. *Arculf.* 2, 5. There is hardly any other writer who wouldn't mention this valley in a clearer way; usually, one wrote in general that Bethlehem, safe for its western side, is surrounded by valleys. Undique ex omni parte vallibus circumdato…Valleculis hinc et inde circumjacentibus. *Arculf.* 2, 1. Sideways with deep gorges. *Baldensel*

bends to the north, at the very exit of the village, into a less imposing ridge called Kilkel, which is cut on its north side by the road to Mâr Elias, and continues northwards[i] to where the so-called King David's Wells have been hewn into it, before gradually descending eastwards into the Wadi al-Kharoobeh opposite the large Temple of Mary and the three Christian monasteries, whereas westwards it slopes down into an irregular hilly terrain all the way to Rachel's grave. Having begun in the northern part of the town itself, the Wadi al-Kharoobeh runs from south to north under different names: Wadi al-Jamal, Wadi al-Sideh, Wadi al-Tarajmeh and Wadi al-Dchora, all the way to Wadi Samour and Wadi al-Rahib al-Dairi near Mar Saba.[ii] The terrace structure of this wadi in the town makes it reminiscent of an amphitheatre. The entire ridge, not a quarter of an hour long[iii] from west to east[iv] is narrow[v] and not especially high.[vi] The western hill

120. Quod aquilone et oriente et austro vallibus circumdatur. *Fabri* 1, 463. Over two densely cultivated valleys. Hailbronner 2, 298. Wegelin 2, 120. Robinson (2, 378) calls it the questionable valley Wadi et-Ta'âmirah, which stretches North of the Franken Mountain towards the Dead Sea, by merging with the valley beneath Mâr Eliâs slightly further downhill.

i   Et recurvatur contra occidentem versus Jerusalem. Fabri.

ii Extendit (valley underneath Bethlehem against the Gihon) enim se vallis illa contra orientem, usque ad Sodomam et mare mortuum. Fabri 1, 465. Quaresm. 2, 615 (see later David's cistern). Prokesch. At the foot of the hill on which the monastery is located extends the valley of Rephaim. Schubert 2, 35. Robinson (2, 378) says that the valley is broad at the beginning, that it continues northeast and merges with the one under Mâr Elia's (? Mâr Sâ'ba).

iii Quasi M. passibus porrigitur. *Arculf.*

iv Ab occidentali plaga in orientalem. *Arculf. Marin. Sanut.* The length is from orient to occident. Breydenbach 131. From west to east Tschudi says 270. Schwallart says from east to west 302.

v   In dorso (scil. montis) sita est angusto. *Arculf.* Colle aroto et oblongo. *Brocard* o. 9. Narrow. *Marin. Sanut.* Breydenbach. Jugum montis, non multum lati superius, sed longi. *Fabri* 1, 463. Schwallart. Thetmar says (in Waltens Weltk., Feb. 1844, 192) that the city of God is situated lengthwise on a mountain ridge.

vi But not high. Schwallart. High. *Marin. Sanut.* Quite high. Breydenbach. Tschudi.

slopes steeply to the south,[i] less steeply to the north,[ii] to the west not at all, cambering gently toward it instead,[iii] which is also partly the case to the south or rather southwest, toward Wadi Ma'ali, which is a branch wadi that runs alongside Wadi al-Qawas. The eastern hill opposite appears less high, but wider, as it extends into the east side of the Wadi al-Kharoobeh. Northeast of the monasteries it descends precipitously into a branch wady originating near Beit Sahour, but not to such a degree that its ascent should present a hale and healthy man with difficulties. Directly to the east, the escarpment begins only forty-eight paces from the village, where the Milk Grotto is situated. Due to the position of this hill with the small saddle between both domes,[iv] the town cleaves into two parts. This unusual configuration of the ground, which contributed greatly to the town's agreeable positioning,[v] now affords a variety of views to the onlooker, depending on which perspective he chooses, whether he stands on the east or the west side, on the south or the north side. The view overlooking the flat roof of the Latin monastery on the north side extends towards the east, north, and west. Along with part of the Arab Mountains and the Dead Sea one can see the Shepherds' Field, Beit Sahour, Soor Baher, Mar Elias, the Wadi Samoor and at the feet of the town itself a pile of grey houses.[vi]

---

i   When Schubert (2, 492) says that climbing up the steep hill is not possible without much effort he should have added that he was a rather elderly, frail man.

ii   From the western gate (as seen from Jerusalem), the path continues across a heap up to the city. Tschudi 270.

iii   Seen from the West the mountain is higher than the village and then sinks very rapidly westwards towards the Wadi Ahmed. Robinson.

iv   Most people only discuss one mountain (Gumpenberg 463. *Fürer* 65), or a hill (Schwallart, *Surius*: une belle colline en forme d'un croissant [on the northern side, that is].

v   A funny place. Rudolph v. Suchen 842. Everything is funny about that place. Della Valle 1, 157. Sa situation est charmante. Voyage 1699. 79.

vi   One sees the landscape around Jericho, the Dead Sea, and Arab mountains, and a big mountain toward the south. Rauchwolff 645. A lovely view of the Arab mountains and the Dead Sea. Troilo 400. Quand on est sur ces terrasses, on a le plaisir de voir un des plus beaux pays du monde; on voit les montagnes d'Arabie, celles d'Engaddi...on voit encore la montagne des

To complete the panorama of the south and east, of the Wadi al-Rahib, the region of Tekoa or the Mountain of Little Paradise (Frank Mountain), for instance, from this inviting belvedere[i] one turns to the roof of the Armenian monastery, which extends to the crown of the eastern hill. In general, Bethlehem's highland location[ii] among valleys and with medium-high mountains in the greater distance, makes of it not only an airy, well-ventilated place, but one that is both exposed to and poorly sheltered from the winds. The climate is more or less the same as in Jerusalem, perhaps a little milder.[iii] Snow is not unknown in Bethlehem[iv]; both cold and heat are easily endured. Fourteen centuries ago, it was no different: in summer, the shadow of the tree was considered a cool enigma; in autumn, the air's measured warmth and the fallen leaves betokened a place of rest; in spring the field was painted with flowers, and amidst the garrulous birds, psalms were sweetly sung; when the cold and winter snow arrived, one did not buy wood, and it was warm enough, whether one was awake or asleep.[v] Seed is ordered at the beginning of winter, but a lot has to take place for the stalk to reveal

---

François. *Ladoire* 204. Korte 118. Berggren 3, note 147. From the terrace of the monastery one can see far and wide into the calm, rocky gorges and slopes covered with green grass. We had the monastery of St. Elijah to the north 10 degrees, Bethlehem in the west, Arabian Mountains from northeast to southeast, the road to the monastery of Saba east to north, the grotto of the shepherds south 75 degrees, the grotto of the Holy Virgin south 32 degrees. Prokesch 117. One can see all the way to the mountain range of Hebron (scarcely), the hilltops of Thekoa and the Franken Mountain can also be seen quite clearly (as one can fancy from one's office in Munich); to the East the mirror of the Dead Sea and the area around the Jordan river delta, part of the Pisga mountains. Schubert 3, note 34.

i Berggren.

ii E vero che il paese non è pianura, anzì è fatto come il nostro paese di scese e di salite. *Sigoli* 134 sq.

iii A mild climate. Binos note 212.

iv Quæ (calida vallis Bethlehemiata) nives nescit, glacies ignorat. Nec tamen est calidum illud tempus (Winter), sed recens, quo homines affligi possunt frigore. Fabri 1, 457.

v Certe, quod scio, vilius non algeno. Hieronymi ep. ad Marcellam.

its spike in time for Christmas[i]; there is, however, plenty of time for herbs[ii] and it is a favourable season for flocks and shepherds.[iii] When pleasant weather yields suddenly to rain, the temperature in the middle of winter drops dramatically. On the 27th of December 1845 we had thoroughly pleasant weather. On the night of the 28th there was a torrential rainfall, such that by the morning of the 29th the thermometer had sunk to 3° Celsius above zero, on the mornings of the 29th and 30th it read 4°, on the evening of the 29th, 5°. I cannot say that I did not suffer somewhat from this profound chill, and at night I was happy to recover in my warm bed what the day no longer afforded.

---

i   Circa gestum nativitatis Domini incipit habere spicas. Fabri. On May 8, 1581 the harvest was already over. Schweigger 310.

ii   Lingua eorum (of the natives) tempus nativitatis Domini dicitur tempus ad herbas. *Fabri.*

iii   Ideo ex aliis locis mittuntur in eam bestiæ, ut hieme ibi pastum habeant et impinguentur, et emunt ibi certas petias terræ ad tempus sanctum. *Fabri.*

CHAPTER 2

Water, David's Wells

In summer, whatever is not watered dries up from lack of rain, just as it does everywhere.[i] It will come as no surprise to learn that Bethlehem has also had its share of earthquakes. A powerful earthquake, of which I also was apprised, happened not long ago, in 1834. Any claims, however, that almost the entire monastery collapsed into rubble and buried nearly all the inhabitants beneath,[ii] are not warranted.[iii] The Latin monastery did indeed suffer a great deal of damage, and, in 1835, I myself

---

i   Per æsteatem autem fervescente sole est terra arida et adusta, et cum in Septembri solis fervor mitescit, omnia terræ nascentia incipiunt virescere, sicut apud nos in Aprili, nisi quod virgulta non producunt illo tempore flores. Fabri.

ii   A letter in Geramb 1, 326.

iii   The honorable Röser who does not lower himself to being a priest's servant, wrote on November 11 1834 (445) that part of Pasha Ibrahim's residences were reduced to rubble and ruins by the earthquake in June and that he found the monastery in such a state one could have mistaken it for a Roman fort (446). The Duke of Ragusa wrote briefly (3, 46) that as a result of the earthquake, a long (or "wide") opening divided the monastic walls from top to bottom.

witnessed the restoration as it was being undertaken[i]; but from my inquiries to many Bethlemites, I learned that no one had been killed by the earthquake. During the church father Jerome's time, an eclipse of the sun was observed during Pentecost, which led everyone to believe that Judgement Day was nigh.[ii]

There lies more poetry than truth in the words that Bethlehem possesses a surfeit of streams[iii], wells and springs or that overseas there exists no other place with clearer, colder, healthier or sweeter cistern water.[iv] The truth is, that the streams only rush when the rain falls extraordinarily hard. I once saw water flow abundantly in Wadi al-Kharoobeh, but the little stream's life span was short, and it soon fell silent and disappeared. Most water comes from sealed wells and cisterns that feed the aqueducts. It is good, but I also found it mixed with impure things. The women of Bethlehem (the men never are seen carrying water) fetch it from the aqueduct referred to previously, located in Wadi Ma'ali, five minutes southwest of the town. They fill a water skin (kirbeh) with it, and by wrapping the cord that seals the bag around their foreheads, they are able to carry it on their heads. The load, as I learned from my own experiment, is fairly heavy; to avoid its pressing down too hard, the head has to grow

---

i   *Meine Lustreise* 2, 113.

ii   *Hieronymi* epist. ad *Pammachium*. Edition from Erasmus epist. LXI.

iii *Benjamin Tud.* 48.

iv   *Fabri* 1, 453. Similarly Gumpenberg (464) also remarks that there is only water from the cistern. The water is of the highest quality. Browne 430. The water in the monastery is excellent, like the purest, liquid crystal each drop resembling a diamond...It is excellent, even more excellent than the most excellent water in Bethlehem. I have never seen or drunk it so pure. It happened to me often that while I was dining I would interrupt my meal out of sheer enjoyment, that is how extraordinary its purity seemed to me. Geramb 1, 184: "When the water containers and aqueducts that supply water to Bethlehem as well as Jerusalem are in ruins and are dried up eleven months each year (why also not in the 12th month, if they are in ruins?), the women have to walk for an hour to search for water that is needed for the household."

accustomed to it.[i] To the south, just below the Harit al-Najajreh ("Carpenters' Quarter"), a kind of cistern with two openings rimmed with seemingly ancient white marble lies under a vault, where it is fed by water from the aqueduct flowing past.[ii] If in the fourth or fifth century it could be claimed that, apart from a few springs, in the region of Bethlehem there was no water other than the rainfall collected in reservoirs, and that therefore when God in his fury withheld the rain, there was a greater danger of dying of thirst than of hunger.[iii] This is clear proof that the main water lines did not supply Bethlehem with water. It may have been built later or restored, but either way the aqueduct provided a not inconsiderable quantity of water in 1845, even before the heavy rains, and afterwards, Bethlehem's women fetched water from it as before, either because there were not enough cisterns in the little town or because the living spring water from the town's main water lines was preferred to the standing rainwater. Otherwise, as stated, one makes do, at least in the monasteries, with cistern water, and with the Latin cistern, which lies just north of the nave of the Church of St. Mary next to the cloister, and into which several steps lead into depths of not such great significance and holds good water.[iv] On the square directly before the main entrance to the Church of St.

---

i   A quarter of an hour from Bethlehem, Geramb (1, 170) ran into a twelve-year old girl with a water hose; at his request she put the load on his shoulders. Yet the trappist found it so onerous he could hardly walk a few steps with it. That proves sufficiently that he was a very week man who liked to exaggerate, such as when elsewhere (182) he assures us that he is allegedly "blessed with considerable strength" when he was clearing out the Church of St. Catherine in Bethlehem and throwing out the last ones remaining there.

ii   While we were descending from the steep (southern) slope, after some 50 steps we encountered two wells as it seemed to us at first at least; but then it turned out that they were just openings above water pipes which run through a deep vault of sorts, from which the water is then brought up some 20 feet. Browne 43.

iii   *Hieronymi* commentar. Ad Amos IV. Introduced by Bachiene 1, 1, 435.

iv   3 good cisterns in the Friars Minor Monastery. Zwinner 357.

Mary can be found three cisterns,[i] the water of which however is used only for livestock. During my time there the rain filled them quickly, but since that swelling in size, they have not filled up every year. Hence the Bethlehemites regard an abundance of water in these cisterns with delight. Especial mention should be made of David's Wells,[ii] or David's Cisterns,[iii] also called less frequently the Cisterns of Bethlehem.[iv] This reservoir lies to the left as one comes from Jerusalem to Bethlehem,[v] fifty-eight paces to the north of the road,[vi] very near the town,[vii] which is to say, four minutes to the west of it,[viii] on the northerly continuation of Jabal al-Kilkel, across from and to the west of the monasteries and the great Church of St. Mary, and the Wadi al-Kharoobeh in between.[ix] From this quite attractive spot, one can enjoy views of

---

i   One can see these three cisterns on the new ground plan. Tres cisternæ multis aquis affluentes; ad quas hauriendas advenæ et Bethlehemitæ accedunt. *Quaresm.* 2, 623a. Plusierus cisternes. *Nau* 397. The third cistern, which is closest to the gate, used to be closed. *Quaresm.* 1. c. See the last note.

ii   To this day it is known as David's well. Radzivil 169. *Zuallard,* 205. Troilo 386. Thomson p. 48. Korte 117. Berggren 3, 149. The last one had the peculiar name of Ras Etaes, which might refer to the name of the area.

iii   *Fabri* 1, 437. *Quaresm.* 2, 614. *Surius* 522. Zwinner 353. *Bremond* 2, 3. *Legrenzi* 1, 178. *Nau* 394. Robinson 2, 378.

iv   *Quaresm.* Voyage 1699. 79.

v   Rauchwolff 643. Quaresm. Surius. While walking from the tomb of Rachel, one climbs up on a small hill and can see the whole of Bethlehem (correct). Zwinner. En tournant un peu à gauche. Voyage 1699.

vi   1 bowshot. Radzivil 169. About 1 musket shot. Ignaz von Rheinfelden 126. 50 steps. Bremond. From Rachel's grave it is 1.2 mile according to Zuallart or not far according to Zwinner.

vii   Fabri, Fürer, Radzivil, Zwinner. Some distance away. De Bruyn 2, 230.

viii ½ mile. Schwallart. Circa…medium milliaris. Quaresm. Only ½ hour (to the north). Surius. ¼ hour. Thomson, Korte (just a little), Robinson (about). 2 rifle shots. Legrenzi. A une porte de mousquet. Voyage 1699. 1000 steps. Geramb 1, 183. Ladoire says: a musket's shot away from Bethlehem until the point where one turns toward the cistern. Others, like Brocardt, Breydenbach, Tschudi (first, 269) specify the location in the west next to the gate. Cf. de Bruyn for this reason.

ix   Inter hanc cisternam et Bethlehem est magna et profunda vallis, ubi sunt vinea, fleus et oliveta. *Quaresm.* 2, 615a. Beyond the deep valley below the village. Robinson.

the picturesque little town with its temple, and of the Mountain of Little Paradise.[i] There are actually three cisterns,[ii] so situated as to form a triangle[iii]: a southern one, which is nearest the road, a western and an eastern one. They are hewn in the rock[iv] and covered by a wall at the top.[v] Their rather careful construction provides evidence that they were very beautiful in their day[vi]; the cisterns once had marble lids[vii] and were each contained within a square structure.[viii] The southern cistern, the one that was probably used most often by pilgrims and the first to be mentioned, is 17' deep,[ix] and has two openings that can still be accessed and one that is blocked. In the Orient, people use a stiff leather bucket, which is left hanging by a rope in the depths, to draw the water.[x] This cistern is very big[xi]; however, I am unable to report the full dimensions.[xii] Forty-four steps from here to the north, one encounters the eastern cistern with its four openings

---

i   Della Valle 1, 157.

ii   However, writers speak not of three cisterns but of three openings of one single cistern. *Fabri* (tria ora, s. Tria foramina), Tschudi (3 holes, 270), *Quaresmius* (2, 614), *Surius*, Zwinner (3 brick-built well openings), *Ladoire*, Robinson (3 or 4). Nau even says (394): Elle a trois bouches, en memoire peut-estre de ces braves de David.

iii Cette cîterne est au milieu d'une petite place de figure triangulaire. *Ladoire*.

iv   Troilo.

v   Bien couverte. *Nau*.

vi   Zwinner.

vii *Legrenzi*. Voutée des pierres blanches. *Surius*.

viii Lapidibus olim in quadro dispositis circumdata. *Quaresm.* 2, 615. The fact that the wells were covered in lead is Geramb's newly baked assertion.

ix   Deep according to Fabri, Rauchwolff, Quaresmius, Robinson, very deep according to Zwinner and Troilo.

x   That is why people go to get water there, equipped with cords, buckets and ripcords, as it is the custom in these lands, and tend to bring merchants along on their journeys. Rauchwolff. Buchi capaci per penetrare con utri. *Legrenzi*.

xi   Fabri, Zwinner, Robinson. Far according to Rauchwolff, wide below according to Troilo.

xii Ayant de sa longuaur 34. pas et de largeur 11. *Surius*.

and a depth of 21'. The western cistern has a southern and a northern opening. If all three cisterns are viewed as one, there forms before us a large water reservoir, which had to have been of considerable significance. Although the rain during my time there fell abundantly, I found no water in any of the cisterns, and in late spring 1838, others had it no better.[i] The name David's Wells is explained by reference to the assumption — the basis of which I shall deal with elsewhere — that David's three mighty men, after breaking through the enemy army, had drawn water for the king here, near the gate.[ii] I would now like to provide the more recent history or that from tradition and a few memorable events. Already in the time of the Frankish kings, David's Wells, the ones from which he longed to drink,[iii] were a known sight in Bethlehem, but it was not recorded in which part of the town they were located. In 1280, and again in 1310, the cistern was apparently to be found on the west side of Bethlehem, at the entrance or gate.[iv] The tradition had such flimsy roots that in 1320 one locates the cistern in a different place; it was presumed to lie before the façade of the great Church of St. Mary, whose cistern we already discussed, a stone's throw from the birthplace of Jesus.[v] I was unable to find reference to David's Wells again until the late fifteenth century,[vi] and without a doubt it is the same cistern with which one is familiar today. The absence of any gate in its vicinity, however, inspired the pilgrims to put forth the hypothesis that in antiquity the town of Bethlehem

---

i   Robinson.

ii   I. Chron. 11, 17 and 18.

iii   *Phocas* 22.

iv   Brocardt and after him *Marin. Sanut.* 3, 14, 11.

v   In platea que est ante faciem eius ecclesie (St. Mary's Church) est cisterna illa cuius aquam desideravit David dicens O si quis etc. Super cisternam illam ad iactum lapidis est locus ubi natus est Dominus. *Pipin.* 72b. One encounters this opinion in *Quaresm.* 2, 623.

vi   Breydenbach and Fabri. The latter notably says that the cistern was located about a stone's throw away from the path while walking from Jerusalem towards Bethlehem.

must have extended as far as its location.[i] In those days people praised the plenitude, clarity, freshness, and goodness of the water[ii]; and later, too, they praised it for its copiousness[iii] and quality.[iv] In 1738 it was only reported that the reservoir was not an overflowing spring[v]; from then on, I was unable to find the cistern described as anything other than simply containing water. It was never drawn attention to as a spring[vi]; on the contrary, it was expressly described as being filled with rainwater that had flowed to it from the surrounding hills and vineyards.[vii] As long as the reservoir was full, it was quite popular; at least that is how it was reported in 1583, when the stream of those not only from Bethlehem but also from surrounding villages was great[viii]; in the latter half of the last century, the cistern water kept all of Bethlehem alive for the better part of the year.[ix] It has been recounted that in 1483, a very unpleasant occurrence took place. A Saracen woman, attempting to draw water, was so careless that she slipped into the opening of the cistern and fell into the water, and was then pulled out dead. In consequence, the people, especially the Bethlehemites, developed a very strong aversion to the water.[x] It was once believed that over the cistern stood the house of David's father.[xi] My view in this regard is that there was indeed an important building here, but that it was more likely

---

i   Tschudi, Zuallart (205). See also Nau, de Bruyn.

ii Continent aquas copiosas, claras, sanas et frigidas. *Fabri.*

iii Rauchwolff. Almost always full of water. *Quaresm.* Rarely not enough water. Zwinner. Full of rainwater and otherwise unremarkable. Thomson.

iv Tschudi (like Fabri). Zuallart. Fresh and cool. Radzivil. Very fresh and good. Zwinner. Fresh and healthy. Troilo. Elle est bonne et tres saine. *Ladoire.*

v   Korte.

vi More of a water receptacle than a spring. Thomson.

vii *Surius.*

viii Radzivil.

ix Zwinner.

x   It is supposed to have happened ante paucos dies. *Fabri.*

xi *Ladoire* 191.

a monastery than a fortress. Cistern water was obtainable from any number of sources; this water could not have been intended for more distant areas, such as today's Bethlehem encompasses; undoubtedly it served the area in the immediate vicinity. Already in the twelfth century the house of David's father was believed to have stood to the left of the Church of the Nativity of our Lord,[i] and in 1829 a narrow road in north Bethlehem is specified as the site where the house of David's father must have stood.[ii]

---

i *Epiphan.* M. 52. Scheidt was shown (71) Isai's dwelling at the end of town.

ii Prokesch 118. Gumpenberg found David's house before and the small town behind it.

CHAPTER 3

Vegetation

The region of Bethlehem is fertile,[i] and it would be even more so if protections were permitted against roving Arabs who care little about the property of others, thus allowing for the dedicated cultivation of the soil.[ii] It is not well endowed with trees, and with firewood hardly at all, so coal is also burned.[iii] The cultivation of fig trees[iv] is in decline because the trees and their

---

i   Fertilissima est gleba per circuitum. *Fabri* 1, 464. Fruitful hills and valleys; as though everything was smiling at you. Della Valle 1, 157. Amman 120. Sane talibus bonis affluebat Bethlehemitica regio, ut non facile fecunditate alius pluribus Palæstinæ partibus cederet, sicut nec in præsentia cedit. *Quaresm.* 2, 620. Un pays fertile. Voyage 1699. 79. With the best soil in these regions. Bolney 2, 240. *Duc de Raguse* 3, 446.

ii   Schubert 3, 12. Cf. Binos 212 and Geramb 1, 148. The latter, however, fights without need against others who attribute the barrenness of the soil to Christianity, because they do not, and in return he should rather not have said that "everything thrives" in Bethlehem.

iii   Bethlehem has no wood; one can only find it several hours away and this the women have to procure as well. Geramb 1, 171.

iv   Surrounded by fig trees. Zwinner 355. Rauchwolff found great fig trees (645), Boucher discovered terraces covered with olive trees and fig trees (276) and Wittman (7) and Prokesch (112) found abundance. Lovely-tasting figs.

fruits are not safe from the Arabs, whose animals destroy the orchards. A not so very old man once told me that for as long as he could remember, fig trees and vines were no longer planted in many of the places where they had once flourished, and he could not help complaining that the government, instead of protecting the hard work of its countrymen, simply twiddled its thumbs. Olive,[i] pomegranate,[ii] and almond trees[iii] also grow here. While I have to trust reports from other informants that apricot, apple, and pear trees thrive as well,[iv] I can say with confidence that the gardens of the monasteries are resplendent with orange and lemon trees, and cypresses.[v] The grapes are excellent,[vi] but the vines are allotted very little ground.[vii] The fruit is white,[viii] like all grapes in the vicinity of Jerusalem. Bethlehem wine is of superb quality[ix] but evidently does not age well. In 1845 it fared very badly, just as in Ein Karim, so I was served old wine; although I entered several establishments with the intention of finding something of quality, I nonetheless failed. On my last sojourn

---

Geramb 1, 148.

i   Ella (Bethlehem) possiede comunemente assai bel paese e bene ulivato. *Sigoli* 134. Abundant in olives. Gumpenberg 464. Oleo abundans. *Fabri*. (The Wâdi el-Charûbeh below) is full of great olive trees and fig trees. Rauchwolff. Bolney. Excessive amount of olive trees, which is what the inhabitants actually live off. Wittman. Schubert 3, 12.

ii   Wittman.

iii   An abundance of almond trees. Prokesch.

iv   They blossomed in March. Schubert 3, 114. Bolney talks about fruit.

v   Tschudi says (272) that there are many fruitful trees there in general.

vi   Very beautiful vines. *Duc de Raguse* 3, 446. Wine grapes of exquisite taste. Geramb. Schubert.

vii Some like Baldensel (120), Fabri (vino…abundans. 1, 464), Wittman (all the way to the top of the hill), mention many vineyards, the author of viagg. Al S. Sepolcro (F 6a) mentions a few; others like Gumpenberg, Rauchwolff, Amman, Zwinner, Bolney do not mention the quantities.

viii Bolney.

ix   Good. *Baldensel*. Vinum præstantissimum, nec cum ullo ejus regionis comparandum proferunet. *Cotovic*. 239. Somewhat bitter in an earthly way. Palæst. 1831. 23.

in Bethlehem, I had not a single glass of good wine and passably good wine only once. What I was served tasted somewhat [end of page 15] fusty, almost like vinegar, certainly sour. Like other wines from the ancient land of the tribe of Judah, Bethlehem wine[i] can be described as going directly to the head and intoxicating one easily. Fields of grain are rarely encountered in the immediate vicinity of the city.[ii] I heard nothing about sesame still being cultivated today, as it was in the last century.[iii] In the gardens one can see vegetables, such as cabbage; I would have much preferred to have seen that reclusive planter, who besides translating the Holy Scripture watered the vegetables with his own hands.[iv] In the sixteenth century, herbs in the Wadi al-Kharoobeh or in the Shepherds' Field were mentioned, such as wild majoram, Tragoriganum, Roman hyssop, which the Arabs called za'atar, Absinthium santonicum.[v] Bethlehem once had many pastures.[vi] That withstanding, from more than one side the desert now greets one at close range.[vii]

It is no doubt better to remain silent on the fauna than to recount, for example, how a pilgrim in the sixteenth century

---

i   Bolney.

ii   Square. Gumpenberg 464. Frumento…abundans. *Fabri* 1, 464. Around Bethlehem one finds several well-built valleys with corn. Rauchwolff. Wheat nearby. Amman.

iii   Bolney.

iv   Olus nostris manibus irrigatum. Epist. *Hieronymi ad Marcellam.*

v   Rauchwolff. Cf. Belon.

vi   *Fabri.* In the fruitful valley of Rephaim (Wâdi el-Charû'beh) there are meadows that allow for livestock breeding. Schubert 3, 12. Light found (in September) an Arab encampment between Bêt Sâhû'r en-Naffâ'râ and Bethlehem, and made this impractical remark (169 sq.): It appeared the Arabs were eagerly received by the inhabitants of the country for the manure afforded by their cattle: an amicable treaty between both parties ensured safety from pillage. The cattle I had seen in the valleys belonged to the Arabs: they were driven to pasture during the day, and at night were brought back.

vii   Cui succedit vastissima solitudo, plena ferocium barbarorum. *Hieronymi* epist. ad *Dardanum.*

encountered a chameleon,[i] or another, in this century, a European hedgehog.[ii]

---

i   Schweigger 310. Schubert saw some too (3, 16).
ii   Schubert 3, 120.

CHAPTER 4

The Town, Alleys, Size, Houses, their Construction, Numbers

I shall now sketch a picture of the town,[i] which others, perhaps with as much justification, might call a village, given that it is not surrounded by walls.[ii] I have already noted that the

---

i   Pictures of Bethlehem were made e.g. by de Bruyn (2, 222), Wegelin (good), the author of Palæstina 1831 (50. Completely made-up), d'Estourmel (115), Roberts (Sketches part. VIII), Halbreiter (Bl. III, Image 2). De Bruyn's drawing comes in two parts, the first one is of the monastery and the solid openings in the walls to the left (east) and completely separate, with only a few adjacent buildings, and to the right (west) it shows the little village with humble dwellings. D'Estourmel's drawing is by most critical standards almost indecipherable, without showing the village. Seen from northwest, Robert's image shows a bad terrain, an imprecise group of houses, and the church and the monasteries are poorly drawn. Halbreiter's picture is excellent. It shows the Church of the Nativity from northwest, to the right there's the Armenian monastery, to the left the Latin one; only the artist did not count the church's side windows properly, and one can see on it neither the burial ground nor the little western gate of the Capuchins' monastery.

ii   One should perhaps sooner forgive Döbel the market crier when he proclaims (2, 126): "Solid city walls and deep moats surround the little town in order to protect its inhabitants somewhat from the attacks of thieving Bedouins," as opposed to Robinson when he says (2, 381) that the town is supposedly surrounded by one city wall with gates in it. Already Korte (117) and Ignaz von Rheinfelden (127) found the little town to be without any city

town is separated into two parts: an eastern part comprising the church and monasteries and just to the south, a residential neighbourhood known as Harit al-Anatreh, and a western part encompassing the remainder of the dwellings on the ridge as well as both northern and southern flanks of the hill[i]; indeed the houses continue down and along the western slope of the Wadi al-Kharoobeh, near its beginning, whereas the Latin monastery is nestled along the valley's eastern slope on the opposite side, so that the town's two parts face each other, albeit obliquely. If one does not also consider the temples and monasteries as a Harit al-Dair, despite their being the town's most important buildings, then Bethlehem has seven neighbourhoods:

1. Harit al-Anatreh, to the south of the Armenian and Greek monasteries, the eastern neighbourhood, located entirely on the southern slope of the ridge.
2. Harit al-Quawawseh,[ii] which begins to the west of the church square and lies partly on the ridge.
3. Harit al-Najajreh ('Carpenters' Quarter'), to the west of Harit al-Anatreh, in the southern part of the town on the southern slope.
4. Harit al-Farahieh, to the west of Harit al-Quawawseh at the top of the hill.
5. Harit al-Tarajmeh, to the west of and somewhat higher than Harit al-Quawawseh, as it is mainly on the northern slope.
6. Harit Hreizat, to the west of the previous neighbourhood.
7. Harit al-Fawaghreh, the neighbourhood farthest west and highest up.

The Harit al-Quawawseh is the largest neighbourhood. Harit

---

walls.

i   The houses are located on top of the hill and on the slopes. Binos 207.

ii   A learned man wrote to me wondering whether the word Chowâ'si denotes the female sex, about which Burckhard (Arab. Sprüchw. 495) reports.

al-Anatreh is home only to Greeks, carpenters, and journeymen; the Armenians have their dwellings in Harit al-Najajreh, the Moslems in the neighbourhood highest up; and the Roman Catholics live dispersed amongst the other neighbourhoods.

The town is not large[i]; its length from west to east exceeds its width from south to north by a significant margin.[ii] Its size amounts to about sixteen hundred paces,[iii] which equal no more than a quarter of an hour, the length being about eight hundred paces and the width slightly more than two hundred paces. There are a number of streets. The route from Jerusalem does not transect the whole town. It leads down along the Wadi al-Kharoobeh from the west, rises suddenly towards the south or southeast, then turns back in the earlier direction (eastwards) as it continues downwards to the Monastery Square. Where the market stalls in the Harit al-Quawawseh, Al Farahieh, Al Tarajmeh and Al Hreizat are located, is actually the main thoroughfare, which is also called Bazaar. Not quite in the middle of the town, it is divided into three lanes, the most northerly of which is called Jerusalem Way. There is a goodly number of narrow cross-streets,[iv] many resembling staircases, along with those leading over house tops, as there is also a lane running south to north from the southern slope of Harit al-Anatreh all the way up to Harit al-Fawaghreh. The dwellings of the western hill are split apart from those of the eastern hill only enough so that the space between them forms a broad street,[v]

---

i Not very big. Palæst. 1831. 48. Cette petite ville. *D'Estourmel* 2, 113 sq.

ii Many writers, such as Baldensel (120), the author of Palæst. 1831 (49), remark that the village was built in an elongated way.

iii Legrenzi, who is the only one known to me to have a precise measurement, even though it is not from our century, writes (1, 185): E di brevissimo giro von più estendosi che un miglia in circa, which rather corresponds to my own measurements.

iv Narrow streets. *Light* 165. Röser 445.

v Robinson's remark (2, 379) that the monastery is located 200 steps east from the village, is imprecise. "The village lies across from the top of a sizable hill, some 100 steps away from it; the monastery lies on another hill." Mayr

which then, more on the southern side, turns eastwards and as a somewhat narrower streets runs between the Armenian and Greek monasteries to the north and the Harit al-Anatreh to the south all the way up to the east end of the town and the Milk Grotto of Mary. Very few streets are paved, and when it rains the muck has no equal.[i] What I marvelled at, however, was that even before the rain began to fall, with everything otherwise parched to the bone, the road leading to Jerusalem already had puddles of water in it.

Although I must admit that Bethlehem today has nothing of its former beauty, not to mention greatness,[ii] those sojourners who perceived the town as a poor, miserable backwater,[iii] as little more than a heap of rubble,[iv] would have made my detailed description of it and its constituents considerably easier if only I had trusted them enough to follow in their footsteps. For alongside various ruins and dilapidated structures, which are by no means the most attractive sight for the newcomer, one still notices many residential structures that we should deem worthy of our attention. As far as the design of the houses is concerned, their lateral boundaries make them look like city dwellings. Yes, in some places they press up against each other with such insistence that they might have been built directly into each other, had it been possible. As in many places in Palestine, the

---

v. A. 330.

i   Dirty streets. Röser.

ii Cf. Geramb.

iii Mayr v. A. Currently a truly ugly nest. Rutzegger in the prize book Morgenland [Orient], 1839, 39.

iv The piles of rubble of this so-called…town…The misery and poverty which live here underneath the ruins. Schubert 3, 11. The earthquake of 1834 certainly caused some destruction (Röser), in 1835, however, I did not find it quite as bad as suggested by Schubert's fanciful style. Already before the earthquake, Geramb (1, 166) wanted to portray the town as having consisted only of a disorderly pile of houses and dilapidated walls, probably in order to project "the misery and subordination" (under the Franciscans?) onto the ruins.

building material comprises small blocks of stones[i] which make the dwellings look quite solid.[ii] Needless to say, stones from old, destroyed buildings were also used in new constructions. Thus, one finds fragments of old columns directly in the houses. There are also quite large stones with carved edges and on one house a very beautifully crafted cornice of polished red marble, probably from the so-called school of Jerome. The houses are rectangular in form,[iii] their roofs flat[iv]; only the relatively numerous little bakehouses, on account of which the uninitiated view the town as a pile of shacks, have vaulted roofs. For as many low[v] and crooked mounds as there are, there are others that are tall, truly well-built, and more attractive. The stairs are always mounted on the outside,[vi] where they go up one or two storeys; where the lodgings, and there are many of them, are level with the ground, the stairs lead downwards, of course. Windows of glass are as good as non-existent; one finds instead window openings and other small apertures looking here and there onto the street so that the houses, albeit according to oriental notions, resemble dwellings rather than prisons.[vii] Windows are only very rarely kept closed by shutters, and for most buildings the doors perform that function. These thick wooden doors are held fast with a wooden lock into which a wooden key fits; although iron locks are not uncommon. Camels and other domestic animals are kept in vaults or cellars or caves, but unless one was driven by curiosity to look inside, the stalls would remain undetected.

---

i   Mud huts, in one of Schubert's sentences. After the earthquake, Röser also saw smaller houses.

ii   Massively built. Robinson 2, 381.

iii   Borsum 145. De Forbin 124. Geramb.

iv   Terrace-shaped. Geramb. With domes. De Forbin. We shall verify this later.

v   Borsum, de Forbin. Robinson mentions smaller houses, while Röser mentions bigger ones, which seem to be growing out of the rocky ground.

vi   De Forbin, Geramb.

vii   As Röser would have it.

Something unusual on the fronts of the houses, specifically those facing east, as in Beit Sahour, is a vault or rectangular room which is left open for the reception of bee pots. The houses also have on one side a single — only seldom is it more than one — protuberant stone, onto which flowerpots are placed. To read some travellers' descriptions, one would scarcely believe that here and there are houses in which gestures toward the symbolic or higher arts were ventured. Crosses carved into the wall, usually over the front door, as a friendly sign for Christians, are the most common symbols in this Moslem region. One also sees frescos and bas-reliefs of St. George and likenesses of Mary, wife of Joseph, and Mary Magdalene. The houses and little bakehouses must be distinguished from the shopkeepers' and workers' stalls, which, separated from them by the street, belong either to the eastern or northeastern quarters of the western hill. I would like to enumerate the number of houses; but not even the residents here could tell me what it is, and I am not interested in embellishing. According to some, there are about one hundred fifty,[i] if not almost three hundred.[ii] To provide a portrait of a house and its interior that is as close as possible to the truth, I shall introduce the report of a pilgrim, who visited Bethlehem in 1832[iii]: 'After crossing through an extremely dirty entrance, I came to a vaulted, windowless room of a house owned by the most prosperous of families; daylight penetrated only through the doorway, the only opening through which the smoke from the hearth could escape; the walls were completely blackened by it. Living there were two brothers busily employed with crafting mother-of-pearl; farther on, the wife of one was suckling a child, and nearby was her mother-in-law doing the same; she was surrounded by three other very young children. Two cradles were the only pieces of furniture. All together in one room slept

---

i   Salzbacher 2, 166.
ii Borsum 145.
iii Geramb 1, 172.

the father and mother, the son and daughter-in-law, and the little children, on the (blanket-covered) floor, along with fowls that occupied one corner of the room'.

CHAPTER 5

History of the City
a. pre-Christian and
b. post-Christian

Before we go any further in our description, let us first cast a glance into the halls of history. By what strange feelings are we overcome when the millennia suddenly unfurl before us. The earliest reference is in the First Book of Moses,[i] with Rachel's death and burial on the way to Ephrath, which at the time the words were written was already called Bethlehem, meaning 'house of bread'.[ii] It was the intention of Jacob and his wife to reach Ephrath.[iii] To distinguish this Bethlehem from another Bethlehem, at least from that of the tribe of Zebulon,[iv] it was called Judah's Bethlehem[v] or Bethlehem Ephratah.[vi] Ephratah,

---

i   35, 19. Cf. 48, 7.

ii   E.g. Jerome (comm. in genes. 35), Quaresmius (2, 619), Surius (523), Robinson (2, 38). Brothusen. *Fabri* 1, 463.

iii 1. Mos. 35, 16.

iv   Jos. 19, 15. It is notable that the Hebrew codex does not cover Juda's Bethlehem, but does cover the LXX. Cf. *Reland.* ad. voc. Bethlechem.

v   Richt. 17, 7. Sam. 17, 12. Matth. 2, 1.

vi   Mich. 5, 2.

however, means 'fruitful'.[i] From Bethlehem came a young Levite and a concubine with whom another Levite[ii] sojourned on Mount Ephraim. When the day was drawing toward evening, the latter two left Bethlehem, and when it was very near its end, they arrived at Jerusalem, and when the sun set they were near Gibeah.[iii] Elimelech and his wife Naomi emigrated from Bethlehem to the land of the Moabites during a famine. One of their sons married a Moabite named Ruth there. When both of their sons had died, Naomi went with Ruth from there to Bethlehem as the barley harvest had begun; the return caused a commotion throughout the whole city. Ruth went to the field belonging to Boaz, and among the sheaves, she gleaned after the reapers, and there she stayed by the women of Boaz until the barley and wheat harvests were over. As Boaz was winnowing barley on his threshing floor, Ruth, after bathing and anointing herself with a fragrant ointment,[iv] went down on the floor and lay at his feet. And in the morning, before the one could know the other, she stood up and he gave her six measures of barley, which she put in her garment and carried into the city. Boaz went (in the city) up to the gate and accorded, in the presence of the ten elders of the city, with the heirs of Elimelech, and took Ruth for his wife, and she bore to him Obed. Obed begat Jesse (Isai), who begat David.[v] Samuel went to Bethlehem, to visit Jesse, the father of David, and the elders of the city met him. None of Jesse's sons pleased Samuel enough to anoint him

---

i   One place in the first book of the Chronicles (4, 4) suggests that the name Ephrata was chosen after a woman called Ephrata, after the mother of Chur, that is, who later became the father of the Bethlehemians. If the word Ephrata or fruitful could still be applied to the area around Bethlehem today, the word would still have originated in relation to this woman after whom the area was later named.

ii   Richt. 17, 7.

iii   Richt. 19.

iv   A type of pomade.

v   In the book of Ruth, which represents the actual chronicle of Bethlehem.

king, until they fetched him the youngest, David, who tended the sheep. At Saul's request, Jesse sent David, who brought to the king a donkey and bread and a skin full of wine and a billy goat, and a harp to bring him cheer. When a war broke out between Saul and the Philistines, in which the three eldest sons of Jesse from Bethlehem also fought, David departed from the king's court to tend his father's sheep in the desert of Bethlehem.[i] But at Jesse's urging, David took an ephah of parched grain and ten loaves of bread for his brothers and ten fresh cheeses for the captain to the camp, to see how they were faring; and David slew Goliath the Philistine, and became king of the tribe of Judah.[ii] Hence is Bethlehem also called David's City,[iii] like Zion. One day, this king desired water from the cistern in Bethlehem by the gate,[iv] which the eponymous well was later proclaimed to be,[v] and the three mighty men he sent forth brought it to him, although the valley where the troops of the Philistines were pitched stretched all the way to the city of Bethlehem. Bethlehem was also the home of David's field captain Joab and his brothers Abishai and Asahel[vi]—all three of them sons of Zeruiah, David's sister.[vii] Asahel was buried in his father's grave, which was in Bethlehem.[viii] Rehoboam, a son and successor of David and Solomon, fortified Bethlehem, gave

---

i   1. Sam. 17, 4 ff.; 17. The fact that David drove the sheep out into the desert follows from the 28th verse of the same chapter.

ii 2. Sam. 2.

iii 1. Sam 20, 6 (However, here it could help with the city of origin). Luk. 2, 4 and 11. David's town does not seem to have been a popular expression but rather a literary, academic one, the way one would say about a famous citizen of Eisleben: He was from the city of Luther, so as to recommend him to someone by doing this.

iv 2. Sam. 23, note 13. 2. Chron. 11, 17 ff.

v   P. above p. note 12.

vi 2. Sam. 2, 18.

vii 1. Chron. 2, 13 ff.

viii 2. Sam. 2, 32.

the inhabitants a captain and a store of victuals, oil, and wine.[i] From the Babylonian exile one hundred-and-twenty-three souls returned to Bethlehem.[ii]

I have here a great treasure of historical notes before me, and it is now the task to illuminate some of them. Topographical sketches, which would allow one to conclude with certainty that the Bethlehem of today is one and the same as the ancient Bethlehem, are in rather short supply; and it is the name, preserved unspoiled through writing and tradition, that is the primary argument for their being the same, something that to my knowledge has never been contested.[iii] From the Levite's journey with his concubine from Bethlehem to Jerusalem, it can be deduced that Bethlehem was not far from Jerusalem and perhaps in the southern direction as well. A valley stretching as far as Bethlehem where the Philistine troops pitched their camp can be befittingly identified as either Wadi al-Qawas or al-Rahib, because apart from Wadi al-Kharoobeh there is no other valley that stretches to Bethlehem, and to place the Philistines in the latter valley would be nonsense.[iv] Since the three mighty men who brought water to King David from the cistern of Bethlehem had to force their way through the Philistine army, it is evident that both the gate and the cistern were occupied by the latter. Without wanting to counter the comparatively recent tradition,[v] I must say it seems quite unlikely to me that the well

---

i Chron. 11, 6 and 11 ff. Whoever wants to know more than is said in the Bible can check Geramb (1, 166).

ii Esra 2, 21.

iii Cf. Robinson 2, 380.

iv If I understand him correctly, Schubert calls the Wâdi el-Charûbeh the valley of Rephaim, and has the audacity to claim that it stretches from Jerusalem to Bethlehem (3, 6), which is not once mentioned by Flavius Josephus (1. 7, 12, 3); incidentally, I know of no such valley that would be 20 stadiums away from Jerusalem and would stretch all the way to Bethlehem.

v Quaresmius also contests (2, 614 sqq.) this tradition, but partly out of scholarly reasons, which I cannot condone. He misplaces the location of the cistern to the eastern side of Bethlehem (615 sq.), similar to an older

was located to the northwest of Bethlehem.[i] When the mighty men left David, he was in Adullam, probably today's Beit Ula, which in accordance with an old report was located about eight Roman miles east of Eleutheropolis. The most direct route from there led to the south side of Bethlehem, where Boorak (pools) is today. If the Philistines were encamped in either the Quawas or the Wadi al-Rahib, and if the well had stood on the northwestern side of Bethlehem, then the three envoys would have bypassed the enemy without difficulty and reached the cistern without breaking through their ranks. It is therefore more likely that the cistern was located on the southern slope, the valley in which the Philistines encamped, and the opinion that this cistern was connected to the Boorak (pools) water supply, just as it is today, is not without foundation; built only as far as Bethlehem, the water pipeline was of an unremarkable construction that no doubt had existed for a long time before it was extended to Jerusalem. Having advanced thus far in our conjecture, we can see clearly that the Philistines must have laid siege to the southern side of Bethlehem, where they could cut off the town's water supply. We inquire now about the field where Boaz had his reapers and granary floor or his threshing floor and where Ruth gathered among the sheaves. The Bible does not indicate the exact location; undoubtedly it lay not far from Bethlehem, and we can well concur with earlier speculations of its being the field where, according to Christians, the shepherds rejoiced at the Saviour's birth.[ii] The desert where David grazed sheep and to which a lion advanced, must have been quite far to

tradition of which he is unaware. By contrast, it is particularly Nau (394 sq.) who wants to rescue the newer and viable tradition.

i   As soon as one connects Joseph with Samuel and the Chronicles, the great difficulty of interpretation arises; but if one were allowed to regard the Bible alone as authoritative, then one could certainly follow tradition, and in general look anywhere for a gate and a cistern, without taking the valleys into consideration.

ii   Fabri (Reyßb.) 259.

the east of Bethlehem.[i] This ancient history also tells us that the land surrounding Bethlehem was cultivated. Wheat and barley flourished; they were harvested collectively and winnowed on the threshing floor. Bread was baked; for the loaves that David brought to Saul and to his brothers on the battlefield were evidently baked in Bethlehem. Grain kernels were also eaten directly, as is still done today. Not only sheep but goats, too, were grazed and cheese was produced, probably goat cheese. For the fresh cheese that Jesse gave his son David can only have been produced by the industry of Bethlehem, just like the wine, which leads us back to the vineyards of Bethlehem. That Bethlehem was a town in antiquity is well known, but it seems to have been of small dimensions.[ii] It undoubtedly had a wall around it, as gates are mentioned: one gate at the top of the town, to which Boaz went up, probably the western gate, and another near the cistern, probably the southern gate. Bethlehem would not have had more than three gates, with an eastern or northeastern gate being the third. The first gate mentioned above[iii] led to the western environs, namely to Jerusalem; the southern gate led to Hebron and Tekoa; and through the eastern or northeastern gate one reached the fertile valleys nearby and the Plain of Jericho. That a somewhat higher intellectual culture was already established during David's youth is proved by the fact that this son of Jesse, the Bethlehemite, could play the harp.[iv] One might ask: 'Was there not a kind of school in Bethlehem

i   When David was a boy tending sheep, he slew a lion and killed a bear in that field (of shepherds).

ii   And thou Bethlehem Ephrata, which art small among the thousands in Judah. Micha 5, 2.

iii   Although they were only discovered much later, the ruins of the rampart ditches lead me to believe that the ancient Bethlehem, like the present one, stood on the western hill. Vaults, caves (for cellars and stables) were certainly always welcome during each new construction, and the ruined stones were being used as close as possible to the building site. How could they have been carried further away? On the other hand, Tschudi says (272) that the new village was located a stone's throw away from the old town.

iv   1. Sam. 16, note 17.

without which David later would not have gotten so far with his poetry?' Today one would search in vain for the grave of Asahel and his father in David's native town. That in his day the graves of Jesse, Job, Asaph, Ezekiel, Solomon, and David could not have been far from Bethlehem, I will report on elsewhere. Anyone who notices the many burial caves in the environs of Jerusalem and even in the great valley between Qalonieh and Beit Hanina, in Beit Sahour al-Atika, in Ein al-Shibrieh, will be surprised by the rarity or absence of such rocky caves in the confines of Bethlehem. In the fourth century, the burial mound of Archelaus, a former king of Judea, is indicated as being near the site of the Nativity, directly at the head of the footpath that led from the highway to the caves of Jerome.[i] This tradition has disappeared without a trace.

According to a prophecy, he who would be Lord in Israel would come from Bethlehem.[ii] There, Jesus Christ was born.[iii] The first two Evangelists, from whom we have the story of this world event, do not connect it with any other topographical observations except that Bethlehem was located within the tribe of Judah. In the beginning of the second century, Jews still lived in Bethlehem, and Evaristus, who lived at the time of Domitian and Nerva Trajan, was the son of a Jew and was born in that

---

i   Sed et propter aendem (Dominicam nativitatem) Bethleem, regis quondam Judææ Archelai tumulus ostenditur: qui semitæ ad cellulas nostras e via publica divertentis principium. *Hieronymi* onomast. (2, 411). Adrichomius has the Tumulus Archelai northwest and the "cisterna" southwest from Bethlehem.

ii   Micha 5, 1. Math. 2, 6. In Echa Rabbati fol. 72 one reads that a Messiah was born in Birath Arba in Judah, and the glossator adds that Birath Arba is supposed to be a place name in Bethlehem, Judah. *Reland.* ad voc. Bethlehem. If the so-called David's well did indeed consist of four cisterns, one would not be embarrassed to continue a hypothesis.

iii   I disregard the recent critics who claim that Jesus was born in Nazareth.

town[i]; Hadrian, however, forbade the Israelites to live there.[ii] Beginning in the fourth century, when the town's exact position was described for the first time,[iii] removing any doubt about the identity of the place then with the Bethlehem of today, the town is cited more often. In the fourth century, Bethlehem was a small town.[iv] At the time of Christian rule, the place must have come under the influence of some monasteries and overwhelmed by the easy pilgrimage. Emperor Justinian rebuilt the walls.[v] In the year 600 it was a splendid place, with an outlying district a half a mile away, and there lived many servants of God.[vi] Around 670 is the first more detailed description of the town's disposition. It was not so much large as much as it was famous because of its church that was admired by people everywhere. Atop the plain, or rather along the exterior of the narrow hill, a low wall without towers ran from west to east, encompassed by valleys on either side, and the space between the walls was occupied by a rather long row of domiciles belonging to the townsmen.[vii] In 1099 the Saracens destroyed everything, with the exception of the Church of St. Mary, leaving nothing inhabitable in their

---

i   Anastasius in the vitæ Pontif. Romanor., introduced by Reland ad voc. Bethlechem. Justinus Martyr mentions Bethlehem; Origenes in the following year Origenes. Cf. Robinson 2, note 284.

ii   Tertullian, introduced by Reland (647).

iii   See note 5 on p. 1 and note 1 on p. 2.

iv   In Christi vero villula. Paula and Eustochium's letter to Marcella. In opp. *Hieronymi*, probably copied from his letter to the latter. In onomast. *Euseb.* civitas David.

v   Prokopius, Lib v. p. 41. secunda.

vi   Locus splendidissimus. *Antonin. Plac.* XXIX.

vii   Quæ ciuitas non tam situ grandis…quam fama prædicabilis per uniuersarum gentium ecclesias diffamata (I chose a freer translation). In dorso sita est angustoIn cuius campestri plaicie superiore humilis sine turribus murus in circuitu per eiusdem monticuli extremitatis supercilium constructus. Ualliculis hinc et inde circumiacentibus supereminet mediaque intercapidine intra murum per longiorem tramitem habitacula ciuium sternuntur (cernuntur?). *Arculf.* 2, 1 (Cod. St. Gall. 267). The nativity cave was located in the eastern and the most remote corner of the town.

wake, as they did in all the holy places outside Jerusalem.[i] Once the Crusaders had taken possession of Bethlehem, it did not take long before another city, in name at least, had been erected.[ii] One may also give credence to the story of their having built a castle at the monastery; not, however, to that of the man who, after Saladin's conquest of the city, defended it for four years against the Saracens, surrendering only because of the lack of provisions, so that the conquerors led him into that very church and cut off his head, which leapt onto a stone, leaving traces that in 1449 were still visible.[iii] The back of the hill on which Bethlehem lay was paved with stones in later years.[iv] In 1187 the town suffered no physical damage[v]; in 1217 Christians lived there, and despite superstitions that Saracens could not stay in the town, some of them, albeit they did not reside there, nonetheless stood at the entrance to the monastery and demanded a bounty from the pilgrims and from anyone who wished to enter.[vi] In 1244 Bethlehem was devastated by the wild hordes of the Khwarazmians.[vii]

I will now outline the period from 1244 until the fifteenth century. The city was small and compact,[viii] but secure and well

---

i   Ibi nihil a Saracenis est remissum habitabilis. *Saewulf.* 35.

ii   Villam etiam Bethleem (year 1110). *Guil. Tyr.* 11, 12. *Phocas* 22.

iii Gumpenberg 464.

iv   *Phocas.*

v   Is intact and not destroyed by the Saracens. Thetmar in Malten's Weltkd., Febr. 1844, 192. Jakût Ham. called (lex. geogr. in *Schultens* Index geogr. ad voc. Bethlehem, behind in Bohadini vita Saladini) Bethlehem a small town, ennobled by the birth of Jesus, over whom peace reigns.

vi   Thetmar a. a. D.

vii Robinson 2, 381, after Wilken 6, 635.

viii Monteuilla 773. *Baldensel* 120. In Abulfeda (f. Schultens a. a. D.) Bethlehem appears as a village where Jesus, the highly blessed, is supposed to have been born. Questa città è molta disfatta, e per antico fù molta grande: ora è molta piccola, e le case che vi sono la maggior parte sono casolari. *Sigoli* 134.

fortified[i] with very good, secure moats and walls,[ii] an entrance and gate, the latter beside a cistern on the way from the west, at the foot of a hill where one descends.[iii] And in the town was a square called Flower Field (*Campus floridus*), named after a miracle that happened there. A girl was accused of having lost her virginity, and was therefore threatened with death by fire. Knowing that she was innocent, she begged God to protect her; the flames were extinguished and the thorns bore roses.[iv] In the fifteenth century, Bethlehem had to lament its decay.[v] One no doubt saw that it had walls and moats,[vi] but the people did not take care of them.[vii] On the west side of the town, moats, walls, and towers were still visible in 1483.[viii] The village or little town, rising continually (towards the west)[ix] from the monastery, and extending eastwards,[x] long and narrow,[xi] to the end of the mountain, had dilapidated houses that had surely once been noble and beautiful.[xii] The hill of Bethlehem exhibited broad protuberances of rock and cliffs and under them large caves that served as dwellings for the poor and those wanting lodgings of

---

i   Maundeville, Rudolph von Suchen 842.

ii   Mandeville.

iii Brocardt 869.

iv   Maundeville.

v   Betleem è una bella citade. Libro de' Viaggi (15. s.). *Fr. Poggi* in his Lezione on Sigoli's edition (37).

vi   Three small ones. Gumpenberg 464. Bena affossata. Libro de' Viagg. l. C.

vii *Fabri* 1, 463 sq.

viii Habuit fossata, muros et turres, sicut hodie etiam patet. Circumivi oppidum, et curiosius ejus perspexi situm. *Fabri* 1, 463.

ix   Gumpenberg.

x   Fabri (Reyßb.) 260.

xi   Ed è piccola, ed è lunga, ed è stretta. Libro de' Viagg. l. C. Quello che si abita si è (lunga) per una balestrata, e larga per una gittata di pietra. F. Nicolò da Poggibonizzi bei Poggi (Gigoli) l. c. Gumpenberg. Rit says big, but long. Fabri.

xii Gumpenberg.

their own.[i] In front of the churches there were vaults under which were shopkeepers' stalls.[ii] In 1449 Bethlehem had two castles, between which it lay. The one, Castle Bethlehem, stood high up in the west, near to the Jerusalem road, to the north of which lay David's Wells[iii]; and the other was next to the monastery, with the most beautiful towers, moats, dungeons, and walls.[iv] In 1489 the sultan demolished the sturdy fortress, razed the city wall, smashed walls and towers, and destroyed the (castle-like) monastery adjoining the great church.[v] I was very attentive to whether traces of the moats could still be seen, even faintly; this seemed to me most likely in the west.[vi] In the sixteenth century, the village[vii] or town[viii] was small,[ix] almost completely destroyed[x] and deserted,[xi] and of dire appearance[xii]; very few houses,[xiii] poorly and small ones at that,[xiv] scattered hither and thither,[xv] made up

---

i *Fabri* 1, 458.

ii Unde (since Bethlehem was so populated in Jerome's time) hodie ante ecclesias sunt testudines, sub quibus fuerunt partegæ mercatorum. *Fabri* 1, 471.

iii Gumpenberg. Fabri (Reyßb.) 258.

iv Gumpenberg.

v *Fabri* 1, 474.

vi Cf. 18 above, note 4.

vii Hodie permodicus est viculus. *Georg.* 557. Tschudi 272. (Flecken) Seydlitz 476. Urbs...in pagum redacta. *Fürer* 65. Radzivil 169.

viii *Anshelm.* 1290. Viagg. Al S. Sepolcro F 6.

ix *Georg., Anshelm.* Ecklin 756. Helffrich 718. Rauchwolff 643.

x La città è quasi distrutta. Viagg. al S. Sepolcro. Tschudi. Seydlitz. *Fürer.*

xi This Viagg.

xii Tschudi. Seydlitz. Villinger 92. Luffy 36.

xiii Several houses on a pile. *Anshelm.* Helffrich. The old buildings, city walls, towers, have deteriorated to such an extent that today it (the town of David) is completely open, and apart from the monastery and the fountain, there is nothing but a few ramshackle little houses to be seen. Rauchwolff 643. Some huts. Schwallart 303. It must be very disconcerting that Radzivil was able to specify 50 houses.

xiv Belon 268. Cf. the last note.

xv However, no house was close to the other, but all of them were scattered

the open locale,[i] which was situated a bowshot to the west of the church.[ii] In the seventeenth century, although some found it quite small[iii] and desolate,[iv] Bethlehem apparently increased in size; the number of houses was given as between sixty and eighty[v] or even one hundred.[vi] The town was as little protected by a ring wall as it had been in the previous century,[vii] and the gate, too, was missing.[viii] From the many ruined, large, and stately buildings one concluded that Bethlehem had once been expansive and very beautiful.[ix] The influence of seventeenth-century writers seems to be at fault for the description of the condition in the previous century having been repeated. This best explains why in 1719 it was possible to refer to Bethlehem as a very small town[x], in 1725 and 1738 as a large[xi] village or hamlet denuded of its wall and with crude houses,[xii] likewise in 1751 as a large village with decrepit houses,[xiii] and in 1778 as a

---

back and forth. Helffrich. Cf. note. 13 on the last p.

i   Seydlitz, Rauchwolff.

ii   Radzivil. Similarly Viagg. al S. Sepolcro.

iii En peu d'heur nous l'(ville) aurons toute veuë, d'autant qu'elle est fort petite et mal bastie. *Boucher* 276. *Gering* Dörflein. Amman. Little village. Della Valle 1, 157. Zwinner 355. Cf. note to p. 20.

iv   The (old?) town is completely devastated. Della Valle. Before him, Scheidt (69) did not find over 40 houses.

v   Ignaz von Rheinfelden 127.

vi   Troilo 388. According to this, Nau (395) fancies himself to have found a rather large and populated village and Mirike (66) a village with few houses. Of a village assez simple speaks the author of voyage 1699 (79).

vii Sans murailles et fortifications. *Surius* 522. Ignaz von Rheinfelden.

viii Ignaz von Rheinfelden.

ix   Della Valle. The city was quite large in the past, and as can be seen from the collapsed walls and foundations, it extended in size to 1 German mile, but today it does not seem to be equal in size to that city. Troilo 388. Similar in Ignaz von Rheinfelden.

x   *Ladoire* 205.

xi   Neret 111. Korte 117.

xii Korte.

xiii Hasselquist 166.

place that appeared to have lost much of its size since the time of Christ, to judge from the empty spaces between the houses and the remains of the old ramparts.[i] In the first quarter of the same century, before arriving in Bethlehem from Jerusalem, one passed very near to one of the town gates, which lay five hundred steps from the monastery square.[ii] Even in the present century, it is referred to as a gate.[iii] What is true is that in the last decade one passed under an arch in order to enter the town. In 1845 it still lacked a gate. It had instead, on the west side, on the road to Jerusalem, an entrance beneath an arch, to the west of which are now houses that I do not remember having seen ten years earlier.

According to more recent historical accounts, Bethlehem was destroyed in 1099, then rebuilt by the Franks, before passing from them to the Saracens in 1489, when the storm clouds of devastation broke again, since which time the town has recovered only slowly, mostly in the seventeenth and eighteenth centuries, and, as far as I know, in the nineteenth. It is a pity my quill has been condemned to the writing of such a fragmentary history, and to make the gaps less glaring, I shall add some warlike events which will cast a sad light on the stormy Bethlehem. In 1719 a war broke out between the Hebronites and Bethlehemites, and the journey to Bethlehem was not without danger; at harvest time, which required the men to return home, peace negotiations were initiated, to which end each village and town sent delegates to Bethlehem. In July the peace indeed transpired, admirably mediated by the curate, a well-known Spanish priest respected by both parties. To confirm the peace agreement, a great meal was held, a cow, a ram, and a lamb were slaughtered,

---

i   Binos 205.

ii   *Ladoire* 191.

iii One enters through a gate half barricaded with rubble. Röser 445. We entered the village through a deep gateway. *Bartlett* 206. The artist also gave (p. 205) a view of the arched entrance, which has a gate-like appearance. Cf. 18 above, note 4.

prepared and eaten according to the customs of the land.[i] As for the peace, it did not last long. In the middle of the last century, the Bethlehemites lived in almost continual strife, either with themselves or with the inhabitants of Jerusalem, Hebron, and other nearby places, rarely without bloodshed. Around 1745 the Bethlehemites and the Hebronites fought such a bitter war with each other that the better part of the finest citizens of both places remained and the area around Bethlehem was devastated, the wheat crops burned, and all but a few olive trees were cut down, the stumps of which were still visible in 1751. The Bethlehemites almost never came to Jerusalem; in particular, they were wary of entering the gates when they had business with the government or with inhabitants who might very well seize the opportunity to revenge themselves against an enemy that they otherwise could not so easily handle. On the other hand, the Jerusalemites had to be especially careful and dared not venture too near to Bethlehem during troubled times. An innocent person, one who merely lived in Jerusalem, could in such a case meet with misfortune. The internal disputes of the Bethlemites were caused especially by the right to lead the pilgrims about and to demand kaffara of them. The Bethlehemites were, like the other inhabitants of Palestine, divided into two parties, the white and the red devils, and one of these parties of Bethlehem possessed said rights, while the other party strove to appropriate them.[ii] Around 1760 a civil war drove away the Orthodox Greeks. It arose because of the kaffara, which the Roman Catholics were illegally required to pay. In 1767 the Moslems, together with the Orthodox Greeks, declared war on the Latins of Bethlehem and its environs, thereupon it truly came to bloodshed.[iii] In 1814

---

i   *Ladoire* 181 sq., 212.

ii   Hasselquist 166, note 170. He also says that Bethlehem is under the jurisdiction of Mecca, and therefore is not governed by Jerusalem, but Jâfa, which also belongs to Mecca.

iii   *Mariti* 2, 365 sq. and 362. Binos says (206) that the Christians of Bethlehem waged difficult wars against the peasants of the neighboring villages, the Bethlehemites, in alliance with Abu Ghosh of St. Jeremiah, were constantly at war with the Christian Arabs of St. Philipp.[i] Around 1815 an Arab family in Bethlehem had presumed to rule over the Christian and Mohammedan inhabitants of the town, so that they levied arbitrary dues on marriages, visits to sanctuaries and the like. The Moslems and Christians therefore conspired together to murder the tyrannical family. Some men fled, and this led to further discord; there were Arabs who demanded that the refugees should repossess their land. There were plans to storm Bethlehem and the monastery.[ii] In 1829 the Roman Catholics killed four of the pasha's thirty soldiers and chased away the remainder.[iii] During a riot in the spring of 1831, the Christians of Bethlehem expelled the Moslems from the city when they refused to pay a new tax[iv]; and in 1834, following an insurrection, the Moslem quarter was destroyed at the command of Ibrahim Pasha.[v]

Having described the little town and conveyed its history, I shall now describe the inhabitants. The Bethlehemites are, on the whole, a pretty big and strong breed.[vi] Their complexion is dark yellow and generally tends towards a shade of tan, but

---

but never cut corners.

i *Light* 167. The Bethlehemians were supposed to have a red flag and the Phillipians a white one.

ii Richter, note 41. He was just in Bethlehem, when someone shot into the windows, and he does not tell the outcome of the incident.

iii Prokesch 113. Ils (Bethlehemians) sont terribles, quand on les irrite, et ils n'épargnent pas mesme, à ce qu'on m'a dit, les gens du Bassa, quand ils veulent leur faire quelque tyrannie. *Nau* 396.

iv Palæst. 1831, 49.

v Robinson 2, 381. Half in ruins due to Ibrahim-Pasha and an earthquake. Rußegger in Preiswerk (Morgenland), 1839, 73. Meanwhile, in 1834, the Duke of Ragusa (3, 446) did not find merely Christians. According to Hailbronner (2, note 297.), (a few years ago) the Christians and the Mohammedans wanted to pillage the convent; the solid walls and Ibrahim-Pasha saved it.

vi The men were young, strong. Whiting in Calw. Missionsbl., 1842, 26.

some even have white faces.[i] Red cheeks may be attributed to rouge; bright red cheeks, at least, are artificially so,[ii] but their appearance overall is healthy. Their faces tend toward curvature; most, therefore, have full faces with a rounded chin.[iii] The taste for blackened eyelids was one that the Franks did not share. As for the beauty of the women, I cannot agree with the praise that is commonly made.[iv] I have seen many Bethlehemite faces, certainly a larger selection than most travellers, and even if now and again some beautiful, black, and fiery eyes have attracted attention, most women were just mediocre, and one sees ugly people quite frequently. Those women who are truly beautiful possess grace and poise.[v] Meanwhile men almost never look beautiful or noble.[vi]

Since there is no reason to deny that the region of Bethlehem, which is only too exposed to wind, is healthy,[vii] so it must be disconcerting to strangers that among the population of Bethlehem the mortality rate is recorded with such large numbers. I am grateful to Father Curato of the Latin community for allowing me access to the death register, and although it does

---

i   Braun, almost completely black. Wittman 71.

ii   Wegelin praises (2, 124) the radiant facial color, which is supposedly worthy of any artist's brush. Hailbronner was (2, 297) amazed by the brimming health, the blossoming coloration and the whitest complexion.

iii   Geramb says the opposite (1, 171): The women are emaciated, haggard, with miserable features.

iv   The inhabitants have a very beautiful appearance and are beautifully grown. The women in particular are beautiful, have noble features and an unaffected demeanor. Berggren 3, 147. Naturalness, perfectly beautiful growth, noble physiognomies. Wegelin. Flavius Josephus (a. 5, 2) speaks of a very beautiful Bethlehemian.

v   Usually grace and regularity; the arms bare and most beautifully formed. De Forbin 124. Women are generally distinguished by the regularity of their facial features; only impurity disfigures and alters their features. Geramb 1, 173. The latter is untrue.

vi   On our walks through the little town and in its vicinity, we often encountered beautiful people with noble facial features. Schubert 3, 16.

vii   Della Valle 1, 157. Un bon air. Voyage 1699. 79. The air of the highest quality. Browne 430.

not contain the most accurate figures, it is nonetheless possible to glean many instructive things from it. No overview covers the ten years up to 1835 and including 1844. During this period, 435 people died. On average, 43 ½ per year; the fewest died in 1846, only 26; and the most, 93, in 1839. An even worse death rate occurred in 1832, with 108. Plague prevailed in 1828, 1832, and 1833, 1835, and 1839. In 1828, from May 25th to July 28th, 15 died of the plague; from May 28th, 1832, to May 14th, 1833, 105; in 1835, in June, 16; the many cases of plague in the year 1839 fell mainly in the months of June and July. In 1831, from August 5th to mid-October, epidemic vomiting killed 25 persons. In 1835, many children succumbed to the genuine human pox. Without excluding the plague, I will list a number of years with the deaths. In 1821, died 57 (born 67); 1822, 51; 1823, 34 (born 60); 1824, 42 (born 65); 1825, 48; 1826, 64; 1827, 42; 1828, 53; 1829, 36; 1830, 52; 1831, 69; 1832, 108; 1833, 39; –1835, 54; 1836, 26; 1837, 39; 1838, 36; 1839, 93; 1840, 50; 1841, 42; 1842, 31; 1843, 32; 1844, 32; 1845 (to December 30th), 33. Of those 435 persons who died, 216 were under 5 years of age; 42 between 5 to 10; 23, 10 to 15; 16, 15 to 20; 15, 20 to 25; 7, 25 to 30; 17, 30 to 35; 6, 35 to 40; 9, 40 to 45; 6, 45 to 50; 5, 50 to 55; 4, 55 to 60; 24, 60 to 65; 14, 65 to 70; 10, 70 to 75; 8, 75 to 80; 6, 80 to 85; 4, 85 to 90; 3, 90 to 95. In 1840, Anna Handal from Nazareth and Azize, daughter of Moysen Abu Hamut, died 'anno 90 circiter', and to mention a few more names, a Sara Daud reached 75 years of age, an Elisabeth Sadat (1835) 80 and a Rosa Zablat (1839) 85. Proportionally, there are more than a few old people, but no very old ones; whether the record is accurate, however, remains to be seen. It is an incontrovertible fact that the mortality of children is very high; half of the total number of deaths are children that could not even reach the fifth year of life. If it goes well, a child's probable life span is 6 years, and the average life is not much higher than up to 18 ½ years old. Therefore, whoever lives in Bethlehem can make the probable calculation that he will have a shorter life there than others in many places in the West.

Based on this information, it would be possible to figure out the approximate population with the help of an analogy. If one assumes, for instance, that with the high mortality rate, and the numbers are most likely higher, that every year a 24th portion of the Roman Catholic community dies, then that means a total of 1,044 members of the community. But this result differs still very much from the information communicated to me in Bethlehem, without thinking about it for a long time, but which I do not trust: 1,600 Latins, 1,200 Greeks, 200 Armenians and 300 Moslems, together 3,300 inhabitants.[i] If we now turn our attention to the movement of the population, I do not want to hide the fact that the results appear credible only in a very general sense, because the data were mostly drawn from estimates, out of which contradictions necessarily arose. We encounter the first contradiction right at the beginning of our presentation, namely in the last quarter of the fifteenth century. In 1483 the town was quite populated[ii] and, in 1491, not very much.[iii] It is not necessary to assume a contradiction in this case, because in 1489 Bethlehem was laid to waste to a significant degree, which could easily result in a significant decrease in population; in 1491 the town was, in fact, also in a state of destruction. Around the middle of the seventeenth century, there were 130

i   In 1835 (Lustreise 2, 114) I found out that the population of Bethlehem was approaching 4,000. "The population consists of 1,800 Catholics, just as many Greeks, 50 Armenians, approximately 140 Turks. These figures are accurate; I learned them from Catholic priests, and I am passing them on to you for this reason, because the majority of travelers are very mistaken about this point; there are those who put the number of inhabitants as low as 100." Geramb 1, note 166. Obviously, he and I drew from the same source. The population was about 400 to 500 strong. Döbel 2, 126. The Christian population was about 800. Skinner 2, 46. 1,000 to 1,500, mostly Catholics. Röse 452. 800 Christians. Schubert 3, 12. An estimate of 800 taxable men, which indicates a population of more than 3,000 souls. Robinson 2, 381. Roughly 3,000. Rußegger in Preiswerks Morgenland, 1839, 73. A little more than 3,000 souls. Whiting in Calw. Missionsbl., 1842 (1841), 26.

ii   Hodie vero villa est satis populosa. *Fabri* 1, 463 sq.

iii   Kapfman 10: There are not that many people anymore.

families or about 650 persons[i]; in 1725 a populous village[ii]; in 1738 about 200 families,[iii] which equals about 1,000 persons; in 1778 not more than 800 Latins, Armenians, and Maronites, and 7 to 8 Mohammedan families[iv]; in 1784, 600 men, among them 100 Latin Christians.[v] In 1821 one pilgrim estimated 1,500 Orthodox Greeks and 100 Roman Catholics[vi] and another a little over 3,000, including 600 armed Christians.[vii] In 1827, one noted that there were 7,000 inhabitants[viii] and in 1829 only about 1,000 Roman Catholics, 1,000 Greeks, 30 Armenian and 40 Moslem families.[ix] From this historical overview, it is clear that towards the end of the fifteenth century the population was weak in number, that the greater increase falls in the period from the middle of the seventeenth century to the year 1725, but that also from the year 1784 to 1845 there was a considerable increase, whereby an approximate doubling of the population took place. If from 1725 or 1738 to 1784 the numbers stayed nearly the same, the natural explanation for that is found in the fact that at the time the Bethlehemites had been depleted from wars.

---

i   *Surius* 522. Ignaz von Rheinfelden wrote 10 years later: 200 inhabitants (127). Probably a transcription error.

ii   Neret 111.

iii   Korte 117.

iv   Binos, note 205.

v   Bolney 2, note 240. When Richardson some thirty years ago said (Raumer 308) that Bethlehem had more than 300 inhabitants, he deserves to be trusted on account of his imprecision about just as much as if he had said this: more than three souls; both are true.

vi   Scholz 194, 206.

vii   Berggren 3, 145.

viii *Failoni* 116. Hailbronner (2,298) says the same thing.

ix   Prokesch 113. Copied by Salzbacher (2, 166).

CHAPTER 6

Inhabitants, Race, Mortality Rate, Population, National and Confessional Diversity, Traditional Dress, Foods

From the foregoing, one sees that the population of Bethlehem is a rather mixed one; only the national and denominational components need to be explicated in more detail. It goes without saying that the Moslem from here could not be indifferent to the place where his prophets Dawood (David) and Issa (Jesus) were born, and we find him again and again as an inhabitant of the city, even if he disappeared more than once. One can declare as an established fact that at the time of the Frankish kingdom no Mohammedans were settled in Bethlehem ; even after 1187 they did not actually live there, though they did set up camp there from which they could threaten the Christians. Towards the middle of the fourteenth century, only a few Bethlehemites professed Mohammedanism.[i] In 1483, the Moslems, i.e., the Saracens and Arabs, were a small portion of the population.[ii] Even in the first quarter of the sixteenth century, there were

---

i   Rudolph von Suchen 843.
ii   *Fabri.*

few Saracens.[i] In 1565 a number of 'Moors' (Arabs) lived near or not far from the place.[ii] In 1586, however, the Arabs or Mohammedans seem to have constituted the largest part of the population.[iii] That was the case at least in 1613.[iv] A few decades passed, however, and the crescent faded a little in Bethlehem and then more and more. As early as 1646, the Mohammedans constituted only half of the population,[v] and it was about the same in 1673.[vi] In 1719, there were poor Moslem families,[vii] and by 1734, they were already outnumbered by Christians.[viii] The wars that were fought later seem to have decimated the Mohammedans; for in 1751 only Roman Catholic Christians and Mohammedans were named as inhabitants of Bethlehem.[ix] In twenty-seven years, however, the ratio was reversed, such that only seven to eight Mohammedan families lived there, in contrast to the eight hundred Christians.[x] The many feuds therefore seem to have taken on a more-or-less confessional coloration of Islam and Christianity, and the latter finally emerged victorious; for from then on, the Mohammedans only grouped themselves into a small cluster; for example, in 1818 they numbered only two families.[xi] That in 1831 the Christians,

---

i   Viagg. al S. Sepolcro F 6. Tschudi 271.

ii Helffrich 718.

iii Schwallart 302.

iv Amman 120. Scheidt (69) also said that the inhabitants were mostly Arabs. Cf. Ignaz von Rheinfelden (127), who probably copied an older pilgrim.

v   *Surius* 522. Zwinner reports (355) only "Turkish" peasants, Greeks, and Roman Catholics, without mentioning any reciprocal relations.

vi Habitata da Turchi, ma forse da Christiani in maggior numero. *Legrenzi* 1, 185.

vii *Ladoire* 206. *adoire* 206.

viii Thomson p. 89.

ix Hasselquist 166. Admittedly striking, because the Greeks had a monastery (167).

x   Binos 205. Cf. above on p. 45.

xi Sieber 45. De Forbin says he apparently only met Christians (123 in

and, in 1834, Ibrahim Pasha, drove out the Moslem portion of the population, we saw above.[i] Thus, in 1834 and 1838 only Christians were to be found.[ii] Since then, however, the Mohammedans have crept back again among the population,[iii] so that their number is large in relation to the period of the new immigration. Apparently, the immigrants were mostly people who had been expelled; for I was informed that the Moslems, who alone inhabit the Harit al-Fawaghreh, had immigrated from the area of Hebron, from Faghour. When they arrived is not known.

In the eleventh century, only Christians lived in Bethlehem.[iv] What kind of Christians lived here after the capture of this city by Saladin, history does not say, but probably they were Syrians, who also guarded the Church of the Holy Sepulchre. They were, of course, under the jurisdiction of the Saracens.[v] Nor is much more provided in 1336, beyond that the majority of the inhabitants were Syrian Christians; one was content to state: Christians who did not belong to the Roman Catholic Church.[vi] Later, it was deemed sufficient to consider the Christians in a general sense.[vii] In 1483 the greater part of the inhabitants was Oriental (or, what must have at the time been one group, Syrians) Christians, who were allied with the Saracens 'and' Arabs.[viii] In 1519 there were a

---

Joliffe). More in 1829. See p. 46.

i   P. 41.

ii   Robinson 2, 381.

iii   It is doubtlessly a transcription error when Strauß (Sinai and Golgotha. Berlin 1847. P. 287) says that Bethlehem is supposedly only inhabited by Christians.

iv   *Guil. Tyr.* 1, 6.

v   Thetmar in Maltens Weltkd., Febr. 1844, 192. I will return to the treacherous agreement of the Syrian Christians with the Saracens later.

vi   *Baldensel* 120. Rudolph von Suchen's expression is even more general.

vii   La città (Betlemme) siede quasi guasta tutta, e le case dove i cristiani stanno se l'hanno rifatte. F. Nicolò da Poggibonizzi in Poggi, Sigoli's edition (37).

viii *Fabri* l. c. Medschir ed-Dîn says (135) in general that most of the inhab-

lot of St. Thomas Christians,[i] who could be easily confused with the Syrian Christians. In 1565 it was only said that Bethlehem was inhabited mainly by Christians.[ii] One may consider these all the more likely to have been Syrian, as such, many of whom lived among the poor Moors, and whose presence was certainly made note of in 1586.[iii] The Christians mentioned in 1613[iv] were undoubtedly also Syrian Christians, of whom some were reported for the last time, as far as I know, after the middle of the seventeenth century.[v] The decrease of the Syrian Christians in Bethlehem coincides with their diminished importance in Jerusalem. Besides the Syrian Christians, as far as my research indicates, it was first the Greeks who had a permanent home in Bethlehem; perhaps among them were some defectors from the side of the Syrian Christians. I could not find the Christians from before the second quarter of the seventeenth century.[vi] From that time on, the Greeks remained, as far as the original findings that were accessible to me indicated, until the middle of the last century,[vii] when they were at least not recalled.[viii] In 1778 the Greeks again resided in Bethlehem,[ix] and in 1800, along with the Armenians, they constituted the majority of the population.[x] That the Greek community was later a significant one and still is today, we know from what has already been said. The example of

---

itants are Christian.

i   Tschudi 271. Before him the author of the Viagg. al S. Sepolcro spoke only of Christians in general.

ii Helffrich 718.

iii "Christians called Surians," while there is absolutely no mention of any other Christian community. Schwallart 302.

iv Amman 120.

v   Christians known as Surians. Troilo 388.

vi *Surius* 522.

vii Zwinner 355. Troilo. *Legrenzi* 1, 186. (Mirike ignores this. 66.) *Ladoire* 206. Mostly Greeks and Armenians. Thomson p. 89.

viii Hasselquist 166.

ix Binos.

x   Wittman 71.

the Greeks must have impacted the Roman Catholics. In 1646 the Franciscans had thirty Greek converted families[i]; prior to that, no writer mentions a Latin community, and its emergence apparently occurred between 1625 and 1646. This community could not enjoy an uninterrupted existence either,[ii] although there were many 'popes' around the year 1670.[iii] In 1674 at least fifty families of good Catholics were counted according to the Roman rite.[iv]

In 1719 it was reported that the population consisted of Turkish, Greek, and Maronite families,[v] without so much as a word uttered about the Roman Catholics. In 1734 others were noted, but not these Christians.[vi] No light is shed until 1751, when alongside the Mohammedans and Arab peasants,[vii] the Roman Catholics were made mention of, as if they were the only Christians of Bethlehem. Later, the pilgrims more often[viii] remembered the native Roman Catholics, who henceforth form the main Christian community in Bethlehem, and who maintain control.[ix] To those who like to gaze at constellations, we do not want to begrudge the pleasure he might have in asserting that the Bethlehemites originate from the tribe of

i Les autres (80 families) Grecs, desquelles 30. Familles sont converties par nos Religieux à l'Eglise Romaine. *Surius* 522. Mirike says that Maronites were united with their church through the diligence of the Roman-minded (66).

ii Zwinner. *Legrenzi*.

iii Troilo 388.

iv Les Chrestiens etoient preque tous Grecs autrefois. Mais la charité des Peres de la Terre-Sainte, et leur vie plus exemplaire, que celle des autres Religieux des diverses Nations Chrestiennes de cet Orient, en a converty un grand nombre. *Nau* 396.

v *Ladoire* 206.

vi Thomson p. 89.

vii Hasselquist.

viii Binos, Berggren among others.

ix Prokesch 113.

Judah.[i] They themselves judge much more soberly, even if not with the necessary impartiality. According to the legend I heard from Roman Catholics in Bethlehem, descendants of Tekoa live in Harit al-Hreizat; descendants of the Crusaders in Harit al-Farahieh, the Bahri family; in Harit al-Tarajmeh descendants of Venice, who serve as Turjman (interpreters), preferably speak Italian, and are also preferred when employing the service personnel in the Latin monastery. The example of the Greek and Roman Catholics does not seem to have been lost on the Armenians either.

I was not able to find reference to an Armenian community in the Holy City prior to 1673.[ii] In 1734 they made up a significant portion of the population.[iii] In the middle of the last century, the Armenians seem to have disappeared for a while, but in the last quarter of the same century they were in Bethlehem,[iv] and from that time on they have a continuous history in this city, but they never managed to increase to a considerable number. It is said that the Armenians, inhabitants of the Harit al-Najajreh, came from Hebron. We have already met the Maronites, and to what little has been said, I can only add that they also lived in Bethlehem in 1778.[v] Since Hadrian forbade the Jews a permanent settlement in this city,[vi] they rarely settled there, as they had in the time of the Frankish kings.[vii] Later, we learn that in 1565 no Jews came there.[viii] A fondness for Bethlehem drove the Christians to overrun it; with

---

i   Geramb 1, 166.

ii   *Legrenzi.*

iii Thomson. Ladoire also touches upon the Armenians.

iv   Binos.

v   Ladoire and Binos.

vi   See above on p. 32.

vii *Benjamin. Tud.* 48. In the collection of travelogs by Jewish pilgrims, put together by E. Carmoly (Itinéraires de la Terre Sainte. Bruxelles 1847), there is not a single one who visited Bethlehem.

viii Helffrich 718.

their intolerant stance, they seem to have been responsible for the fact that the Jews always had to remain at a distance. Jews from Jerusalem characterize the Christians from Bethlehem as treating them badly. During my visit to Bethlehem, I took a Jew with me, who, without much ado, found an inn in the Mohammedan quarter, but I noticed how unwelcome he was by the Christians in Bethlehem. It is for this reason, and also that of his expendability, that the following day I was moved to send back to Jerusalem the Jew, the appearance of which is a rare occurrence in this holy place for Christians, who I had brought with me.

The traditional dress of the Bethlehemites is very simple.[i] Because after the description[ii] of the city Jerusalem, I also covered in detail the dress of the people, I cannot be reproached for not going into the matter extensively here. I therefore limit myself to only a few descriptions. The woman or girl wears a blue shirt, over it a red tunic,[iii] a sooty white veil,[iv] and goes about with her face uncovered[v] and barefoot.[vi] Apart from the veil, I cannot claim that the people were dressed in an unclean way or that more could be found there than in other places. Clothes of ragged appearance still stood out.[vii] On the contrary, people are

---

i   Extremely easy. Wittman 71. Completely uniform. Hailbronner 2, 297. The copyist 2, 124.

ii   In MS.

iii   A long robe of cotton, tied together with a belt. Wittman. A blue skirt and a red coat, or a blue coat (incorrect). Geramb 2, 175. Light blue shirts with belts, red throws with tunic-like coats. Hailbronner and his copyist.

iv   A large, white veil that hangs down the back. Wittman. Geramb.

v   Berggren falsely remarks (3, 148) that the women only cover themselves with a veil outside of the house.

vi   Somewhat poetically, Hailbronner describes the jewelry as follows: About the forehead and from the ears hangs a garland of real silver coins. Together with bracelets, and these are her few (is this few?) pieces of jewelry.

vii   The lack of water (falsehood) ... causes an extraordinary uncleanliness, which makes the poverty even more daunting. People very rarely wash, which is evident from the linen and the rags that serve them as coverings; everything around here is disgusting. Geramb 1, 172. In rags, hardly covered

dressed quite neatly, and on Christmas there were women in splendid attire. I do not doubt that the cut is a very old one, and it may well be that Ruth of Moabit and Mary of Nazarene were dressed exactly as the Bethlehemites are today, and just as the Virgin is usually depicted in paintings.[i] I therefore in no way envy the fanciful who, at the sight of a Bethlehemite with a small child in her arms, believed that they were seeing Mary with Jesus coming towards him,[ii] though I am not persuaded that the women of Bethlehem can be justly compared to the many women of Europe in their manifold habiliments.

Like the clothing, the diet is more-or-less simple. As it happens, it hardly differs from that of other Palestinians in the vicinity. It was claimed that in his time that Bethlehem actually lived on olive trees.[iii] The prices of food were:

	20 years ago piaster	1845 piaster
1 cantar grapes	9	100
1 rotl wine	1	3[iv]
1 rotl aquavit	2	10
1 rotl honey	8 to 9	24

with some lousy shreds. 1, 168. The uncleanliness is not greater than in other places.

i   Geramb asserts this, adding that even the color is correct. A longer stay would have probably led to the observation that the women in the different parts of Bethlehem, into which people immigrated from different places, did not quite have the same costume. Incidentally, I note that European artists, when depicting our Lady, were hardly thinking of the women of Bethlehem, otherwise there would not be so much distance on the one hand and so much diversity on the other; for example, at a Venetian church I once saw Mary of Nazareth dressed almost entirely according to the new French fashion.

ii   Geramb.

iii   Wittman 71.

iv   I bought ¼ liter for 2 kreutzers.

One must not, therefore, be surprised, when one hears the Bethlemites praise the days of yore before the prices rose nearly beyond belief.

CHAPTER 7

Employment, Crops, Livestock, Beekeeping, Guilds and Trades

The Bethlehemites, although not a very large contingent, once engaged in farming and animal husbandry.[i] In Christian antiquity it was said: In Christ's little town, farming is everything and, apart from the singing of Psalms, there is silence; wherever you turn, the ploughman, with his star in his hand, is singing the Hallelujah, the sweating reaper is refreshing himself with the Psalms, and the vine dresser, pruning the vine with a crooked knife, intones with David.[ii] The tending of the grapevines, which is believed to be reliable, is still a sedulous endeavour. The preparation of wine is carried out this way: With the feet, the grapes are crushed in a large stone trough or pot, and then everything, juice and stems, is put into jars, where it is left to stand for fifteen days. Then the clear or the wine is decanted without pressing, and the rest is distilled into spirits.

---

i   Helffrich 718. Bethlehemians live from agriculture. *Fabri* 1, 463 sq. Some farmers. *De Bruyn* 2, 223.

ii   Paula et Eustochium in letters to Marcella, in the opp. *Hieronymi* and possibly from his letter to Marcella. Cf. *Reland.* 286.

The latter is valued more than a little as is evident by the fact that an excellent fig-wine brandy is made from it.[i] To distil the brandy, a fairly common still with a cooling barrel is used. The wine is stored in large jars (Jara). The brandy is also praised as very good. In the Roman Catholic monastery, the wine is not as strong as it is in the local homes, because the grapes are most likely pressed there. From the wine must a great quantity of dibes (grape syrup) is also prepared. Without letting the must stand, it is put over the fire with a white soil, which is called huwar, in order to remove all impurity and astringency from the juice, and after the first boiling, it is foamed and put aside. Then the decoction is again boiled until the juice reaches the consistency of honey or syrup. Dibes is eaten with bread and other dishes. Beekeeping is an industry of not little import, though in 1844 and 1845, it declined significantly, due to the lack of water and land that had, as a result, suffered. Many bee pots, for which the houses are especially equipped,[ii] are thus seen empty, which previously had been occupied. The bee houses themselves are not baskets but pots (barrels) of about 1' diameter and 2 1/3' length, which are at the back, that is, on the side opposite the entrance, shut with a round closure, and at the front open, but blocked with an earthen disc that has a small opening at the bottom to allow for flight by smearing horse manure on the joint between this and the pot rim. The bee pots are, of course, placed one on top of another, several rows above each other. Where the bees had died out, they were open, and where they were still living, they were closed with the disc. The biggest flight takes place in spring, in the months of March and April, when the flowers are the most plentiful and in August the honey is harvested. In 1778 one noticed the abundance of bees; along

---

i   The last one according to Berggren 3, 146.

ii   See 23 above. The picture I drew of the house shows circles at a niche on top, above the long stairs to the left, which indicate the horizontal bee cylinders.

the cultivated heights, apiaries were seen in great numbers.[i] The honey is extolled as delectable.[ii] That it is white,[iii] I cannot confirm. It is very common in this region,[iv] at least in the most bountiful years. Apparently, flour is mixed with honey and a sort of dough is made with it that the locals serve as a dish.[v] In Bethlehem, there is also more than a little farming of poultry.

Whoever claims that the Bethlehemites are indolent[vi] has not taken the trouble to survey all of its trades. After everything that I saw, I concluded that the Bethlehemites cannot be counted among the lazy, even if it is true that they liked to be served by the women, who tend to the meals, the preparation of the flour, the baking of the bread, the fetching of water for the household's needs,[vii] which in the end is only due to the, I admit, somewhat rigid customs of the Orient in and around Jerusalem. The survey of the trades will provide evidence that something is done after all. Of all the trades the most popular was the making of trinkets from the cave in

---

i   Binos 213.

ii Binos.

iii The honey is especially celebrated for being white and delicious. Scholz 143.

iv Binos.

v   Binos.

vi Geramb calls (5, 167) the Christians in Bethlehem very indolent, because mostly the Turkish tyrants profit from the fruits of their labor. "I do not believe," he then continues, "that a theater play can ever excite more abhorrence and disgust than to see these people…to see them strolling about idly in the square, or sitting by some dilapidated house, ridding themselves of the vermin which nearly consumes them (168)." Highly exaggerated. Yes, indeed, the Bethlehemians are, especially if one takes into account their Palestinian origin, rather industrious than sluggish. I saw neither any disgustingly idle strolling in public places, unless on a feast day in the Latin monastery, nor any vermin hunting. Geramb should have trusted the influence of the Franciscans more. Cf. Johann Adam Henßinger in the Swabian Merkur, 1844, Nr. 48. Alongside with me, Whiting (Calw. Missionsbl., 1842, 26) also calls Bethlehemians industrious.

vii Nowhere have I seen women work so much as in Bethlehem. They alone take care of everything in the house. Geramb 1, 169.

which Mary took refuge[i]: red, yellow, white, green, black rosaries; medallions; crosses; crucifixes; images of Christ; the depictions featured the birth of the Lord, the visit of the heavenly hosts to the Shepherds' Field, Christ in the cradle, the adoration of the Wise Men from the East, the flight to Egypt (with a barbaric Italian inscription), the Annunciation, the sacrifice in the temple, or scenes from the Advent and Passion, the Way of Sorrows as well as the resurrection and ascension of the Lord; in other instances the image of the stepfather Joseph, the twelve apostles, each within a circle; St. Jerome[ii] and other saints; also the crib,[iii] the Burial Chapel,[iv] even tables for supping.[v] The workers borrow the drawings from copperplate engravings that they receive from the Latin monastery.[vi] I have heard extolled the erudition and skill of the people of Bethlehem in these artistic matters, and indeed, commemorative carvings of a very delicate, delightful sort are made.[vii] The majority of these are very clumsily done, and the nose, especially, exceeds all measure. The sculptural representation

---

i   It is not correct what Sieber says (119) that the countrymen in Bethlehem live exclusively from the production of crucifixes, rosaries, etc., when their little field work is done; likewise Schubert (3,13): The inhabitants' activities are completely directed toward the preparation of Christmas gifts. This time Geramb was being fair, noting (1, 169) that the production of rosaries and the like is the main, not to say the only, occupation. Cf. *Nau* 396, *Light* 168. Hommes, femmes, enfants tout le monde y travaille...Les femmes et les enfants enfilent les grains de chapelets, les rangent ou plutôt les entassent autour d'eux. *Marmier* 2, 301.

ii   Schubert 3, note 13.

iii   De Forbin 124.

iv   Robinson 2, 382. In the past they also carved the Church of the Holy Sepulchre, the Church of the Virgin Mary, and the Cave of the Nativity avec tant de justesse, qu'il n'y manque pas un pillier, ny la moindre colonne. *Nau* 396 sq.

v   Schubert 3, 13.

vi   Sieber, Berggren.

vii   Among the jars, boxes, bowls, and plates, one sees many whose semi-sublime works reveal real talent and artistry; especially those made for the Latin monastery in Bethlehem and Jerusalem by Latin Christians. Schubert. An otherwise competent judge, Prokesch (118) saw diligence and effort, but no artistry.

of the Chapel of the Tomb of Christ, I liked best. Whoever comes
to possess one will not only remember very vividly the real chapel
but will also have an accurate picture of local artistic endeavours.
In any event, the best or most contrived works from among such
articles come from Bethlehem.[i] The Bethlehemites may not always
be guided by the best taste, since the Armenian pilgrims pay more
attention to how colourful a work is than how refined.[ii] The main
material used for artistic objects, mostly of cross or shield shape,
are the shells of the oriental pearl or mother-of-pearl. For more
expensive things, gypsum is used; instead of black coral, mineral
pitch from the Dead Sea, whose raw materials are also used to
make beautiful drinking vessels inscribed with sayings from the
Koran,[iii] or wood from fig trees that has been stained black.[iv] The
workers make a point of laying out the artefacts so that the black
colour stands out against the white. For small works, they use
black coral from several species of horn coral, even from the
expensive, genuine *Antipathes gorgonias*.[v] They are very adept at
putting mother-of-pearl on everything they make of wood, such
as on the base of the oriental dining table that is something akin
to a footstool.[vi] In the century before last, only wood was used.[vii]
Fruits were rarely used as art objects; the colourful beads of rosaries
are usually made from the fruit of the doum palm or from the
seeds of the small brown date. Only rarely do we see them made
from an animal tooth substance, from ivory or the teeth of
manatees. For the crucifixes, more frequent use is made of a

---

i   Robinson.
ii Schubert.
iii Prokesch 118. I own one of those vessels with a beautiful Arabic script.
iv Les habitants du village se livrent à l'innocente industrie de polir le fruit du zaccoum et de l'olivier pour en composer des rosaires. *Reynaud* 227.
v   Schubert 3, 14.
vi Berggren. Schubert 3, 13.
vii Le travail est plus cher que la matiere: car tout n'est que de bois, avec quelques ornemens de nacres de perles, et d'os blanc en façon d'yvoir. Tout cela se fait presque avec le coûteau et le canif. *Nau* 397.

pressed animal leather of great durability and thickness and whose origin was no longer recognizable, and allegedly may have been even from horn of a rhinoceros. The seeds of some pod plants from Arabia, unrecognizable in their artificial form, and different sorts of very firm types of wood, including the wood from the olive tree, are also used.[i] The number of craftsmen (sadaf) engaged in this line of work is estimated at four hundred. Once the objects come out of their hands, they are blessed by a priest, either in Bethlehem,[ii] or at the Tomb of Jesus.[iii] If the objects are not sold directly at the site where they are produced, the Bethlehemites, and the women especially, take them to the market in Jerusalem[iv] or peddle them in this city as well, or in the Latin monastery at least. The line of business in question is not very old. I find the first mention of it in 1586. It was the Syrian Christians who made wooden paternosters, little crosses from the olive tree and from the wood of cedars and other such things, decorated them with relics or other strange things and sold them to the pilgrims.[v] In 1595 they made not only crosses and rosary beads from the olive tree, and the latter also from the terebinth, but also other works of art, such as the Church of the Holy Sepulchre and the crib.[vi] If it is true that in 1616 all the inhabitants were shepherds,[vii] then it is reasonable to believe that this occupation was on the decline. Be that as it may, in 1646, the newly converted Latin Christians were busy making crosses, rosaries, monuments, and cribs.[viii] A few decades later, the Arabs learned from the Christians, who made little crosses out of the wood from olive and cedar trees, rosaries,

---

i   Schubert 3, note 14. Cf. Robinson.
ii And sprinkled with holy water. Korte 126. Cf. *Nau* 396.
iii Korte and de Forbin.
iv Schubert 3, 13.
v   Schwallert 302.
vi *Cotov.* 239.
vii Della Valle 1, 157.
viii *Surius* 522.

the model of the Tomb of Jesus and the crib, and the latter of which was inlaid with mother-of-pearls and turtle shells in an extremely graceful and delicate manner, because they saw before them the lucrative nature of the trade, such that they even taught the craft to their wives and children; for the Mohammedans also used rosaries of a hundred pearls.[i] The zeal of the Moslems seems to have soon cooled down again[ii]; at least it was expressly noted in 1681 that only the few Christians of Bethlehem earned their living by making crosses, Tombs of Christ and even, owing to their fortitude, knew very well how to depict the entire Church of the Holy Sepulchre.[iii] Over a century ago, this line of work was so profitable,[iv] and sales were so high,[v] that probably too many Christians and Mohammedans[vi] were tempted to turn to it.[vii] Hence, in the middle of the last century, there was a surplus of manufactured goods, and Bethlehem's population, consisting of Christians and Moslems, compelled the local Franciscans to buy rosaries, models of the Tomb of Christ, and the like from them. In fact, this unhappy state of affairs, that not as many goods (rosaries) would be sold as were produced, made it necessary, not long after, for the people of Bethlehem to turn their creative forces more to

---

i   Troilo, note 388. Ignorant of history, Geramb writes (1, 168): "The price of rosaries has increased because of the increase of Greek and Armenian pilgrims...and also since the Turks have taken to wearing a rosary of kinds, which seems to have become necessary to complete their attire, and which they even use in the streets as a kind of toy."

ii Nau (396) even counted the Mohammedans among the makers of rosaries.

iii De Bruyn 2, 223. This critic, an artist, is competent, and since that time, the craft seems to have made little to no progress. A few years later, Mirike (67) wrote that the inhabitants, by which one can also understand the Arabs, made their living partially by making crosses and rose wreaths etc. from olive and terebinth wood; he and his traveling party bought many such items and brought them to Constantinople.

iv Quite profitable. Thompson §. 89.

v   Neret.

vi Neret.

vii Manufacture is supposedly the sole occupation of all the village inhabitants. Hasselquist 171.

agriculture again.[i] The high point of this industry seems to have been during the first half of the last century,[ii] in which, among other already known art objects, the Tomb of Our Beloved Lady was made from wood from the Shepherds' Field, of white bones like ivory[iii] as well as the Grotto of Bethlehem from wood with pristine arrangements of mother-of-pearl.[iv] As far as I know, Bethlehem does not trade in anything other than these commodities. Sales are not particularly high but are nonetheless significant. In the third quarter of the seventeenth century, the Mohammedans, in particular, took pains to provide an outlet for these industrial goods. They amassed large quantities of rosaries and built trade connections with Cairo in order to promote them during the great caravans to Mecca.[v] Even today, the rosaries of Bethlehem or Jerusalem are so well subscribed by the Turks in Constantinople that they are brought there as merchandise. As for the Christians, in the last century, ordinary merchants in Akra bought the devotional wares, packed them in a box, delivered them to Venice, and from there they went to the rest of Europe, especially to the German countries.[vi] Some of the goods were sold directly to the pilgrims who were visiting Bethlehem. Monconys bought 50 rosaries, 2 sanctuaries and 56 crosses.[vii] The prices, it is said, were set unequally at various times; after the middle of the [end of page century before last, very low.[viii] Later, it was said, that crosses had a price of 3 to 4 thalers, the Burial Chapel, a price of 15 to 20 thalers, and that, though it is hard to believe, Bethlehem

---

i   Bolney 2, 241.

ii   Great many things are made in Bethlehem, from small to big crosses. Korte 125.

iii   Neret.

iv   Korte.

v   Troilo.

vi   *Mariti* 2, 369.

vii   1, 315. Cf. p. 62, note 2.

viii Sold at low, negligible price. Troilo.

delivered devotional goods for 3 to 4000 thalers annually.[i] In our century, the prices may very well rise somewhat higher than they were at the time when the trade,[ii] because of the glut of goods and because of a reduction in sales, came to a standstill; one may not claim that they are only expensive, especially when the great pilgrimage is over. A very small cross is given away for 2 fuddah, i.e., not even a penny. I do not want to leave unmentioned that the Minorites now sell the keepsakes almost as cheaply as the workers themselves do.[iii] We now leave this strange industry, for which Bethlehem is certainly the main place in Palestine, to have a look at the gunsmiths. Few Bethlehemites make rifles and sabres, and the shotguns of Bethlehem are prized, perhaps because of the dainty stock. Moreover, one finds carpenters, joiners, stone builders, masons, potters, shoemakers, cotton beaters, butchers. Large mills are not found in Bethlehem, and the housewives are, as stated, the millers. For the preparation of flour, a hand mill is used, which consists of two stones. The lower one is stationary, while the upper one is turned around in a circle. To prevent the runner from deviating during this movement, the lower stone has a [end of page long iron pin, like a fishing rod, which engages through the opening of a short wooden crossbar fixed in the middle of the upper stone. The rotor has not only such a little wooden piece to guide the passage of the pin but also two, half disc-shaped openings next to it, which allow the grain to fall into the mill.[iv] The rotor that I measured was 15 ½" in diameter and 1 ½" thick. And to make the turning of the rotor or grinding easier, on one side on top, a 6" long wooden handle is left vertically in the stone for the hand to grasp. The lower stone is set in baked clay and has a small low depression on one side into which the flour slides. The grain is ground twice until it is suitable for baking.

---

i   *Nau* 397.

ii Geramb in note 6 to p. 61.

iii Schubert 3, 15.

iv Robinson also describes (2, note 405) the hand mills near Bethlehem, and says that between both stones there is a small arch.

The whole mill came from near Gaza, and such a mill costs 60 to 80 piasters. I observed a woman milling on Sundays without incurring offense. A related task that belongs to women is the baking of bread. The bakehouses, as I mentioned above, are constructed in such a way that is unique to there. They are vaulted, to a height not as tall as a man, but with a low entrance, such that the person entering is forced to duck their head. Inside, in the middle, the stove, which stands on the floor, occupies so much space that at most there is room for six to eight people. This stove has the shape of a half-spherical cap with a peak. Its circumference is 9' and its height to the lid is 7". This hollow hemisphere is made of pottery without a bottom, and with a lid that has an upright little piece of wood at the top centre for touching, for picking it up and down. The floor in the oven is covered with small, angular limestones about a few inches high that are not secured firmly with mortar. They not only give the bottom of the loaves an angular appearance, but when the latter are removed, they probably stay attached and thus go along with them. Bricks that have burnt out are replaced by others. Dung is used to heat the oven, but it is not on the inside. It is instead placed around the outside of the entire oven pot, as well as over the lid, and allowed to burn in this position, which heats the oven, even the stones on the bottom, to such a degree that the bottom of the cakes or breads burn easily. For baking, the dough is placed in a wooden bowl, the oven lid is lifted up, the cakes (round) are shaped alike and placed one after another in the oven until its bottom is covered, whereupon the lid is put back on. There is room for seven to eight cakes or loaves on the bottom. After three minutes, the bread is baked, it is taken out, and the baking continues in the same way as long as there is dough, or the oven is warm enough. I can affirm that the bread of the Bethlehem women tastes good. In 1738 a traveller observed something particular about the ovens, and the comparison of his report with mine is too interesting for me to resist the thrill of adding to that more than hundred-year-old report here. It reads: '(In Bethlehem) the ovens are generally built deep into the earth and covered with a transversal arch. On a staircase with a few steps, one descends to the door, through which one enters. In the middle, there is a pyramid of hot ashes, which are usually brought there from the houses. This is placed on a large earthenware dish, which is covered and half full of small stones, which, I believe, have turned fire-red by the heat. Once a week, the ashes are all taken away, and replaced with others, which are kept at a certain degree of heat and are frequently (?) changed. When one wants to bake cakes, one puts away the ash on top, lifts off the lid and puts the dough on it, puts the lid on top again, and covers it with ash on top. I was told that the Arabs once kept a captured pilgrim very warm in such an oven'.[i]

It is said that the inhabitants of Bethlehem roam about as carters and riding messengers and that it would be rare to find a guide bolder than a Bethlehemite,[ii] the latter of which I would not doubt. There are more than a few shopkeepers, and for one's needs they provide quite a bit. At their shops one can find not only finely cut tobacco and cloth goods, but also victuals, figs, raisins, dibes, oranges, flour, rice and so on. Bethlehem is the uttermost place of provisioning for the sons of the desert. Nowadays, in Bethlehem no one is engaged in tattooing (tâk), as they were in the last and previous centuries, nor are there, as there were in the twelfth century, any dyers, of which twelve Jewish ones were then counted.[iii] I may have passed over another tanner because I remember having seen an animal skin spread out on the market street, which probably had to endure the shortest process of tanning possible.

---

i   Pococke 2, par. 53.
ii Berggren 3, 146.
iii *Benjam. Tud.* 48.

CHAPTER 8

Language, Manners and Customs, Moral Character, Public Authorities

It goes without saying that the inhabitants speak Arabic, but it is noteworthy that some Latin Christians express themselves reasonably well in Italian. This is attributed to the influence of the Roman Catholic monks, but that can only be justly said in relation to the more recent past. It is curious that the inhabitants spoke Italian before they had converted to the Roman Catholic Church. In 1586 almost all Syrian Christians spoke some Italian, which they called 'Franco', taught it to their children, and thus transplanted this language from children to children's children, so that they could later serve as interpreters for the foreigners.[i] Towards the end of the sixteenth century, it was the same or similar.[ii] After the middle of the century before last, not only the Syrians, but also the many Roman Christians spoke Italian, some of whom were designated as interpreters for foreigners.[iii]

---

i   Schwallart 302.

ii *Cotov.* 239. Similar in Amman (120), Surius (522).

iii Which you must have with you and use often while you travel or go anywhere. Troilo 388. Il n'y a gueres d'hommes parmy ces Catholiques, qui

I cannot say enough about how friendly it is for the foreigner when he hears the Frankish language from the mouths of the natives.

In a place where property is not very secure because of bad government, where feuds and wars are not rare, where now and then there is a lack of sufficient rain, where industry is also subject to its vicissitudes, when, for example, if for some reason only a small number of pilgrims come, one cannot take for granted the prosperity of the inhabitants. It is very credible when, especially in the sixteenth century, people complained about the poverty of the people of Bethlehem.[i] In our times, it has been stressed that the population is particularly poor,[ii] but this assertation comes partly at the expense of the truth. Although one cannot deny that poverty resides in Bethlehem, the misery is not so terribly great. That some have made themselves poor through their inordinate generosity towards friendly visitors[iii] should not be believed without question. Under the current government, the population of Bethlehem is obviously too large to be supported by the land. Industry led to an artificial increase of the population. When the farming sector is hit by a bad year and the industrial sector by poor sales of manufactured goods, poverty can reach an alarming level. It is highly probable that this confluence of misfortunes is rare, and it often happens that the luck of the farmer and the worker changes, so that the one may reach out to the other in misfortune.

If one opens the chapter on customs and traditions, there

---

ne sçavent l'Italien, et qui ne servent de Truchemens. *Nau* 396.

i Helffrich 718. At least the Arabs. Schwallart. Very poor. *Cotov.* In the last century, Ladoire (206) called the inhabitants poor.

ii Geramb 1, 173. Indeed, the misery that lives here under the ruins, looking out of the mud huts, seems to say: We are finished (it takes time, Professor). And yet the people are cheerful (Because - they seem to be finished, "all his miserable families"). Schubert 3, note 11.

iii Whiting in Calw. Missionsbl., 1842, 26.

would be much to learn, and for good reasons I will be brief here. About a decade and a half ago, one could not find enough words to describe the pressure that women have had to endure.[i] The woman, it was said, had to fetch the man's water from far away, warm it, wash his feet, then prepare the evening meal, serve him and the eldest son standing up, without taking the least part in the meal, and wait until they are finished in order to be allowed to move to the side and eat the leftovers alone.[ii] I was witness to the latter scene, against which the feelings that I brought with me reacted so mightily, but I would not like to remain silent about the fact that, generally speaking, oriental customs prefer it to be this way. Also, disconcerting is that parents betroth their children when they are only two or one year old or even younger.[iii] An Arab had a daughter who was not yet even fifteen days old that he had betrothed to a four year old. The boy's father buys the girl, agrees on the price, and immediately pays part of it as a premium. The more daughters the father has, the richer he is. One often hears the words: 'My wife cost me so and so much; that is probably a high price'. A maker of rosaries answered to inquiries: 'I paid 800 piastres for my wife. The price of the mother? 400 piastres; but back then the piastres were worth more'. Part of the premium is used by the recipients to purchase some cleaning equipment for the betrothed daughter. At the wedding, people dress up gaudily in brightly coloured robes and abandon themselves to dancing and other amusements.[iv] The funeral services have something

---

i   Cf. above on p. 57.

ii   Geramb 1, 171.

iii   Geramb (whom I follow here) 1, 176. Wittman says (71) that the Bethlehemians are betrothed when they are in their cradles, and marry at the age of 12.

iv   A crowd of peasantry was assembled to celebrate a marriage…The females were chiefly girls, dressed in a profusion of colored garments, with uncovered faces, displaying great beauty, and features not entirely Syrian… They ceased their concert of voices, accompanied with clapping of hand and quick motion of the bodies, on my arrival. *Light* 166.

strange or pagan about them, as I learned on my first trip to Palestine.[i] On the day of the funeral, the women come to the grave to dance, cry, jump, scream. On certain days of the month in which the funeral took place, at the cemetery they repeat their movements, their cries, and their lamentations. One of the women speaks for two minutes, while the others listen in silence; then, at a certain signal, they start the movements and the screaming again, which lasts until exhaustion forces them to stop. Latin speakers, who are very well acquainted with Arabic, say that this is a language particular to women, which even their husbands do not understand. Despite all the admonitions from the Franciscans, this practice has not ceased.[ii] I saw and heard something very similar in the Moslem village of Silwan. In 1483 all the Saracens, both men and women, followed a female corpse with a marvellous and terrible screaming and howling, and they wrung their hands together over their heads, believing that the dead were very hostile to the living.[iii]

As for religious or moral character, it is somewhat difficult to judge. In terms of true Christian piety, however, Bethlehem's Christianity seems to be oriented more externally than internally[iv]; the pressure that stems in part from the Arabs or Moslems who surround them, must not even slightly mollify judgment of them. The restless[v] or uncouth nature probably arises from the position they have to or had to take up in the face of antagonistic enemies, and from the wars themselves which they sometimes waged. The campaigns or expeditions

---

i   Lustreise 2, 175.

ii   Geramb 1, 179.

iii *Fabri* 1, 479 sq.

iv   Christians by rote only. Johann Adam Henßinger in Swabian Merkur, 1844, Nr. 48. All the inhabitants of Bethlehem currently profess to be Christians, but what do they know about Christ? They know no more about him, the savior, about sin, about the retriever of the lost divine image, than the Mohammedans around them. Herschell 154. Zelotisch.

v   Prokesch 113. Turbulent. Hailbronner 2, 298.

have awakened a certain self-confidence in the Bethlehemite Christians, who are, as they were in 1829,[i] still allowed to bear arms today, and no one will deny their bravery.[ii] When I went with Bethlehemites to Khirbeit Khraitoon and the three ponds, they appeared everywhere with a marked confidence against the Mohammedans, and my prejudice, which I had harboured in the beginning, as if they would not be brave enough and would not provide enough protection against possible re-enactments from the side of the Moslems, I soon put aside. They say that in 1778 there was a family of one hundred-strong persons with such unity and courage that they alone repulsed four hundred enemies who had attacked them.[iii] If in our day friction between the various Christian communities, which is most likely incited by idle clergymen, is not uncommon, and was not particularly so in former times, history preserves for us traces of harmony, of accord, among the various co-religionists,[iv] especially in the last century, that are very beautiful.[v] Especially the Roman Catholic Christians, whom I have visited in a number of homes, are less bigoted than some other Christians of Palestine[vi]; they are even friendly towards the foreigner, and I have become fond of them.

Christians in Bethlehem made it known[vii] that a closer bond

---

i Prokesch.

ii Kühn. Whiting a. a. D.

iii Binos 206.

iv Ils (Christians and Mohammedans) vivent entre eux de bon accord pour se maintenir dans leurs droits. *Nau* 396.

v Familles Turques, Grecques, Armeniennes et Maronites, lesquelles, quoique de differentes Religions, vivent de bonne intelligence. *Ladoire* 206. The Bethlemians argue among themselves, but not because of religion; that is why Mohammedans and Christians live peacefully next to each other. Hasselquist 170. Bolney 2, 241. Around 1778 the Christians held together faithfully. Binos. Light was told (167): that they (three parties) lived in great harmony among each other.

vi And more independent than the inhabitants of Jerusalem. Whiting a. a. D.

vii Schubert 3, 16.

connected us and how they observed that I breath more freely.[i] When I was amongst only them, I was imbued with a pleasant feeling. The peculiar vigilance over the chastity of the virgins or over the virtue of the women has to be discussed in a little more detail. In 1738 it was generally reported that the women behaved well and better than in other places.[ii] These days, if it was said that touching a girl or a woman, taking her hand, was a crime that would roil the entire place,[iii] I think that would be going too far; it could be the case, though, if it were a Mohammedan who did the touching. According to my inquiries, unchastity is punished inexorably with death by the people's court; the disgrace must be extinguished by blood[iv]; the belly of the fallen girl is cut open with a khanjar.[v] Around 1822, one Mohammedan was noticed in one of the neighbouring caves. Unfortunately, the widow of a Roman Catholic Bethlehemite, who was famous for her beauty, was also there. That is why such a clamour was made. The Moslem turned tail, and the young, frightened woman fled to the Franciscans. The crowd that had been locked out forced their way into the monastery. Despite the monks' efforts to protect the woman, she was snatched away and dragged to a public place. There she sought to caste off suspicions; the father and brothers who were present were the most insistent that she meet her ruin; the father kills her, and the brothers dip their hands in the blood, thinking that in this way they will erase the stain from the family. The twitching remains are torn apart by the mob.[vi] Nowhere else in the world do they praise

---

i Where one can certainly enjoy and refresh oneself, because one can exercise a greater degree of freedom here than in Jerusalem. Troilo 400. It is the only place in Palestine where the Christians enjoy a certain freedom. Binos 206.

ii Pococke 2 par. 51.

iii Sieber 46.

iv Geramb 1, 177. Cf. above p. 35.

v Sieber.

vi Geramb 1, 177 ff. This might have been exaggerated.

moral purity,[i] the chaste seclusion of the women and virgins,[ii] like they do here today; I see little virtue under the crushing force of barbarism. True virtue without freedom is impossible. But where is freedom possible when suspicion can so easily kill? Faced with such severe punishment, is it any wonder that the women of Bethlehem withdraw? It could also be said that a thief who sits in a dungeon is a good man because he does not steal there. More astonishing is that the women of Bethlehem still commit indiscretions, even if very rarely, as generally, in accordance with the prevailing moral rigidity, the virgins of the Orient only very rarely allow the flower of their honour to be plucked; death would potentially await those who did. Not long ago [end if page the people of Bethlehem had a feud with their neighbours, because one of the latter had committed adultery with a woman of Bethlehem, and it ended with revenge and bloodshed. A custom to the contrary is also reported about Bethlehem; fornication, particularly around Christmas, takes place under the cloak of sanctity.[iii] I will return to this intimation in the Chapel of the Nativity, and here I will only add that I did not notice any fornication, but perhaps because I did not choose more solitary hours to visit the chapel on Christmas Eve, did not go to the great Church of St. Mary at all, and did not attend the Greek Christmas festival. As a side note, it is said, as if it were an indubitable fact, that during Holy Week the women of Bethlehem visit the Church of the Holy Sepulchre in Jerusalem at night time and there gladly betray the chastity that at home is so strictly guarded.[iv]

In 1821 a number of counterfeiters were arrested without

---

i   Geramb 1, 177.

ii   Schubert 3, 16.

iii   Scholz 225.

iv   Noting that the facial features of the Bethlehem women were not entirely Syrian, Light presses the heavy charge: Scandal account for this by the numerous strangers who visit Bethlehem during the holy week (166).

disturbing the peace.[i]

Let us now turn to the authorities of Bethlehem. The highest command is entrusted to a Molsem shah who lives at the uppermost part of town in the west. In 1814 three groups of Christians and the rest of the Mohammedans were under a Christian shah and did not experience too much pressure from the Turkish authorities. He was allied with Abu Ghosh of St. Jeremias, and on demand, he was able to put in the field a hundred men equipped with firearms.[ii] In addition to a shah today there is still a Christian governing body of sixteen members. Members are replaced by a sort of succession. If the father dies and leaves sons behind, one of them always takes his place, the selection of which is left to the governing body or the community council. The government does not get involved in this matter. The newly elected person or successor takes office on the day of his father's funeral, which he does by putting on a new robe at his father's grave. A kind of church council, presided over by the father of the Roman Catholic community, meets from time to time in the Latin monastery.

It cannot be denied that the tax burden of the inhabitants is very heavy, but, as I was told, is somewhat less oppressive under the Turkish government than it was under Ibrahim Pasha. Per male head, from fifteen years of age on, one pays annually, as Fardeh, 55 (20, 25 and 30)[iii] piastres; another head tax, called Ia'na or support, 50 (36) piastres; for land ploughed in one day with a team of cattle, 30 piastres; for a yoke of cattle, 70 (150) piastres; for a camel, 40 (30) piastres; for a mule, 10 (20) piastres; for a goat, 1 (1) piastre; for an olive tree, 1 (1) piastre. In addition, quartering fees are paid for the soldiers and Arabs passing through, the number of which is indeterminate. The cost

---

i   Berggren 3, 147.

ii   *Light* 167.

iii According to Robinson (2, 576), the numbers in parentheses refer to Bêt Dschâla in 1838 under Ibrahim Pasha; to facilitate comparison, I added the Olim and Alibi immediately in parentheses.

of quartering a man is set at 50 piastres a week. In 1821 it was said that the Franciscans paid every year the land tax in the amount of 1,000 piasters for their parishioners.[i] Let us look even further back, first to 1598. The poor people of Bethlehem did not have anything subject to taxation at that time; they paid 1 maidin for a sheep or a goat, and 2 maidins for 8 plants or trees of any kind; annually they paid the fourth part of the harvest. Furthermore, the married men had to pay a gold zecchin annually, but often, they flee, forsaking everything, which is why not so infrequently the place became so desolate that only the Minorites remained.[ii] In 1679 poverty and oppression were equally present: annually the head tax of married men was 1 zecchin, every piece of cattle, small or large, 1 maidin and so on.[iii]

---

i   *Scholz* 198.
ii *Cotov.* 238.
iii *Laffi* 361. So similar that it seems to be translated from Kottwyk.

CHAPTER 9

The Church of the Nativity, its Chapels and Monasteries

Church of St Mary

Ground plans:

1552 to 1559. Ritrato in Pianta. Natal Bonifacio F. Copied by Zuallart, and even in 1738 almost everything exactly as Pococke (p. 25), with the difference that the northern chapel (D) next to the high altar is designated as the chapel of the Armenians, and that of the northern part of the Latin monastery itself.

1596. Bernadino Amico. Its ground plan was copied by Quaresmius (2, 677) and, on a smaller scale than that of the latter, by Zwinner (fol. 375), who added only trees to the gardens and slightly reduced the cisterns on the forecourt. With scale and Boussolle.

1844. Because of disagreements between the Latins and Armenians, the English architect Chrisblow was commissioned by the pasha in Jerusalem to draw up a new plan of the church. This Englishman did not comply with my request to see this work, excusing himself by saying that it was in Constantinople. It is possible that the ground plans are not so old, and that one would prefer to shield it from the Franks. A view of the

Church of St. Mary was given by de Bruyn (2, 222), Wegelin (from R.W. and good), d'Estourmel (115, barely recognizable), Bartlett (205, bad), Kalbreitern (Bl. III, 2; faithful) and others. The interior of the basilica by Roberts (part. VIII) and Bartlett (210) is worth looking at. The choir (Chancel of the Church of St. Helena) and in Roberts the entrance to the Nativity Chapel is very beautiful.

The Church of St. Mary,[i] the Church of Our Lady,[ii] the Church of the Crib[iii] or the Church of the Mother of God,[iv] is situated at the top of the northern slope of the second hill, which faces eastward the hill bearing almost all the harat of Bethlehem.[v] Above the Wadi al-Kharoobeh,[vi] such that the central axis of the cruciform structure[vii] runs parallel with the back of the hill from west to east, while one arm extends to the north and the other to the south. Moreover, the shape is that of a basilica, similar to the gabled Al-Aqsa Mosque in Jerusalem. Before arriving at the church from the west, one passes through an oblong,

---

i   Sanctæ Mariæ ecclesia. *Arculf.* 2, 2. Ecclesiam… in honore s. Mariæ. *Bernard.* 16. *Saewulf.* 35. Basilica s. Mariæ. *Fulcher. Carn.* 17 (397), 24 (406). *Marin. Sanut* 3, 14, 11. Templum est D. Mariæ. *Fürer* 65. Ecclesia S. Mariæ Bethlehem. *Quaresm.* 2, 622.

ii Ecclesia cathedralis in honore beatæ virginis consecrata. J. de Vitriac. e. 59. *Perdicas* 76. Honoring our Dear Lady. Alexander 74. Tucher 667. Zwinner 371. Tempio della vergine. *Legrenzi* 1, 181.

iii The Church of the Holy Manger. Radzivil 169. It is called the birthplace of Christ or Christ's Manger. Troilo 392. The church of Mariæ de præsepio. Raumer 309 and after him Schubert 3, 13. Also in Bartlett (208), as well as in Troilo, the Church of the Nativity.

iv *Epiphan M.* 52.

v   Ab altera urbis parte versus Orientem. *Fürer.* A l'opposite de la Ville de Bethleem 2. Traits d'arc du costé du Levant. *Surius* 524. Outside Bethlehem, in the morning. Troilo 392. A rifle's shot away from town. Della Valle 1, 157. Cf. above on p. 37.

vi Just outside Bethlehem, on the other side of the heap, towards the mouth of the river (where the town used to be). Rauchwolff 644.

vii *Quaresm.* 2, 643. *Surius* 525. Troilo. *Ladoire* 192. Prokesch 114. Geramb 1, 149. Schubert 3, 19. Hasselquist found (166) a church built according to a special design, which is said to be the same one as the Church of St. Paul in Rome.

flat,[i] rectangular plaza, bordered to the south by the Armenian monastery. It seems that in the past it had been closed[ii] and had an entrance or arch on the west side, just towards the town.[iii] In the sixteenth century, it was thought that hardly half of the original church remained, as could be assumed based on the old foundation wall, remnants, and arches found outside.[iv] For more than a century, with a pipe in the mouth and the khanjar in the belt, some even armed with shotguns,[v] the city's Arab thieves, sometimes joined by Christians, camped in front of the arches. Nearly two centuries ago, closer to the church, an even greater spectacle took place there. In the 'forecourt' three dervishes, who had assembled for a Moslem feast, sat naked on the ground, and

---

i   Hæc tota est marmoribus quadratis delapidata. *Quaresm.* 2, 622. II y a une belle plaine quarrée. *Surius.*

ii   This is how the square is at least drawn on the ground plans of Bonifacio and Zuallart (cortile), of Amico, Quaresmius, and Zwinner. The three cisterns are walled-in on all sides, and an alley leads crookedly toward the monastery, first to the east, then to the south. Ignaz von Rheinfelden writes (128): As we approached the town, through a vaulted high arch in the forecourt. ... we thus approached the church. Une grande court. *Nau* 397.

iii   A 50. pas de cette porte (de cette ville), l'on passe sous une ancienne et haute arcade. *Ladoire* 191. Elsewhere he says (206) that from one gate eastward up to the ancien portail qui reste encore, et qui fait l'entrée d'une grand cour qui est devant la grande Eglise de la Nativité, an unoccupied place 250 steps away, and from the other or western gate to David's cistern, there is supposedly no other house within a 100 step radius. This gate can be found on the ground plan of Bonifacio and Zuallart (Prima entrata), as well as on that of Amico and Zwinner, twice as far from the door into the present vestibule as the length of the nave. In Bonifacio, the Prima entrata is just opposite the Seconda (today's outer entrance). Vous trouvez d'abord une grande porte, dont les murailles sont fortes et epaisses. *Nau.* Cf. the last note (Ignaz v. Rh.)

iv   Rauchwolff. Surius says about his plaine quarrée: Qui estoit jadis embellie de belles colomnes et galeries, qui de leurs lustre n'ont laissé autre chos g'aucunes pieces et fondemens. In the courtyard Bonifacio drew at least 10 columns on the plan. According to Georg (523), judging from the location and the ruins, there must have once stood many more columns. Ex Aquilari erat magna porticus, quam pulcherrimæ marmoreæ rubeæque perlucidæ columnæ fulciebant, ut bascs superstites præ se ferunt, nec non alia ædificia. *Quaresm.* 2, 622.

v   *Ladoire.*

made a great clamour throughout an entire night.[i] The forecourt is now poorly paved.[ii]

As is often the case, the church does not grant a panoramic view, because on its north and south side, monasteries were added and because the choir is surrounded by a high wall, including a garden, and in its crevices it makes the most woeful impression, not the sort of which we receive when a worried mother lays her protective hands over a child, but rather the impression it gives is that of a Christian temple surrounded by hostile Mohammedens who despise it, and thus out of sheer fear it is not allowed to show itself properly; thus the western façade, in particular, still the most open side, has little that is inviting.[iii] It will not further excite the pilgrim's already excited expectations; its somewhat gloomy, old-grey colour, and its lack of ornamentation, is much more likely to cause disappointment; very few are those who are blinded by the passion of anticipation of what is soon to come.

The portal may perhaps catch one's attention? It is neither large, nor handsome.[iv] For centuries now, the small size of the gate has been a source of complaint, but the opening was deliberately left small so as to prevent Arabs from leading their horses into the temple.[v] Small doors for entrances to ensure the

---

i   Ignaz von Rheinfelden.

ii   The entrance to the monastery is paved with broad stones, accompanied by fountains, wide and handsome. Prokesch.

iii   La facciata di questo glorioso Tempio è più considerabile per la smisurata grandezza de marmi, che la compongono, che per la conditione del lavoro, poiche sudarono più gl' arteflei nel collocarli, che gl' ingegni per scolpirli ond' è che riesce più soda l'opera, che vaga, e di comparsa all' occhio. *Legrenzi* 1, 179.

iv   Une petite porte basse (la principale a été bouchée) nous introduisait. *D'Estourmel* 2, 115.

v   *Zuallard.* 205. Two large high portals, one of which is walled, the other one open to the waist, through which neither horse nor camel could enter. Ignaz von Rheinfelden 128. The entrance alone was 4' 5" high, closed by a strong, double iron-barred door, and from there one proceeded through 5 large, handsome gates, now all walled-up except for the largest, 18' high and 12' 5" wide. Troilo, note 392. Per picola, ed angusta porta, obligato ogn' uno a chinarsi. *Legrenzi.* De Bruyn 2, 224. *Ladoire.* Schubert 2, 492. He saw an

safety of the occupants of a house are, however, common in the Orient, and not only among Christians.[i] Once we have entered the church, we will then experience a second deception. We had hoped for a panoramic view; instead, we stand in a vestibule.[ii] Is it separated from the church by a wall, just as the church itself is concealed by a wall.[iii]

Another door in the middle of the eastern wall of this vestibule leads into the nave of the church. Opposite to the east, are three doors next to each other, the middle one leads up a few steps[iv] to the apse and the choir. The choir has been closed off from the nave for a long time,[v] apparently to better prevent desecration by Mohammedans.[vi] Next to the entrance door to the nave and to the north is an entrance to the Latin monastery[vii] and another to the south of the Greek monastery; the Armenians have their

---

Arab gatekeeper; I did not.

i   Questa angustia, e bassezza di porte è accostumata non solo in queste parti, mà anco in tutto il Dominio Ottomano artificio particolare de Christiani, come li più soggetti allo strappaccio de Turchi, li quali di passagio prendono volentieri allogio appresso loro qualunque volta vedono una buona fabrica senza il riguardo, che sia Chiesa, introducendo anco li loro Cavalli, che però ritrovando anguste, e picole le porte si ritirano. *Legrenzi.*

ii   A small, lower gate led to un vestibule élevé, construit en partie de grandes pierres; cette portion m'a semblé la plus ancienne des bâtiments. *D'Estourmel* 2, 115, who then had en face a door to a church or to a nave. This vestibule is found on the ground plan of Bonifacio and Amico.

iii Medschir ed-Dîn distinguishes (135) between three parts, the nave, the eastern side (choir) and the rock caves (Sachrah). 81. The altar and transepts…are separated from the nave by an unsightly wall, which entirely destroys its architectural effect. *Bartlett* 209.

iv   Le chœur est plus élevé que la nef de 4. marches. *Ladoire.*

v   The church is walled at the point where the stem joins with the arms. Prokesch 114. Geramb 1, 150. *D'Estourmel.*

vi   Il Coro…è murato interno. Viagg. al S. Sepolcro F 6a. Le grand Choeur enclos en ses murailles. *Surius* 525. Separé par une haute muraille. *Ladoire.* On the ground plans the separation does not appear as strong, and one can count five entrances between the nave and the choir.

vii One sees this entrance on Zuallart, Amico, Quaresmius, and Zwinner's ground plans. On the other hand, these do not show the special outer entrance of the Latins, except for the ground plan by Amico. Upon his arrival, Helffrich was led through the large church into the monastery (717).

entrance on the south side of the vestibule.[i] In addition, there is a special entrance to the Latin monastery, closed with a solid iron door, next to the main entrance but more to the north. The actual monastery door is usually locked, and the Latins prefer the entrance through the church, because they have already been deprived of some rights by the Greeks, and because they believe they are protecting their old rights by asserting the passage through the nave. In one respect, one cannot object to the behaviour of the Roman Catholics ; but taken from another perspective, one cannot but accuse the Franciscan fathers of being partly to blame for the desecration of the Christian temple. Needless to say, the Greeks should also be forbidden from using the church as a general entrance to their monastery.

The basilica is large.[ii] It measures about 170' from the door of the vestibule to the foremost part of the choir and about 80'[iii] from one side to the other in the nave. The nave is, from its lofty aspirations, still an imposing structure,[iv] but it is no longer beautiful, as it was once referred to in 1719.[v] The walls are made of blocks of ashlar,[vi] while the floor is covered with stone slabs

i   One can see this on the aforementioned ground plans. At Zwinner's time, this entrance was shared by the Greeks and Armenians.

ii   Quite large. Seydlitz 474. Large Wormbser 409. Helffrich. By no means inferior to any church in France as far as size is concerned. *Ladoire*. Palæst. 1831. 49.

iii   My calculation adheres to Amico's ground plan. Otherwise the data varies significantly. Fürer (66) estimates the length to be 78 steps, Schweigger (122) says 40 steps (maybe if one does not take into consideration the choir), in Surius (525) it is 82 steps, in Troilo (393) 204 feet; Schweigger gives the width of 45 steps, in Surius it is 40, Troilo says 193 feet. Amico and Surius deserve the most credit. Quaresmius (2, 644) communicates bizarre measurements.

iv   A true splendor. Mayr v. A. 330. A majestic nave. Hailbronner 2, 298. It is a venerable and magnificent Basilica. *Bartlett* 208. Ladoire says about the choir (193): Il a un certain air de grandeur, qui frappe et qui étonne ceux qui le considerent avec quelque attention.

v   The church does not yield in beauty to any church in France. *Ladoire* 192.

vi   Bastie de belles pierres de taille. *Surius* 525. Bâtie d'une tres belle pierre

lacking in grandeur,[i] and which have for centuries been deprived of marble decoration.[ii]

The side walls (of the substructure) look rough now at the bottom and above. Over the columns are preserved on each (of the narrow superstructures)[iii] indistinct, old depictions or pictures in mosaic that are barely recognizable.[iv] On these side walls of the recessed, high[v] superstructure are found ten large, arched windows,[vi] which throw quite a lot of light into the church. The ceiling of the central building, which rises above the central nave is formed by simple beams of wood, probably from cypress,[vii] that had never been painted,[viii] so too are the aisle-way balconies and the rafters too, that is, the entire wooden frame

---

de taille. *Ladoire.*

i   The pavement is in such a dilapidated state that it is impossible to walk on it without having to worry about injuring oneself by falling. Geramb 1, 150. Only a shameless dreamer without any respect for the truth can write like this. Quaresmius found (2, 643b) the Ecclesia delapidata… ex quadam mixtura ex attritis lateribus calceque compacta…punicei coloris.

ii   Hoc templum olim totum marmore et stratum fuit et contabulatum. *Fürer* 65. Tout le pavé comme une grande partie des murailles estoit autresfois couverte et revestüe de marbre blanc, et d'autres pierres precieuses, comme on remarque encore en aucuns endroits. *Surius.* Troilo 393.

iii   Neret found (112) the wall above the columns of wood to be very beautiful, and Richter (38) discusses some Byzantine wooden paintings on the walls.

iv   Some damaged pieces of mosaic. Geramb 1, 150. Des débris de mosaïque, épars sur les murs attestent l'ancienne magnificence du décor. *D'Estourmel* 2, 115. Röser 446. Destroyed mosaic walls. Hailbronner.

v   Les murailles de la nef du milieu sont fort hautes. *Surius.*

vi   On each side 11 windows through which the light comes in evenly. *Quaresm.* 12 grandes fenestres. *Surius.* Neret (very large) and Joliffe only discuss windows. Whether my predecessors counted incorrectly or whether there has been a change in the construction since their time, I do not know. 7 northern windows can be seen on Wege and Halbreiter's drawings.

vii   So it appeared to the sober Prokesch (114). Surius says: Toute la charpenterie est bastie de bois de Cedre et Cypres. Others, such as Troilo, Ladoire, Binos, Wegelin (2, 120), recognized only cedar; Röser relies on Soll. Troilo says: The church is not vaulted, but only covered with visible beams made of cedar wood.

viii The unpainted beams look like new. Röser.

of the gabled roof,[i] which did not make the best impression on me. The roof is covered with lead, and according to available information, always has been.[ii] In 1845 it was in such a state that it rained in the temple while I was there. The superstructure or its stone walls rest on the inner row of columns in the nave, that are situated more or less vertically below.[iii] It seems to have escaped my attention that the knobs supported a wooden architrave[iv] on which the stone walls of the superstructure were built. The marble columns[v] are placed in four rows,[vi] eleven on each, forty-four in total.[vii] Thus, the nave is divided into five

---

i   This is of architectural interest to Bernardino Amico, whose drawings, however, look different from what it looks like today.

ii Thetmar in Maltens Weltkd., 1844, 192. Rudolph von Suchen 842. Anonymous in Allat. 15. (Churches and choir) Gumpenberg 463. Seydlitz. Wormbser. *Fürer.* Radzivil 169. *Surius.* Ignaz von Rheinfelden. Troilo. *Legrenzi. Ladoire.* Binos.

iii Cette charpente… est appuyeé sur une muraille tres mince. Cette muraille est soûtenuë de part et d'autre par une frise (from wood) ..; 50 colomnes .. à chaque côté de la nef portent cette belle frise. *Ladoire* 193.

iv Hailbronner. A beam, says Quaresmius (2, 643a). La frise..d'un bois bien travaillé. *Nau* 398.

v   Alexander 74. *Anshelm.* 1290. Wormbser. *Fürer.* Rauchwolff.

vi Breydenbach 131. La Chiesa ha.. 4. filare. Viagg. al S. Sepolcro F 6a. There are four rows. Tschudi 274. Rauchwolff. Schwallart 306. *Ladoire.* Richter 38. *Duc de Raguse* 3, 46.

vii Alexander, Georg (523), Tschudi, Helffrich, Schweigger (122), Surius, Monconys (1, 314), Binos, Richter, Wegelin all counted this many; by contrast, Anshelm, Schwallart, the famous ground plans by Mayr (330), Hailbronner all counted 40; counted 46 (81); 48 das Viagg. al S. Sepolcro, Prokesch, Palæst. 1831 (49), Geramb (1, 149), d'Estourmel (2, 115), the Duke of Ragusa (3, 46), Schubert (3, 19); 50 Medschir ed-Din (135), Fürer, Quaresmius (2, 642b), Zwinner (371), Troilo, Ladoire; 52 Ignaz von Rheinfelden (129). If the number of columns changed or varied over centuries, one would have reason to assume that structural changes had taken place; but since the present number 44 goes back to the fifteenth century, we are right to declare the other numbers to be erroneous, with the exception of number 50, because there used to be 6 columns in the choir, which could be counted among the 44 (See Monconys).

sections,[i] of which the middle one is by far the widest,[ii] so that
two wings are formed.[iii] The ceiling of the side aisles is flat and
barely higher than the tops of the columns.[iv] The columns, which
as I recall are brownish-red,[v] are no longer really beautiful[vi]; they
are one-piece columns,[vii] 18' high, including base and capitals,[viii]
2' 6"[ix] in diameter at the bottom, and stand 13' from each other
from east to north 7' and in the two rows from south to north
13'apart.[x] If in the past, the fine work of the bases and the knobs
had been praised,[xi] it is certain that these columns, which belong
to the Corinthian order,[xii] are of poor workmanship.[xiii] Some
people attached a strange superstition to the columns and to the
marble panels, which were 7' wide and 12' long and smooth as a

---

i Cinque archi, overo coperti. *Viagg. al S. Sep.* There are five vaults. Ignaz
von Rheinfelden. È in 5. Navate. *Legrenzi* 1, 182.

ii Quella (navata) di mezo si dilata a 9. braccia, le laterali sono la metà
meno. *Legrenzi.*

iii Qui (the four rows) font 2. aîles. *Ladoire.*

iv *Quaresm.* 2, 643a.

v Yellowish. *Medschired-din.* Di marmoro rosso e bianco. *Viagg. al S. Sep.*
Of many colors, red, yellow, and white. Schwallart. D'un marbre brun, ou
pour mieux dire, d'un porphyre taschetté, et d'autres belles couleurs. *Surius*
525. Colomnes de marbre rouge. . Ces colomnes estoient toutes peintes par
dessus. Monconys. De differentes couleurs, parmi lesquelles le rouge semble
dominer. *Ladoire.* Roth. *D'Estourmel.* Troilo also saw porphyry.

vi As Breydenbach (131), Alexander (74), and Schweigger found it.

vii Schwallart, Mayr, Richter.

viii Richter 38. Prokesch 114. Nearly 18'. Binos. 14'. *Surius.* 22 feet 1 inch,
from which the shaft measured 17', the base 1' 5" and the capital 3' 8".
Troilo. Nearly 30'. *Ladoire.* High. Rauchwolff.

ix Richter. Prokesch. 9 spans thick. Rauchwolff. 6 palm. 6 unc. (= 5' 9") in
circumference. *Quaresm.* 2, 644. 8' *Surius.*

x Schwallart. Cf. note 2. The distance of 9½'. Prokesch. According to other
ground plans as well as my own, the relationship is significantly different.

xi Fort joliment travaillez. *Surius.* Very artfully hewn. Troilo.

xii Quaresmius, Richter, Prokesch (a kind of Corinthian knobs), Palæst.
1831, Geramb, the Duke of Ragusa, Hailbronner.

xiii De Forbin (123), Prokesch.

mirror,[i] which can be traced to the pilgrimage books from about 1280 to 1583. One source claimed that the sultan had taken away the pillars in order to use them for a building in Cairo but after the sudden appearance of a snake, he set aside his plans in horror.[ii] Another said: 'When a serpent of incredible size bit the first marble panel with which the church was clad, it split it in two, and so it continued with forty other panels. As soon as the sultan dropped his plans, the snake disappeared, but its traces, like something that had been burned, remained'.[iii] From the year 1320, we hear something additional. A certain sultan had many marble tablets brought to his palace, until a snake stopped him from carrying out his plan.[iv] In the last quarter of the fifteenth century, this superstition persisted in a far more refined state.[v] It was after the expulsion of the Christians from the Holy Land that the Egyptian sultan partially destroyed the church in Bethlehem, at least the altars and images. At the sight of the marble slabs, with which walls and floor were covered, he had ordered the removal of those that were next to the entrance to the Grotto of the Nativity until a terrible snake[vi] sprang out of the whole and scatheless wall, through which not a needle seemed to have penetrated,[vii] first with a fiery tongue and biting on one

---

i   *Fabri* 1, 476.

ii *Brocard.* c. 9.

iii *Marin. Sanut.* 3, 14, 11. He also touches the columns.

iv Sed quidam Soldanus multas ex hys tabulis (marmoreis) removeri fecit et ad suum deferri palatium. Sed Christi faciente virtute. quidam serpens multis videntibus de sub lapidibus illis egressus cucurrit ad illas super tabulas marmoreas parieti applicatas. et sicut ibat ita sue vie vestigia tabulis imprimebat, que vestigia hodierna permanent die in signum miraculi. Soldanus autem propter hoc miraculum ab incepto destuit neque amplius illos lapides removere presumpsit. *Pipin* 72b. For a few decades, the Saracens assumed the role of a sultan. Rudolph von Suchen 842.

v   Mira res, et fidelibus prædicandum prodigium. *Fabri* 1, 475.

vi *Fabri*. A mighty dragon. Kapfman 9. A cruel dragon carved here for this purpose. Tschudi 283. From a marble column jumped a dragon. Lussy 37.

vii On the other hand, Kapfman was shown a large crack from the snake on the painted wall.

side until the slabs split, then it shot over to the other side of the Epiphany Chapel and there ran along the smoothest marble, upon which a spider could not have held fast. The vestiges of the passage looked as if someone had struck the stones with a red-hot iron, and as if the stones were burned like wood.[i] In 1341, after this incident, the Saracens came to carry away those valuable columns. But when they laid hands on them, they were so frightened by a terrible face that they were paralyzed and could do nothing,[ii] and then fled in terror. Years later,[iii] a sultan let the church again be destroyed and the floor panels in the Grotto of the Nativity to be taken away. But during the attack, everything decayed like rotten wood, so that no spoils remained for him.[iv] It is not said who the temple-desecrating sultan was,[v] nor in which year the so-called miracle took place that, later on, was greatly embellished and repeated. In the stories about it there is a lack of cohesion; sometimes the sultans play a role, then the Saracens, then the marble columns, then the marble tablets on the church walls, or sometimes both, then a snake, then a worm that is sometimes a monster. It seems to me that the burnt marks on the marble were very likely caused by lightening that were then used to light the path into a labyrinth of superstitions. That a sultan or the Saracens might have attempted to steal precious artefacts from the Church of St. Mary's may be possible, but precisely because the story is so bedizened with miracles, it remains doubtful whether any part of it is true. It is conceivable that the tales about it were originally a deliberate attempt to

---

i *Fabri.* The bloody traces of the snake, as if burned by fire. *Georg.* 523.

ii *Fabri.* Rudolph von Suchen speaks about a face.

iii *Fabri.* Meggen reckoned (125) shorter; one showed him the traces of the terrible snake that 30 years before had chased the sultan. Rudolph von Suchen says it happened before his time.

iv *Fabri.* Cf. also *Anshelm.* 1291, *Salignac.* tom. 10 c. 3, *Anthonius de Castilio* in Ignaz von Rheinfelden 130. Surius refers (526) to Salimgiaque (Salignac) because of a broken column base originating from the snake.

v Only Antonius de Castilio mentions "Saladinus Bassa (?)" in the Great Cairo.

prevent the Moslems from tampering with church treasures by frightening them.

On the right (southern) side,[i] near the wall, stood a magnificent baptismal font of porphyry.[ii] In 1449 it was described as red and cross-hatched. In this beautiful, marble stone, Christians baptized a child by pouring oil into the water, after which the children threw ashes and stones into it.[iii] In 1507 the baptismal font to the left of the door belonged to the Greeks, who during Christmas also baptized older children in it.[iv] Around 1620 the marble baptismal font was eight-sided, the inside in the shape of a cross or a rose, the outside with crosses and inscriptions.[v] In 1754 the baptismal font was still referred to as an exquisite porphyry, in the shape of an open rose, one-and-a-half cubits high and three-and-a-half cubits in diameter at the top.[vi] In the last century, near the baptismal font, some Greeks of Bethlehem indulged in a strange superstition. In the first nave, a column on the right-hand side had five holes. The Greeks blindfolded themselves and turned their bodies quickly in circles to see if they could hit the five holes with their fingers; if not, they would be damned, so they believed. In the middle of the church, there is a column with an apple on the top.[vii] What this may have meant in the sixteenth century,[viii] I cannot say.

The choir towards the east, the outermost part of the church,[ix] is

---

i   The location of the baptismal font can be seen on the oft-cited ground plans.

ii *Anonymous* in *Allat. 15.*

iii Gumpenberg 464.

iv *Georg.* 524. *Surius* mentions (526) only au bas de l'Eglise the fonts baptis-maux.

v   Totum integrum, altera parte excepta, quam Mauri fregerunt. *Quaresm.* 2 643.

vi Schulz 7, 8.

vii *Legrenzi* 1, 182 sq.

viii Viagg. al S. Sepoloro F 6a.

ix *Anshelm.* 1290. Schwallart 307.

large[i] but no longer beautiful,[ii] because too bare, and disfigured by the Greek altars.[iii] Instead of marble, one sees whitewash on the walls, instead of beautiful paintings,[iv] the whitewash or Greek incompetence. The pillars[v] have disappeared, as have the canons' chairs.[vi] The friendliest thing seems to be the bright lighting.[vii] The high altar in the centre of the chapel,[viii] almost immediately above the Grotto of the Nativity, has such little appeal that we turn to the sides, where in the arms of the cross, side chapels are found.[ix] The southern chapel is now deserted, and from here a staircase leads up to the buildings of the Greeks, along which on this side, but closer to the chapel, the old staircase[x] went

---

i Viagg. al S. Sepolcro. Schwallart 306. 39 steps long, 16 wide. *Surius* 525. According to Amico about 80' long and at the cross arms, and with these over 110' wide.

ii Like in Schwallart's time.

iii Wittman already noted (70) that the beauty and symmetry of the temple had been compromised because the Greeks were allowed to use a part of it for a special chapel in return for an annual fee.

iv Viaggio, whom I cite here, mentions a picture of the Madonna and the image of Abraham next to the high altar.

v Schwallart says that there is a large pillar and two columns standing behind the choir (?), Medschir ed-Din (135).

vi At the beginning of the sixteenth century, they were all destroyed (guaste. The same in Viagg.); on the other hand, in the century before last, it was said: Il maggiore (Altare) recinto da molte sedie di noci ingegnosamente lavorate, le quali vengono a comporre il Choro a commodo de Religiosi per salmeggiare, e servire alle Messe solenni. *Legrenzi* 1, 182. Viaggio also says that the church (more likely the choir) had 3 altars: east, south, and north.

vii Schwallart.

viii Cf. Viagg., *Surius*. The ground plans give the best idea in this respect. According to Fabri (1, 468 sq.) there were some steps leading from the choir up to the sanctuary and presbytery, and from there again some steps leading up to the high altar.

ix On each side there is another choir, which makes up the sanctuary of the church, in each of which there are three altars. All three choirs are vaulted. Schwallart, note 306. According to Surius, the church had 7 altars, just as Helena had them built.

x Like it still is on the plans of Amico, Quaresmius, and Zwinner. According to Viaggio, 12 steps led towards a chamber here, which had once been the sacristy.

down. The chapel on the northern side is not very attractive.[i] West of it, if I remember correctly, a door opens into the Church of St. Catherine.[ii] In this chapel, we will point out some more curiosities for the pilgrim.

First, the Altar of the Circumcision, which, like the subsequent altars, belongs more to history. At the beginning of the fourteenth century, on the left side of the wall of the Church of St. Mary was the place where Christ's navel lay and where he was circumcised.[iii] In the last three decades of the same century, the place of circumcision and of the navel were shown on the southern side.[iv] From that time on, the latter was not mentioned; only the place of circumcision was always shown on the south side,[v] next to the high altar,[vi] often until the end of the last century.[vii] In this place, which was reached by climbing

---

i   To enter the smaller choir, doors have been made in the walls. Schwallert 307. On the ground plans, the side choirs also appear to be closed off.

ii   Ha tre usci. The Viagg. Above (east of) the stairs leading down into the Cave of the Nativity, a door led into the choir. Also on the plans of Bonifacio and Zuallart, the eastern part of the choir next to the stairs of the Nativity cave is closed off ; the ground plan of Amico and others show 3 entrances here. Où (in the whole choir) on entre par 3. portes, sçavoir: du costé du Levant, du Septentrion et du Midy. *Surius* 525. Prokesch says (114) that the entrance to the church (choir or nave?), that had formerly been designated for Roman Catholics, was walled up during his time. Cf. Geramb 1, 150.

iii   *Marin. Sanut.* 3, 14, 11. Pipinus says (72) less assuredly: Et vidi et tetigi locum ubi (Christus) circumeisus est (in Bethlehem).

iv   In the churches (Bethlehem) against the south there is a statue of the circumcision of the sweet infant Jesus. Rechtenstain 98b. E dove (in the Church of St. Mary on the right, not on the left as Marinus Sanutus claims) Cristo fù circonciso; ed evvi una capella al lato all' altare maggiore. *Frescobaldi* 139. Appresso (the Nativity Chapel) suso nella detta chiesa. *Sigoli* 166.

v   To the right, outside the choir. Gumpenberg 464. *Albert. Sax.* 2110. Tucher 667. *Fabri* 1 440. Ad partem autem dexteram chori respectu orientis. *Anshelm.* 1290. *Surius* 525 sq.

vi   See the last note Nr 3. See also Tucher. See particularly the famous ground plans.

vii   (A little away from the altar of the 3 kings) Si riverisce il terze santuario, ed é il luogo dove Christo otto giorni doppo la nascita giusto la legge hebraica fù circonciso. *Legrenzi* 1, 181.

up from the church floor,[i] there was a chapel with an altar[ii] or just an altar.[iii] After the middle of the sixteenth century, beneath this, as an addition to the lore, lay a stone slab, upon which the circumcision was performed,[iv] and the blood[v] could still be seen but around 1620 only a built-in cross on the grey marble floor.[vi] If we consult the Gospel about the place of circumcision, it does not provide us with any definitive conclusion. It only says that when it was the eighth day, the day of circumcision, the baby was given the name Jesus; but since it says that after the purification was completed, it was brought to Jerusalem to present it to the Lord,[vii] it is very likely that the circumcision took place in Bethlehem, otherwise it could or should have been said that Jesus was brought to Jerusalem to be circumcised. The theologians do not, by the way, agree at all about the place of the circumcision.[viii] St. Epiphanius and St. Bernardus have the opinion that Jesus was circumcised in Bethlehem,[ix] and in his time the opinion was that it took place in the Grotto of the Nativity.[x] The Roman Catholic Church granted complete

---

i   *Fabri.*

ii *Frescobaldi* in the final, third note. *Surius.*

iii Gumpenberg. The famous ground plans have only one altar of the circumcision, the older plans show one that is closed; the newer ones show a fairly open altar; both are located East of the Eastern aisle toward the Nativity Cave, in the corner between the central chancel and the Eastern aisle.

iv Ehrenberg 512. Lussy 39.

v   Ehrenberg.

vi *Quaresm.* 2, 637. He attributes the oral tradition to the Armenians, and not others.

vii Luk. 2, note 21.

viii As one hears in Quaresmius (2, 636 sqq.).

ix In the words of Epiphanius (as cited in *Quaresm.* 2 637a, Ignaz von Rheinfelden 130): Christus natus est in Bethehem, circumcisus in spelunca, oblatus in Jerusalem. To this I can only add that it seems that the old legend has the circumcision happening in a cave, which is no longer the case later on.

x   *Quaresm.* 2, 637. He also thinks it is more likely. Nau adopts his view (408 sqq.).

indulgence of sins at the Altar of the Circumcision.[i] In 1583 the altar was owned by the Roman Catholics; however, because the Mohammedans were free to move in, it was stripped bare.[ii]

Opposite this altar, on the north side of the church,[iii] there was an altar, where in the past it was said[iv] that the Three Kings (shahs) offered sacrifices, or where, as it was better considered later on, they readied themselves to offer gifts.[v] The Roman Catholics obtained a seven-year indulgence here.[vi] In the beginning of the twelfth century, probably on the south side, there was a marble table in the Church of St. Mary on which the mother of Jesus ate with the Three Magi after they had offered their gifts.[vii] It was assumed in the fourteenth century that the star went as far as the Altar of the Kings and then stopped here,[viii] or as far as the cistern

---

i   *Anshelm.*

ii   Radzivil 170.

iii   Ad partem sinistram versus est altare innixum parieti orientali. *Anshelm. Surius.* According to Neret (112), an altar was dedicated to the three Kings in the cloister where they arrived.

iv   *Frescobaldi* 139: "If you enter from the side where the three Kings made their sacrifice", there are 16 steps down to the Chapel of the Nativity (north). Gumpenberg. Next to the chancel on the left. *Albert. Sax.*

v   Although Frescobaldi and Sigoli visited Bethlehem at the same time, they saw the matter differently; for the latter says: Appresso (the site of the circumcision) si é il luogo dove gli Magi ismontarono da cavallo quando andavano a offrire a Gesù Cristo (167). The altar is located where the Three Wise Men spread out their cotton sacks, took out their gifts which they wanted to offer, and prepared them so that they would signal devotion, culture, and honor to the child and his mother. Fabri 259. *Anshelm, Surius.* Binos says (207) that the altar in the choir where the three holy kings descended to worship the Messiah, was built by Helena. The newer plans briefly show the altar of the Three Wise Men on the eastern side of the north chancel. If it were true, as Chateaubriand writes (1, 301), that the manger of Jesus was located vertically below the altar of the Three Wise Men, then the legend must have displaced the location further to the south.

vi   *Anshelm.*

vii   *Saewulf.* 36.

viii E insino (The altar of the Three Wise Men) gli accompagnó la stella e poi ispari. *Frescobaldi* 139.

next to it.[i] In the fifteenth century, near the altar there was a deep cistern from which, it is said, the servants of the Three Kings drew water for the camels, dromedaries, and horses.[ii] Later (in the sixteenth century), next to the altar of the Three Kings, a spring[iii] or a cistern[iv] was indicated, thereafter a deep hole for it,[v] in which the guiding star had fallen; in the present century, the image of the star is in jasper-like marble or the zenith point at the altar of the choir in a marble stone,[vi] above which the star is said to have remained.[vii] From this example can be seen how a story that had been put to rest had then been revived. In its time, one used to see the star even in the cistern.[viii] I will return to the Three Kings and their guiding star in the Chapel of the Nativity. In the sixteenth century, on the left side of the church, there was an altar covered with marble, in which the figure of Simeon, carrying the boy in his arms, was admired.[ix]

The chapel is used for worship, but not the nave,[x] and has not been for a very long time, if you do not count the baptismal

---

i Appresso (where the Wise Ones descended to the east) si è una cisterna dove la stella si posoe, e apparve a' tre Magi; there the Roman Catholic received a complete remission of sin. *Sigoli* 167.

ii *Fabri.*

iii *Anshelm.*

iv Viagg. al S. Sepolcro F 6b (on the left-hand side when descending into the Nativity Chapel).

v Tschudi 276. The more recent plans have the cistern of the Three Wise Men just east of their altar. Quaresmius mentions a cistern north of the Cave of the Nativity; it was dry and the aqueduct was closed; the opening pulverized by ropes, suggesting that there was once much water and a large inflow (2, 638b).

vi Joliffe 118.

vii Röser 447. According to Raynaud (229), there was a chapel of the Armenians there, with a marble star on the floor. Wolff says (134) that in the middle of the choir, at an altar belonging to the Greeks, there is a niche underneath the altar: a white marble stone with a star-shaped hole.

viii The Viaggio.

ix *Georg.* 523. At an altar. Wormbser 409. Rauchwolff 644. See later the picture of Jerome.

x Geramb 1, 150. *Duc de Raguse* 3, 46.

service. Worse than this abandonment of the nave as a place of worship, is the fact that it has been defiled so much and so often. I do not mean the thoughtless and insensitive ransacking of the church that took place previously, but this time something else, which the pen resists recording. I ask the reader not to ascribe to me a lack of decency, if words fail me completely. Indeed, in describing a Christian temple, for which the Christian heart of the West is filled with respect and admiration, the truth will not be concealed. After seeing it frequently, I must attest that the floor of the church or the nave, specifically the northwest corner, was contaminated with urine and human excrement, which I noticed especially after the Latin Christmas Eve. When I once read that the ancient Greeks did not keep their temples particularly holy, that they satisfied the same needs, especially in the great temple of the sun at Rhodes, I was horrified. Now I experience the astonishing cynicism of Christians, not in a despised corner of the world, but, according to the faith of so many Christians, in the Church of the Nativity of the Saviour. The temple has also already been defiled by the hatred of those who take pride in the faith and religion of love.

Truth be told, in a place where different Christian communities need to share a temple, one has to assume that enmities prevail. It is sad that here, too, Christians do the dishonour of quarrelling, as they do in Jerusalem. In 1818 there were manifest scuffles, in which many were wounded, and several were slain, and later the Christians fought with swords for the right to read Mass at the door of the sanctuary.[i] During my stay in Bethlehem (1845) there was an outbreak that truly disgraced the Christians. One evening, a group of French singers of considerable reputation, led by a certain Mr. Roland and allegedly supported by the former Queen Adelaide, wanted to return to the monastery through the usual entrance of the church. The Greeks had closed it already and did not want to open it again. There was an exchange of words,

---

i   Palæst. 1831, 58.

not carried out with love of course, as the exalted founder of our religion had preached with such ardency. In the end, the French, who were perhaps in the right, but who dragged it out beyond all reason because the monastery might have been expected to lock its gate at such an unusual time of day, forced their way in. With a joyful sense of triumph, the Latin partisans told me afterwards what had happened, and an Armenian whom I met later hurled angry words at the French and paid me many courtesies because he knew that I had nothing to do with the incident. It would not be too much to claim that the Christians bring more shame to their temple than the Mohammedans themselves, some of which even worshipped it.[i] Repeatedly, one is told about things that Moslems carry out in their thoughts and actions at other sanctuaries, thus betraying a lack of sensitivity and consideration in matters related to religion. Such behaviour brings them little honour. Robbery was ostensibly carried out to embellish the mosques.[ii] It was not enough that they, or their Christian minions, ripped out the marble stones from the floor and walls of the church. They also used the nave as a house and stable, at a

i   The Saraceni honor all the churches of Our Lady, but especially this one in Bethlehem. Breydenbach 132. The Muslims revered especially the Cave of the Nativity: while we were waiting to offer our prayers there (of which one can never get enough), two Turks came in without their babutzen or shroud, and worshiped the holy site with kisses as if they were Christians... the Turks come in great numbers to worship this holiest of places, knowing that Christ was born there of Mary, the most blessed of virgins. Ignaz von Rheinfelden 129.

ii   If you think back to the time when a miracle always served to frighten the wicked should they attempt to wrong a church, we realize that the myth that the church was inviolable had been invented (*Fabri* 1, 476); it thus seems that the treasures must have escaped from greedy hands. Istis tamen non obstantibus, Fabri himself admitted, multæ tabulæ politæ sunt parietibus detractæ per fures christianos, which they bartered away to the Saracens. According to Belon (268), the Turks took away the marble tiles. Schwallart claims (306) go even further: that it was moved to the stone dome (Temple of Solomon) and to Cairo. Tout le pavé comme une grande partie des murailles estoit autresfois couverte et revestüe de marbre blanc, et d'autres pierres precieuses, comme on remarque encore en aucuns endroits, que les Turcs ont enlevez pour orner leur grande Mosquée. *Surius* 525. This account is echoed by Troilo (393), Prokesch (114) and others.

time when it was more in a state of decay. In 1583 the pilgrims met the 'boluchus' with some janissaries and his horses in the church; because it was always open, the Mohammedans moved in with their cattle whenever they pleased.[i] In 1586 the nave was the dwelling of the kadi or the judge presiding over Bethlehem, who also slept in it; when pilgrims arrived, he sat directly in front of the choir stairs on carpets that covered the floor, according to the custom of the Orientals, who use neither bench, nor chair, nor table.[ii] We will learn more later about the manner in which the temple was further contaminated by animals. If one does not want to imitate the example of those Frenchmen, the entrance to the ship and the choir is now effortless and trouble free, and one does not have to worry about encountering a Turkish camp. A free entrance such as this was not something about which the Christians could always boast, without having to admit that the Mohammedans do not surround the Church of St. Mary in Bethlehem with even half the rigor that they would a customs house, such as at the Church of the Resurrection in Jerusalem. In the first quarter of the sixteenth century, a man paid one drachma[iii]; in 1556, entrance could be purchased for one-half a maidin[iv] and in 1565 with a whole maidin.[v] I will now descend deeper into the treasure trove of history. The assurance that there where later the church of the birth of our Saviour rose, the house of David stood,[vi] cannot trouble us here, since it obviously reaches into the depths of the legends without end. We now enter another foggy terrain.

Apparently, the faithful have always visited and venerated the

---

i   Radzivil 169.

ii   Schallart 303.

iii Di muta, ò datio. The oft-cited Viagg.

iv   Ehrenberg 512.

v   Villinger 93.

vi   Quo loco olim domum Davidis stetisse memorant. Fürer 65. According to Gumpenberg (463), one can tell that the charming monastery had once been a beautiful fortress in David's time. Cf. above on p. 15, note 1.

place of birth, indeed already during the era of the apostles and first Christians. They had a kind of church there, but it was destroyed in the year 137 by order of the emperor Hadrian.[i] He is said to have built a temple of Adonis in Bethlehem as a means of insulting the name of the Christians and destroying their faith.[ii] This does not seem very credible, since it was mentioned only around the year 400, and it is very unlikely that the father of the church's history, who also tells us about the church's history in Bethlehem, would have passed over in silence such an important fact and that the temple to idols was destroyed under the emperor Constantine the Great[iii]; the parallels with Jerusalem, where a temple of Venus and a temple of Jupiter marked the place of death and burial of Jesus, permitted the faith and the pen to be misled.[iv] These somewhat shadowy historical accounts were meant to prove that the place of birth had never been lost sight of and that the one they assumed it to be in the fourth century was the real one. In my opinion, as concerns the issue now, such evidence is unnecessary. Either the life of Jesus must be declared a myth, or the place of birth at that time must be declared real. In this case, I am led by very particular reasons, never mind that nowadays one can find three-hundred-year-old houses in which famous men came into the world, as the so-called Lisighaus at Wildhaus in Tockenburg, where Huldreich Zwingli first saw the light of day,[v] shows. The soil in Bethlehem has a thoroughly excellent character. If there were an occasion in which you had

---

i *Surius* 524. Prokesch 117. Surius refers to the old fathers, but does not name them.

ii S. Paulini epist. 2. ad Severum, as cited by Besold 26.

iii On the other hand, Jerome wrote in a letter (49.) to Paulinus (after Robinson 2, 285, Paulina after Reland ad voc. Bethlechem) that Bethlehem was shaded by the grove of Thamus or Adonis, and in the cave where Christ came into the world, the love of Venus was being lamented. Cf. also Surius.

iv Cf. Robinson.

v It might incidentally be about time to start appreciating more the development of tradition or the proofs of authenticity than has perhaps been done so far.

to, you could probably not move back and forth at all on the
northern slope, just under the ridge, and on the east side of the
Wadi al-Kharoobeh just as it begins, nor over this wady towards
Jerusalem, nor further towards the east, nor upwards towards
the water shed, nor even on the south side of the ridge of the
hill at all. If all of the buildings in Bethlehem were razed to the
ground, so that not a trace of a town or even a cave could be seen,
then I could, despite the peculiar configuration of the terrain,
point out, without too much difficulty, by sight, where the
church stands, its position; a more accurate placement, however,
expressed by individual feet and inches, that was in keeping with
topographical traditions, and with the one in question, would
be omitted and would have to be given up in advance. If it may
be assumed that the Christians had a great and sincere interest in
the city of the birth and in the place of Jesus' birth specifically,
and that a chain of believers, connected chronologically took
heed of it with their very own eyes, it would have to have been
impossible to mislocate the site. Why did I not I weigh in the
balance such reasons as regards the question of the authenticity
of Golgotha? Because the historical, topographical, and political
conditions were different. Golgotha had to lie outside of the
city; if the account of the monks be true, then the tradition that
places it between the wady west, next to the area of the temple,
on the one hand, and the mid-valley of the Ben Hinnom, on
the other, where it bends next to the Hippicus Tower toward the
south, there it had no fortified place at which it ended; security
demanded or convenience also suggested that the two holy
sites be surrounded by the city wall. The oldest record does not
delimit the location of the birthplace in Bethlehem; the assumed
site in Bethlehem is not the safest from enemy raids, and if the
need for greater security would have advised moving the site,
it would have been to the heights of the western hill or that of
Jabal or Kilkel. As for the site of the ascension, the site was not
as permanent or fixed as that of the nativity, crucifixion, and
burial; the tradition must have been established later, and this

later one conflicted with the Bible.[i]

After this preparation, I will proceed to the temple history, which offers far greater certainty. Around the year 330, by order of the emperor Constantine,[ii] a basilica was built in Bethlehem[iii] at the site of Christ's birth,[iv] prior to the completion of the construction of the Temple of the Holy Sepulchre [end of page in Jerusalem.[v] Unfortunately, we lack an accurate description of the beautiful temple,[vi] which was not surpassed in splendour by the Church of the Resurrection.[vii] Where are such wide vestibules? one could ask. Where is the gilded ceiling? Where are the basilicas, equal in splendour to a palace, built by the contributions

---

i   A more detailed justification is given elsewhere.

ii   The pilgrim of Bordeaux, who visited Bethlehem in 334, wrote (154): Bethleem, ubi natus est Dominus noster Jesus Christus. Ibi basilica facta jussu Constantini. Near Bethlehem. *Socrat.* hist. eccles. 1, 13. In Bethlehem. *Sozomen.* hist. eccl. 2, 2.

iii   See the last note. *Euseb.* de vita Constantini 3, 40. The usual defiance of the writers, whose ranks Robinson also joins this time (2, 380) has it that the building was endowed by Helena. See Schwallart, della Valle, Surius, Ignaz v. Rheinfelden, Geramb, the Duke of Ragusa, Röser, and others. I note explicitly that the oldest writers cite Constantine as the founder, and only later writers, such as Socrates and Sozomenus attribute this honor to Helena. The whereabouts of the sources of reports that it was Jerome (Alexander 74) or Placidia, sister of Theodosius the younger, and his wife Endocia (see Raumer 309, evidently after Kootwyk, and the copyist Schubert 3, 19) who built the church, are unknown to me.

iv   See note 2 on p. 102. Primum illud (antrum), in quo primum Servator noster divini numinis virtute in carne apparuit, honoribus decenter ornavit (Konstantin). *Euseb.* 1. c. In antro illo, ubi Christus natus est secundum carnem… exstruit (Helena). *Socrat.* Ad speluncam illam, in qua Christus natus est. *Sozomen.*

v   I conclude this especially by means of a comparison with the words of the Bordeaux pilgrim. For the Church of the Resurrection, he uses the same formulation, only by increasing the modo: Ibidem modo jussu Constantini imperatoris basilica facta est (153). Eusebius pretty much predicts the building of the church in Bethlehem. Sozomenus says: Almost at the same time that Helena built the Church of the Resurrection. Socrates writes: As soon as Helena had completed the building of the New Jerusalem (Church of the Holy Sepulcher), she proceeded to build the temple in Bethlehem.

vi   See Eusebius in the last note.

vii   *Socrat.*

of individuals, through which such exquisiteness even the humblest of bodies may wander; because it seems as if in the world there were nothing more magnificent, one might even prefer to gaze at its roof than even the sky[i]? About seventy years after its construction, the church in Bethlehem was called the Church of the Grotto of the Saviour (*ecclesia speluncæ Salvatoris*),[ii] and it was said of Bethlehem: There is the holy church; there are the relics of the apostles and martyrs; there is the true confession of Christ; there is the faith preached by the apostles and trampled underfoot by the pagans, there is the Christian word rising daily to heaven; vanity, prestige, the greatness of a city, the pretence of seeing and being seen, of greeting and being greeted, of praising and scolding, of hearing and announcing, of having to move through large crowds of people, remains alien to the aspirations of the monks and their tranquillity, or they do not seek such things, at least.[iii] The leadership of the church was entrusted to the priest Jerome, whereas the parish was under the bishop of Jerusalem.[iv] Five priests in the monastery had the right to baptize.[v] Constantine's temple lasted only about two centuries. The emperor Justinian did not find it beautiful enough, had it pulled down, and built a church on the same site, which surpassed in beauty all the houses of worship in Jerusalem, and since the imperial envoy did not carry out the order according to Munsch, the emperor had his head cut off.[vi] Around 670 a somewhat

---

i   Ubi sunt latæ porticus? Ubi aurata laquearia? Ubi domus miserorum poenis et damnatorum labore vestitæ? Ubi instar palatii opibus privatorum exstructæ basilicæ, ut vile corpusculum hominis pretiosius inambulet, et, quasi mundo quicquam possit esse ornatius, tecta magis sua velint aspicere, quam coelum? *Paula et Eustochium* in epist. ad Marcellam. See the opp. *Hieronymi*, and also copied from his letter to Marcella.

ii   *Hieronymi* epitaph. *Paulæ*.

iii   *Paula* et *Eustochium* 1. c.

iv   *Sulpit. Severus* in dialog. S. 4 *Reland* ad voc. Bethlehem.

v   *Hieronymi* epist. ad *Pammachium*. In the former's opp. Epist. LXI, Erasmus' edition.

vi   Eutychius (Said Even Batrik), cited by Nau (400). The latter says: Celle

meagre report about the newer church is received. Located at the eastern and farthest corner of the town, over the Half-Grotto of the Nativity, known for the first time by the name of the Church of St. Mary,[i] it rose above the stone dining room[ii] as a large structure.[iii] If one does not want to perpetuate myths, I consider it highly probable that the real birthplace was chosen for construction in the fourth century; it would be downright foolish to accept the notion that the highly venerated site had been moved in a period in which until the year 614 the Christians ruled exclusively and even as late as 670, after having been distinguished with the placement of a temple above it, and that the Church of St. Mary that now towers above that very same place where emperor Constantine had the Temple of the Nativity of Our Lord erected could not plausibly be denied. Around 728 a church and an altar stood over the birthplace.[iv] About a hundred and forty years later, the Church of St. Mary was very large.[v] In 1010 it was said that during the Saracens' attempts to destroy the Church of the Nativity of Our Lord in Bethlehem a blinding light suddenly appeared, and the whole house of the Gentiles collapsed and died, and thus the Church of the Mother of God remained intact.[vi] When in 1099, the Franks entered Bethlehem, they found the church still in one piece.[vii] In this basilica the

---

(Eglise) que nous voyons, est l'ouvrage de l'Empereur Justinien.

i   See note 1 on p. 78.

ii   Probably refers to the part of the church where Maria ate with the Tree Wise Men. Cf. above on p. 95.

iii In eiusdem ciuitatis orientali et extremo angulo...cui (of the cave of the manger) utique semiantro super lapideum cæmaculum sanctæ mariæ æcclesia supra ipsum locum ubi dominus natus specialius traditur. grandi structura fabricata et fundata est. *Arculf.* 2, 2 (Cod. St. Gall. 267).

iv   Et ibi supra nunc est ædificata ecclesia: et ubi Domunus natus est, ibi stat supra nunc altare. Willibald. 20 (after the nun).

v   In cujus medio est scriptura sub uno lapide, cujus instroitus est a meridie, exitus vero ad orientem. *Bernard.* 16.

vi   Abemar in *Le Quien* Or. Christ. 3, 479.

vii *Saewulf.* 35.

conquerors, visiting the birthplace of Jesus, quickly performed their prayer of devotion to God, gave the Syrians (Syrian Christians) the sweet kiss of peace, and then hurriedly returned to the Holy City.[i] We have a very inadequate picture of the ancient church which passed into the hands of the Crusaders; this much is certain, however, that it was large and not lacking in ornamentation.[ii] It is possible that the Justinian temple still existed, which one only improved now and again.[iii] In 1101, on Christmas Day, Baldwin was crowned king in the Basilica of St. Mary near Bethlehem.[iv] In 1110, at the request of Baldwin II, Paschal II raised Bethlehem to the status of a diocese[v] and gave the cathedral to the village of Bethlehem, the municipality of Bedar (in the Affon region), Zeophir and Kai Kapha (Kaifa?).[vi] During the period of emperor Manuel Comnenus, King

---

i   *Fulcher. Carn.* 17 (397).

ii   Ecclesia satis decens et ampla miro opere fabricata (1110). Gesta Francorum expugn. Hierusal. 26 (573).

iii   *Fulcher. Carnot.*

iv   Episcopalem ibidem obtinet (ecclesia) dignitatem. Gesta Francor. exp. Hier. *Guil. Tyr.* 11, 2.

v   *Guil. Tyr.*

vi   *Phocas* 27. Temple inscription in Quaresmius 2, 672; Dositheus (hist. patriarch. p. 1213) in *Le Quien* 3, 643.

Amalric,[i] and Bishop Raguel,[ii] in the year 6677, according to the
Constantinian calendar or in the year 1169, according to the
Christian one, the church had been restored,[iii] most probably
rebuilt, leaving perhaps only a few Constantinian or Justinian
foundation walls[iv]; at the very least a thorough repair and
beautification had taken place, and though he had decorated the
church entirely with gilded stones,[v] the emperor Manuel
Comnenus did not gain any honour for this act of charity.
Efraim oversaw the construction, in general, and the mosaic

---

i   Almerik I reigned from 1163 to 1173, while the reign of Emanuel
Komnenus falls between 1143 and 1180. According to others' opinions,
Edrisi visited Bethlehem around 1155; however, since he only saw the newer
building, we must assume that the visit took place later. Based on Almerik,
Mariti declares it to be between 1162 and 1173. Quaresmius only read the
Greek and translated it as "A. 677", without saying, as the abbate led him
believe, that it was the Year of the World. Mariti erred perhaps even more
when he did not know the correct reading by the patriarchal Dositheus in
Le Quien Or. Christ., copied by Quaresmius, and the same mistake was
made by Chateaubriand (1, 299 sq.), who was being impatient with Mariti,
because he rapped on the knuckles of one of the mad and confused pundits.
Of course, what the Jesuit Nau says in 677 is even more nonsensical (401): Il
parle là de l'année des Mahometans. I must add that in Quaresmius (2, 645)
I found the year 676 (above the porta S. Mariæ) = 1168 a. D. and 624 (on
a gate) = 1116. The difference is no less than 52 years, and one can hardly
assume that the construction lasted that long.

ii Tempel inscription after Dositheus l. c. Quaresmius read (2, 672)
Raulinet. The allusion here is to the Greek bishop; the Latin one was called
Radulph. Le Quien Or. Christ. 3, 1278 sq.

iii Quantum enim possum conjicere, non video, quod tempore beati
Jeronymi sit adificata illa ecclesia solemnis, quæ hodie ibi est, quam tamen
inexperti dicunt ab Helena erectam, quod et ego credebam, sed dispositio
moderna non admittit...Credo ecclesiam illam ædificatam temporibus
novissimis latinorum regum Jerusalem et monasterium hoc similiter... et
alia dispositio loco data, quod et scripturæ, pictura et sculpturæ monstrant.
Fabri 2, 339 sq. What Quaresmius and Dositheus convey from the inscriptions does not contradict Fabrian's view. The church was built by Helena and
renewed by Christian princes. Prokesch 117.

iv I am not at all surprised when Chateaubriand writes that the church is
antique, bearing the mark of its Greek origins, but rather when the sober
Robinson thinks (2, 380) that the church as it exists today was supposedly
founded by Helena.

v   In Greek: *Phocas*.

work, in particular.[i] I also believe that in this new structure, the old form of the Constantinian or Justinian church was essentially retained, out of reverence; or at least the basilica form was preserved. This temple, newly built over the ceiling of the Grotto of the Nativity[ii] was very large,[iii] elongated, and cross-shaped, covered with wood that does not rot, and the altar was topped with a brick dome.[iv] The incomparable splendour was praised,[v] as was the gold mosaic, to which the aforementioned emperor must have contributed a great deal. The first bishop of the Franks was called Aschetinus or Asguitinus. Around 1136 Anselm appointed the bishopric; in the year 1147 Gerald or Gerard; in 1157 and 1167 Ralph, who died in 1173; in 1175 Albert was presented to the church. The latter attended the church assembly in Lateran in 1179.[vi] After Ascalon was conquered by the

---

i   Tempel inscription in Quaresmius. The Greek name is shown and the Latin one is called Efrem. The latter, somewhat indistinctly, reads as follows: Comes nostis et Inretatis et Grecis imperitabat, hic ecclesiame (ecclesia me) docebat. S Efrem fertur fecisse tvavtem. Even Nau read (400) on his first journey (1668) the Greek inscription; but he gives the Latin translation by Quaresmius. Opera Ephraim monachi et historiographi. *Desitheus* I. c.

ii In Greek: *Phocas.*

iii *Phocas.* Edrisi (346) and the monk Epiphanius (52) both wrote "big".

iv *Phocas.*

v   Solid and so delicate that it cannot possibly be compared. Edrisi. Very nice. *Phocas.*

vi *Le Quien* Or. Christ. 3, 1277 sqq. Albert signed himself at the church meeting: Provinciæ Palestinæ I. Albertus Bethleem episcopus, and was given St. Martin's Church near Pisa in 1186. The later, more titular (in partibus) Latin bishops, are the following: Peter I (at least in 1204, a bishop of Bethlehem was among the electors of Balduin I., the Latin Emperor of Constantinople), Regnerius who in 1223 attended a review of the aid to the Holy Land under Pope Honorius III, Thomas Agni de Lentino from 1255 to 1267, Gaillard d'Oursault, Hugo from 1285 to about 1287, Petrus de Sancto Mexentio, Jagard or Gerard under Pope Boniface VIII, Wulfram d'Abbeville from 1301, Gerard de Gisors, Johann Hegescliff, Petrus III from the year 1347, Durandus, Adimar de Rupe, Johann II, Wilhelm de Valen from 1383 to about 1389, Johann de Genence and Hugh before the year 1394. *Le Quien* 3, 1280 sqq. In 1199 the election of canons was disputed. See the relevant document from Pope tom. 1. edit. *Baluz.* epistolar. *Innocent.* III. tit. 27 de restitutione. Idem canonicis Bethleemitanis. Cum super electione

Christians in 1153, it was incorporated into the episcopal see of Bethlehem.[i] In 1187, a disastrous one for the Christians, most of the church was depopulated, but it was not significantly damaged; at most, the altars and some images were destroyed.[ii] We can, therefore, confirm and add to the description of the temple from 1219: The lead-roofed cathedral was very beautiful; the base, shaft, and pommel of the columns were of the finest marble, as were the floor and the vaults; the walls were decorated with gold and silver, with various colours, and even most delicately embellished with all the art and splendour of painting (mosaics). Of course, the Saracens would have destroyed the cathedral many times if the Christians had not prevented this misfortune with heavy monetary sacrifices.[iii] I will now summarize how the church appeared from 1219 to 1449, because it is very probable that it endured no change in this period of two hundred and thirty years, and if it did, it must have been largely insignificant. One can only regret that no single accurately detailed descriptions have been handed down to us. The former

---

Bethleemitensi etc. p. 585 col. 2. *Le Quien* 3, 1280. The Greek bishops had a larger sphere of activity. Elias was the bishop before Raguel (see the following note). Marc the patriarch, who succeeded Jacob in 1482, strangely bore the title: Archiepiscopus Bethleem et patriarcha s. urbis Hierosolymitanæ et sanctæ Sion etc. *Le Quien* 3, 516. Anathasius was a citizen of Bethlehem before the year 1646 (*Le Quien* 3, 643); a bishop was commemorated in 1660 (*Le Quien* 3, 520 B); Neophytus was Bishop from 1661 until at least the year 1672, in which he signed himself under the synod in Greek; Before 1733 Malachias; 1733 Ananias (archiepiscopus) lived in the village of Wallachia. *Le Quien* 3, 643 sq.; 3, 777 sq.

i   S. ecclesiae Bethleem et Ascalonis unitae in *Le Quien* Or. Christ. 3, 1275 sqq. But now it says here 3, 602 B: Anno 6654. mundi juxta aeram Constantinopolitanam, i. e. Christi 1146, sedebat Bethleem, quo sedes Ascalonitana a quibusdam annis translata fuerat, Elias. Dositheus enim…lib. 7 de Patriarch, Hierosol., c. 22. par. 4., refert Eliam, episcopum Graecum Bethleem..

ii   *Fabri* 1, 474.

iii Thetmar in Maltens Weltk., Febr., 1844, 192.

cathedral[i] was located at the east end of the hill[ii] and was large,[iii] sixty feet wide and a hundred wide long to the choir,[iv] and had an oblong[v] or cross shape, like the collegiate churches in the Occident.[vi] Because of its beauty, the magnificent building[vii] was without equal anywhere in the world.[viii] The lead-covered roof was supported by beams and rafters of precious wood.[ix] Colourful marble covered the floor.[x] The side walls at the bottom were covered with marble one-storey high[xi]; further up,[xii] above the columns up to the roof beams,[xiii] the walls of the nave were richly decorated,[xiv] like a royal palace,[xv] with very beautiful, exquisite mosaics,[xvi] some of them shining with gold,[xvii] depicting

i *Vitriac.* e. 59.

ii Brocardt 869. In a place that faces east. Monteuilla 773.

iii Rudolph von Suchen 842.

iv Gumpenberg 464. He does say 6' wide; for the misspelling or misprint alone I put 60 in good conscience.

v *Anonymous* in *Allat.* 16.

vi Gumpenberg.

vii Rudolph von Suchen.

viii Brocardt 869. Ut vix hodie inveniri possit locus sacer illo pulchrior. It is called the church sacellum. *Marin. Sanut.* 3, 14, 11. Ecclesia autem illa de bethlaem...et pulcherrime et devotissima. *Pipin.* 72b. Monteuilla. Rudolph von Suchen.

ix *Marin. Sanut.* On top, it is not covered with fabric, but with exquisite cedar wood and beams. Rudolph v. Suchen. *Anonymous* in *Allat.* The most beautiful beams and ratchets of cypress wood. Gumpenberg.

x *Marin. Sanut.* Brocardt.

xi Inside of a building, lined with marble stones. Gumpenberg 463.

xii All of it is above... Gumpenberg. He especially distinguishes between the fact that the lower section of the walls was decorated with marble and the upper one with mosaic.

xiii *Marin. Sanut.*

xiv Ibid.

xv Rudolph v. Suchen.

xvi Gumpenberg (464) puts it as follows: beautiful pictures and paintings made of gold, "like Sanct Mark's churches in Venice."

xvii Golden mosaic. *Anonymous* in *Allat.* Rudolph v. Suchen says at some point that the "mused" work consists of jasper, marble and gold, and else-the history from the beginning of the world to the Last Judgment,[i] in particular the genealogy of Jesus.[ii] Columns of very precious marble,[iii] astonishing because of their quantity[iv] and size,[v] formed four rows.[vi] The choir itself, eighty feet long and thirty-five wide, was already decorated with mosaics,[vii] and had six marble pillars; the corner pillars of which three hewn sides stood free, were equal in size to three others; each of the two apses, which crossed the choir, measured forty feet in length and twenty-five in width.[viii] Outside, the temple was protected by bulwarks[ix] and many high towers[x].

If the miraculous tales about the removal of the marble columns deserve little credence, it is nonetheless a credibly reported fact that in 1449 the church was already missing many marble stones with which the side walls were lined, and which the Saracens or their Christian accomplices had stolen.[xi] Time also revealed how

---

where that the walls are covered in gold. See Gumpenberg in the following note.

i   *Marin. Sanut.*

ii   *Baldensel* 119.

iii *Marin. Sanut.* Others, such as Brocardt, Monteuilla, Rudolph v. Suchen, Gumpenberg, simply mention marble columns.

iv   *Marin. Sanut.* The number that is given varies, from 40 in Monteuilla and Gumpenberg, to almost 70 in Rudolph v. Suchen, to 50 in the anonymous at Allatius.

v   *Marin. Sanut.* Each 1½ fathoms thick (in circumference) and 3 high. Gumpenberg.

vi   *Marin. Sanut.*

vii Very nicely offset with beautiful pieces and lines. Gumpenberg.

viii Gumpenberg. While he refers to marble columns, but also mentions their hewn sides, I wrote "pillars" instead.

ix   With strong walls and bulwarks, like a mighty castle. Rudolph v. Suchen.

x   (Church) with many high towers, and with strong, well-constructed pillars. Monteuilla. Later the pilgrims frequently mention a tower located southeast by the chancel, which the Greeks used as a monastic building, and on Bonifacio and Zuallart's ground plan, there is under the letter N a Torre rovinata, about two nave lengths from the present outer entrance to the church.

xi   Gumpenberg 463. Cf. above on p. 87 ff. and 98.

it gnashes its teeth. After three hundred years, the roof became dilapidated, and permission was finally obtained to repair it, which took place around 1482.[i] The Duke Philip of Burgundy provided the wood and Edward, King of England, the lead.[ii] The Franciscans saw to it that all the necessary timber was prepared in Venice by craftsmen who had received the exact measurement from the church, and brought on ships to Jaffa, and from here shepherded by camels to Bethlehem. Thus, Venetian craftsmen built the entire church roof, and much effort and expense were required to create what was lacking in wood and lead. The old cedar and cypress wood from Mount Lebanon was replaced by new spruce wood from our mountains. The church also became cleaner as a result of the repair; because before it was full of pigeons and sparrows and nests of various birds, which made messes almost everywhere, especially on the exquisite floor: later, however, this mess was also thwarted by numerous martens who tolerated neither birds nor messes.[iii] In the middle of the sixteenth century, people were already complaining about the miserable structural condition.[iv] In 1542, again, in many places the roof could not withstand the rain[v]; the temple still preserved

---

i   *Fabri* 1, 477.

ii   Alexander 74. According to Jodokus von Meggen (119), the Duke of Burgundy covered the roof with lead tiles. Alexander could have probably said that the church had recently been roofed. – It was without doubt Edward IV (1461 to 1483). Philip III stepped down from actively participating in these affairs as early as 1463; but anyone who knows the slow pace with which authorizations are given in the Orient will not be surprised that the renovation was held up for so long. Mariti says (2, 377) that the church was newly renovated in 1492 by Ferdinand and Isabella of Spain. Hardly; for Duke Alexander, who visited Bethlehem only three years later, would have mentioned this first. I note in passing that wood for a Palestinian monastery was also loaded on the Giusto, Captain Budinich, with which I sailed to Alexandria in 1835.

iii   *Fabri* 1, 477 sq. I translated martrices as marten (martes).

iv   Helffrich 718. *Jod. a Meggen.* The latter mentions that the reason why the temple is dilapidated or close to decay in many places is because the Christian princes used to spend more on these buildings in earlier times.

v   *Jod. a Meggen.*

magnificent treasures from the Frankish period, and it was called beautiful, at least parts of it, until the end of that century[i]. If one looked at a marble panel on the wall, one saw, as in a mirror, everything that was going on in the back of the church.[ii] The mosaics were particularly praiseworthy,[iii] especially on the side walls at the top of the central nave.[iv] In 1586 the figures were still easily recognizable.[v] However, in the previous century, the magnificent work of art deteriorated in a very regrettable way.[vi] As late as 1673, many large and well-preserved paintings in mosaic above could still be seen,[vii] and in 1719, one did not notice

---

i   This is a nice, big church. Tucher 667. I have not yet seen or heard of any man who says he has seen a church as devout and precious as the church in Bethlehem. Breydenbach 131. Alexander. *Medschired*-dîn 135. Magnificent, probably unparalleled worldwide. *Georg.* 523. Very nice. *Anshelm.* 1290. Absolutely magnificent, one of the most beautiful churches in the world. Tschudi 274. A nice, big church. Wormbser 409. Beautiful. Villinger 93. The most beautiful church in Judah. *Fürer* 65. You would have to go a long way without coming across such a magnificent and beautiful one. Rauchwolff 644. There is an especially beautiful church there. Schweigger 122. Helffrich expressed himself conditionally (718): There must have been a beautiful and awfully wide church there in the old times. Similarly (quite identically) Schwallart 306. Cf. p. 83, note 4.

ii   Fabri 260. Tschudi 274.

iii   Of a beautiful, aristocratic, mused work...of marble decorated with many different colors, everything so exquisite that many think it is priceless. Breydenbach, note 131. Richly painted with fine gold. Alexander. There are several beautiful paintings to see, which are inlaid skillfully and artistically with irenic colors. Schwallart. Adorned with a mosaic from precious stones. Ignaz v. Rheinfelden 130.

iv   On the sides, and above in vaults. Schwallart. What is meant here are the vaults above the double rows of columns, and so I myself interpret the words in Viagg. al S. Sepolcro (F 6a): Di sopra, e di sotto è lavorata (the church), ed ornata di belle pietre (mosaic). See also the somewhat obscure passage in Breydenbach. Alexander more puzzlingly says: "The walls of the same church are also painted from the ground up" (mosaic). I cannot agree with this as one knows exactly from earlier times that the lower wall of the church had marble wainscoting.

v   Schwallart.

vi   With age it peeled off in many places. Ignaz von Rheinfelden.

vii   Non ostante il giro di tanti secoli. *Legrenzi* 1, 182. II en reste encore quelque chose, mais il en est bien tombé depuis la premiere fois que je les vis l'année 1668 ... il n'en reste plus que l'Apparition de N. S. à S. Thomas..,

much more beyond that.[i] It is not clear to me how in 1778, one could recognize large figures of crude mosaic representing the most noble stories from the Old Testament,[ii] and also how, in 1818, one was able to judge that the mosaics bore the imprint of the Middle Ages,[iii] however true the verdict may be before the tribunal of history. Of the mutilated remains of the figures mentioned in 1817,[iv] we return to an earlier time to consider them more closely. We learn what we already know — that the stories from the beginning of the world to Judgment Day were artistically rendered[v] — as well as additional details from the first quarter of the sixteenth century. On one arch was the entire genealogy as described in the first chapter of Matthew; to the left of it was the entire genealogical register from the Gospel. It read thus: it happened as they baptized all peoples, etc., and so there were many more lineages. Above the main gate, which faced east (?) and was never opened, stood the genealogical tree that sprouted from Adam's rib, and the first branch bore Ezekiel, the other Jacob, and so branch upon branch the prophets who foretold the birth of Jesus, each with the prophecy in his hand.[vi] In the century before last, the images were no longer clearly discernible, because it was said that the mosaic work showed

---

quelque chose de son Ascension au Ciel, de l'Assomption de la Vierge...*Nau* 399.

i   *Ladoire* 193. From the paintings on the walls Neret saw only a few pieces that were almost erased (112).

ii   Binos 207. This is even harder to do if one hears that on the columns there used to be Latin and Greek inscriptions, and figures painted in glaze and yellow. One can compare this with what Mariti (2, 375) says, that nothing is more strange than glass worked into a mosaic, i.e., the composition of small colored glass parts against a gold background.

iii   De Forbin 123. Even though O. F. Richter (38) recognized the remaining fragments of mosaic as Byzantine shortly before.

iv   Joliffe 118. Cf. note 3, p. 84.

v   Breydenbach 132.

vi   Viagg. al S. Sepolcro. Several beautiful stories taken from the Old Testament. Rauchwolff.

different likenesses of the holy ones,[i] despite the fact that a large section of it had already fallen off or had deteriorated,[ii] which made it impossible to see and evaluate the piece in its entirety. Inscriptions also accompanied the mosaic, as already hinted at just now and previously.[iii] In the first quarter of the sixteenth century, above the aforementioned main gate, one saw a Greek and Latin inscription,[iv] and in 1542 ones in gold, as ornamentation.[v]

In the first quarter of the seventeenth century, one could read Latin, Greek and other inscriptions, which had been handed down for posterity by way of the printed word,[vi] and some of which I will include here. On the doors of the large entrance (facing west) one read an Arabic and an Armenian inscription. Translated, the latter reads: 'In the year 676, St. Mary's gate was made with the cooperation of Father Abraham and Father Arachel, under the reign of Erman, son of Etem Constantine. Christ, the Lord, help their souls. Amen'. Once one entered the temple, one noticed above the gate an image of a tree on whose branches the prophets with their prophecies about Christ were depicted. Thus Joel: 'On that day shall be, etc. (3, 18), Amos: On certain days the sun will set at noon, etc. (8, 9), Micah: From the land of Bethlehem, Ephrath, etc. (5, 2)'. Under the windows, directly above the columns, on the side wall from the entrance

---

i   Troilo 393. Surius says (525) that above the columns, around the windows by the wooden framework, no pieces of mosaic representent au Naturel Nostre Sauveur et la S. Vierge avec les mysteres de son Incarnation adorable, et autres belles histoires de la S. Escriture.

ii   Desquelles une grande partie et gastée, soit par vieillesse, soit par mancquement de reparation. *Surius.* Zwinner 371. Cf. note 3, p. 114.

iii   Notes 6 and 7 to p. 106, note 1 to p. 107.

iv   Viaggo al S. Sepolcro.

v   *Jod. a Meggen.*

vi   *Quaresm.* 2, 645 sqq. I do not quite trust later mentions of the inscriptions, such as the ones by Binos (see note 6 to p. 114), Chateaubriand (on the walls of the nave still traces of Greek and Latin letters) and Joliffe (half-extinct Greek inscriptions from the Evangelists).

of the church to the end of the nave, one could see bust portraits of the Jewish kings and the famous men from whom our Saviour descended, according to the evangelists Matthew and Luke. Above these figures, on the north side, arches or faldstools were inscribed in square areas, under each of which was depicted a pedestal with a book, with an incense burner on one side and with a candlestick and cross on the other. Above it, and partly in two columns next to it, were Greek inscriptions referring to several councils and to the number of bishops involved. For example, one read: 'The Holy Synod of Twelve Bishops, assembled in Ankara a city in Galatia, was held before the General Church Assembly at Nicaea on the subject of priests, etc.'; 'Antioch. The Holy Synod of Thirty-Three Bishops, held in Antioch, a city in Syria, was convened before the General Church Assembly at Nicaea, against Paul of Samos, who claimed that Christ was a mere mortal. The synod condemned him as a miscreant'; 'The holy synod, convened in the city of Serdica, was held to reinstate St. Athanasius of Alexandria, St. Meletius of Antioch, and St. Paul, Antistes of Constantinople, in their dioceses from which they had been expelled by the Arians'; 'The Holy Synod of Fifteen Bishops, convened in the metropolis of Gangra, was held to condemn the heretic Eustathius, who taught that those who eat meat at weddings cannot be blessed. The high synod banned him as a miscreant'; 'Carthage. The Holy Synod of Fifty Bishops, summoned to Carthage in Africa under St. Cyprian, was held against Novatus, who had deprived sinners of the virtuous remedy of penance. The holy assembly expelled him from the community as a heretic'. The dicta of the church assemblies held in Nicaea, Constantinople, Ephesus, and Chalcedon were also inscribed in this way. These inscriptions provide evidence of how much effort was made in the Middle Ages to give human statutes the appearance of divine ones in order to provide an even stronger barrier against false doctrines or free thought.

In the choir, on the vault of the great chapel, was the angel greeting the Virgin; on the arch itself were images of David and Abraham with a Latin inscription referring to them. On the right or northern side, one saw the apostles in a seated position and opposite on the left or southside, the same as they carried Mary on a bier, above which there was a Latin inscription and below it a Greek inscription, both referring to the construction of the church. In the right or northern arm of the temple cross rose a vast palace or throne supported by pillars: here was a door where Christ and his disciples, along with Thomas, stood, and one read the words: 'Ianuis clausis. Infer digitum huc'.[i] Then the Ascension of the Lord followed, and there were the words: 'Ascensio. † Viri Galilei, quid statis aspiciente (s) in celum? Hic Iesus qui assumtus est sic veniet quemadmodum vidistis eum'.[ii] In the left or southern arm there were some not so insignificant fragments. At the vault, towards the south, one saw the adoration of the Wise Men and the angel who led them on another path. There, a panel bore the inscription: 'Ecce virgo concipiet et pariet filium et vocabitur nomen ejus Emoanuel'.[iii] In this arm, on the east side, one saw the Samaritan woman talking with Christ and the inscription: 'Loquitur cum Samaritana Iocachim'.[iv] Further up was the nearly disintegrated image of a man sitting at a table with a book on it. On the image, it read: 'S. Ioh. Evvangelista', and on the book: 'In principio'.[v] Painted below was the transfiguration of Christ in the presence of Moses, Elijah, Peter, James, and John, with the solemn entry of the Lord into Jerusalem on Palm Sunday, and one saw the following scripture: 'Transfiguratio

---

i   Put your finger here (2, 672). Strauß (Sinai und Golgotha. Berlin 1847. P. 287) may himself be responsible for the following words: "The walls are adorned with colored mosaics against a gold background; Thomas placing his hand in the Savior's side, or the disciples as they look up at the Lord ascending to heaven."

ii From the Apostelgesch. 1, 11.

iii From Jesaias 7, 14.

iv Joachim speaks with the female Samaritan.

v   The opening words of the Gospel of John.

Domini. Heliah. ICH CHS (Jesus Christus). Moises. Ramis palmarum. IHS XPS (Christus)'. On the opposite west side, the imprisonment of Christ was depicted, only with the words: 'Petrus und Iudoeorum'. All of these depictions and inscriptions were done in mosaic; between the nave windows there was always a large angel but painted quite simply. Similarly, some images of saints with inscriptions were painted on the columns.[i]

After the middle of the century before last, the temple was described as partially dilapidated; the lead was falling off.[ii] It apparently fell into ruin as the Greeks took most of the lead off the roof and sold it to the Turks for casting bullets when they moved outside of Candia. The Greek monks even seized the wooden beams, tore them down, and cut boards out of them with their long wooden saws. No wonder the church became so completely porous that it rained heavily inside, that it turned into a bird's nest, that jackdaws, starlings, and sparrows, in particular, nested inside, and that these made such a miserable noise that one could barely hear one another speak.[iii] It could not be allowed to continue if tradition or the more external expression of Christ were not to die with it. And it so happened that the church was repaired and consecrated in 1672 under the Greek patriarch Dositheus, on the occasion of a synod held by the Greek Orthodox against the teachings of Calvin and his follower Cyril Lucaris, from Constantinople.[iv] The construction costs were estimated at 25,000 zecchins, of which 5,000 were fees.[v] If the sum is correct, then this repair must have been a

---

i   In columnis. *Quaresm.* 2, 673.

ii Zwinner.

iii Troilo, note 393. Cf. the second, subsequent note.

iv The resolutions of this synod were signed on 16 March 1672. *Harduini concil.* tom. 11. col. 267, in *Le Quien* Or. Christ. 3, 522 sq. Cf. Mariti 2, 378.

v   *Mariti.* Cet édifice tomboit tout en ruine, il n'y a que trois ou quatre ans. Le plomb qui le couvroit, ayant éte derobé en plusieurs endroits ..., la pluye avoit corrompu le bois, et gastoit tout. Les Grecs on fait une dépense d'approchant 100,000. écus, pour reparer ce sanctuaire, et obtenir de l'Em-

rather extensive; however, the shape and side walls of the nave, at least of the middle and upper parts, remained; the roof truss] and roof, in any case, had to be completely rebuilt. If the lead roof had been taken care of at all times, so that the rain did not penetrate and damage the wooden roof structure, one would undoubtedly still see the cypress and cedar wood that was used in the time of the Latin kings. The new carpentry was lauded by the Franconians and experts as the most beautiful one could see.[i] I am not aware of any significant improvements to the church that have taken place since then. My contemporaries rightly complained that the church had fallen into disrepair.[ii] They therefore set to work to save the temple from complete decay. In 1842 the Greeks provisionally obtained someone to repair the temple. It was accomplished at considerable cost and with as much respect for the old building plan as circumstances permitted. Among other things, the northern wing (transept) of the church cross, which was assigned to the Armenians, was also improved.[iii]

If we take a look at the history of the temple, we can see that after the first construction it was rebuilt four times, namely in the sixth century, in the middle of the twelfth, in 1672, and in the present decade, when for the first time there was a complete

---

pereur des Turcs la permission de le faire. On dit que cette permission seule a coûté 20,000. écus. C'est un Boucher de Constantinople, qui a fourni toute cette somme; et l'on m'a raconté, que se voyant riche de 50,000. écus et sans enfans, il s'en est reservé mille seulement, et a sacrifié le reste cette œuvre de pitié; Dieu veüille (the Jesuit adds) que le schisme ne la luy rende pas inutile. *Nau* 401 sq.

i   Sa nef est couverte de la plus belle charpente qu'il soit possible de voir, toute de bois de cedre, cette charpente qui est faite en dos d'âne...*Ladoire*.

ii   Left in ruins. Mayr v. A. 330. In decay, and if help does not come, soon in ruins. Prokesch 113. Stripped of all ornaments and decayed (exaggerated). Röser 446. The magnificent Church at Bethlehem, which had fallen into a state of miserable decay. *Williams*, the Holy City, 438.

iii   *Williams*. In his time, the Armenians' Christian love seemed to want to affect a firmân to undo what the Greeks had done. In my time, everything was still unchanged.

rebuilding, for the second and third time, a new roof structure was erected and for the second time, other important construction works were carried out. Awareness of this history shows how untenable the opinion of even recent writers is that before one stands a Hellenic building, or that the cedar and cypress beams were constructed by the Crusaders to support the roof. The nave that we see today is probably the work of the Franks, even if the interior of the choir has been significantly altered or the outer wall has been newly built. No one regrets more than I do that the historical findings of antiquity are not more favourable, that nothing of apparent value has been preserved from the time of Constantine the Great. I would gladly have celebrated the consecration of the church in spirit if fortune had shown me the temple of the first Christian emperor. One would almost like to renounce sober research for the moment and become a dreamer, to dream of the sweet delight of the ancient Christians.

I can tie together with a continuous thread the history of its ownership.[i] After the expulsion of the Franks in 1187, the Syrian Christians were undoubtedly in possession of the church. After the Franciscans settled in Bethlehem, they seemed to have appropriated part of it without much difficulty. The construction carried out by the Western monks sufficiently proves that in the middle of the fifteenth century they controlled the church. In the following century their lucky star continued to shine[ii]; only in the beginning of the seventeenth century did it begin to fade, and in 1616 it was said that the church was common to all nations, the Armenian and Greek nations most prominent among them.[iii] The Greeks then mulled over a plan to oust the Roman Catholics, and indeed, after the middle of the century before last, the church belonged exclusively to those usurpers.[iv]

---

i   Radzivil goes all the way back (169): they have brought in monks from the Order of St. Jerome.

ii Churches which belong to the Catholics. Radzivil.

iii Della Valle 1, 157.

iv Troilo 392. He expresses himself somewhat differently on p. 394: Said

The construction which the Greeks undertook in 1672 was certainly a triumph of their right of ownership and clearly served to fortify it. It took quite a long time for the Latins to regain possession of what they had lost. Upon the birth of the Dauphin, living in 1738, the French envoy obtained for them the possession of the high altar from the Grand Sultan, and that same year, the Greeks no longer enjoyed the freedom to say Mass at the altars on all sides.[i] Around 1758 the Orthodox Greeks took the sanctuary from the Latins, who allegedly built a wall to separate it from the nave.[ii] If the church belonged to the Greeks in 1813, [iii] the Armenians occupied the nave two years later.[iv] In 1829 the Armenians had the upper hand in the house of God, which had to be abandoned by the Roman Catholic congregation because it could not or would not settle a monetary claim made by the pasha: proof that since the displacement by the Greeks in the previous century, they had newly claimed the ownership or co-ownership. At that time, namely in the decade before last, the central altar and one wing actually belonged to the Armenians and the other to the Greeks.[v] In the last decade, the Greeks and Armenians held onto their money, which they sent to the pasha of Damascus and to the Ottoman Porte, in uncontested possession.[vi] In my time, the Greeks were the least active in the nave.

Greek monks, who also have jurisdiction over part of the churches, against their monastery. Legrenzi remarks (1, 183): Nel tempo, che i Greci havevano usurpato con il Presepio l'antedescritta Chiesa (St. Mary's Church) alli nostri Padri, and de Bruyn, writes possibly even more vaguely (2, 224), that the church was taken from the Latins by the Greeks.

i   Pococke 2 par. 51. He introduced the note with the words: The church in Bethlehem belonged formerly to the Greeks. Binos thought (207) that the Holy of Holies had been in the possession of the Franciscans since time immemorial.

ii   Cf. above on p. 81 and note 3.

iii   Mayr 330.

iv   Richter 38.

v   Prokesch, note 113.

vi   Geramb 1, 150. Cf. Schubert 3, 19.

The Chapel of the Nativity

We have two ground plans:

1586

By Zullart (215), who probably copied it from Boniface. [Edward] Pococke also took up this ground plan (2, 25); only he moved the tombs of Paula and Eustochium to the south side of the tomb, instead of the old plan showing them on the north side, which still looks very flawed.

1596

By Bernardino Amico (Tav. 3). Quaresmius (2, 632) and Zwinner (364), who increased his or their ground plan with the tomb containing the Altar of the Innocents. This plan is still accurate today, except that the narrow gap in the rock is often missing from that altar. The various chapels or caves and passages are also marked (dotted) on the ground plans for the Church of St. Mary, and it is on this dotted plan that the gap in the rock appears. Copies were provided, for example, by Zuallart (208), Amico (Tav. 3), Quaresmius (l. c.) Pococke (2, 25 and 59), Roberts (Part. VIII. Shrine of the Nativity). When looking at the latter picture, one must know that the viewer is standing on the west side of the chapel facing the birthplace of the Nativity, the staircase, the deep recess to the south where the crib is located, the π = shaped trellis to the north in the depth and a canopy above it; and do not forget, the colourist applied the colours incorrectly.

Before describing the entrances, I must, in order to make it easier for the reader to follow my description, note that the chapel lies directly under the large chancel[i] of the church and in the same direction as it. There are currently three entrances,[ii] two next to and opposite to each other from the chancel, and a more remote one on the west side of the Church of St. Catherine, which partially abuts the north side of the chancel with its south side. The first pair of doors, a southern and a northern one,[iii] can close if needed but are usually left open,[iv] at least during church services, and admission is free. Each staircase leads from the space between the high altar and the eastern wing corner, converging westward down into the chapel, as if into a cellar.[v] It is strange that the staircases, which are not very distinctive,[vi] have an unequal number of steps; namely, the southern staircase has only thirteen, while the northern staircase has sixteen, which corresponds exactly to the number that we know from 1449.[vii] Although in 1842 the staircases were repaired.[viii] One would think that such a simple matter would not produce errors, but

---

i   Gumpenberg 464. *Albert. Sax.* 2110. *Fabri* 1, 469. *Georg.* 523. (Underneath the high altar) Viagg. al S. Sepolcro F 6a. Schwallart 303. Justement dessous le grand Chœur. *Surius* 526. Troilo 395, and many others; but one should orient oneself above all by using the ground plans, such as mine.

ii   On entre dans cette sacrée Grotte par trois differens endroits. *Ladoire* 197, among others.

iii   Specus est portis ferreis clausus, *Fürer* 66. Also Schwallart. After 6 floors on vient à la porte qui est de bronze large de 2. pieds et ½, haute de 8. *Surius.* Iron gates. Troilo 395. Deux portes de bronze ornées de tres belles figures en bas relief. *Ladoire.* This proves the, admittedly very insignificant, fact that the doors have been replaced.

iv   According to Rauchwolff, the entrance was closed several times (644), and according to Legrenzi, only the northern one (1, 180: la porta à mane manco nel corno dell' Evangelio).

v   *Anshelm.* 1290.

vi   Marches de jaspe et de porphire. *Ladoire.*

vii   If you walk in via the side where the three kings offered their sacrifices, you go down 16 steps, and if you walk in via the other side when our Lord was circumcised, you go down 13 steps. Gumpenberg 464. A clarity of expression that could serve as a model to our Schubert. Gumpenberg, likewise Quaresmius (2, 644).

viii Among other repairs they (the Greeks) restored...the steps which lead down from their altar to the Holy Cave of the Nativity. *Williams* 438.

this was not so. We already find differences in the number of steps of the north staircase,[i] even more in that of the south staircase,[ii] and pilgrims who did not realize that the number of steps of both staircases was different counted only the steps of one or the other staircase and immediately assigned the sum to both.[iii] Moreover, during that period one often also introduced calculation errors.[iv] The numbers correspond so little to one another that no increase or decrease in the number of steps due to construction from 1449 onwards can be assumed. The first mention of a staircase dates back to the twelfth century. To the left (probably north) of the high altar was an entrance, and it had sixteen steps.[v] One would be tempted to think that only the northern staircase existed at that time, which would also have been very logical because extending into the northern slope the cave had to be accessible only from the north side. Insofar as it still existed, if later, already in the fourteenth century,[vi] the southern staircase was known, as I see it, a shaft was probably sunk through the vault of rock above or more to the south, which then served as an entrance. Such a view, has, by the way,

---

i   Fabri (1, 469), Zwinner (373; on 363 only 13) count 16, unlike Surius (526), who counts 15 steps.

ii   In Tucher (667, to the left from the high altar), 11 steps in Tschudi 276; although he says incorrectly: from the altar of the three kings), 10 in Scheidt (70), 12 in Zwinner, 13 in Surius.

iii   Albert von Sachsen counted 11 steps; Anshelm (1290), Fürer (66), Prokesch (114, for each) all counted 16.

iv   Breydenbach (131) and Tschudi (271) count 10 steps, Ladoire 12, 17, Chateaubriand (1, 301) and Geramb (1, 156: each) 15, and Binos (207: in an apparent mixup with the stairs of St. Catherine's Church) 25 in total.

v   In Greek *Phocas* 27.

vi   Baldensel says (119) that one descends into the cave via 14 steps located to the right next to the choir per paucos gradus, and the anonymous in Allatius (15) that one descends there via 14 steps to the left of the high altar. In Greek: Marinus Sanutus (3, 14, 11) and the Cod. Vienn. 4578 (202d) mention 10 steps: From the same place you get into a chapel via ten steps; 16 like in the past, more recent past, and the present, Monteuilla (773: down by the church tower); Rudolph von Suchen (842) spoke of several steps.

long been expressed.[i] The intention was, of course, to facilitate the entrance and exit of the large crowd, and the architect had to be willing to execute the work for the sake of symmetry.

The third entrance, as already mentioned, is not in the large church or in its chancel, but in the Church of St. Catherine, in its southwest corner.[ii] In three sections of the somewhat narrow[iii] and dimly lit[iv] staircase, ten, four, and nine steps, together twenty-three,[v] lead down in the main direction towards the south into the Chapel of the Innocents, partly through the rock.[vi] This entrance or staircase is more recent and is the work of the Minorites who, in their constant striving for independence, wanted to have even freer access to the Grotto of the Nativity. The underground communication of the Church of St. Catherine with this cave was made around 1479,[vii] and it was done secretly, as the passage was kept secret even from the Latin

---

i   Et videtur una fuisse spelunca continua, quam solum dividit factum ostium, et ascensus, quo de capella ad chorum ascenditur. *Marin. Sanut.* Breydenbach (oder Kja). The rest is gone because of the door that was hewn next to it (the birthplace). Tschudi 270.

ii   See the ground plans. Au bas de l'Eglise de s. Catherine. *Ladoire* 197. Vis à vis de l'entrée de cette chapelle vers le Midy. *Surius* 529.

iii   Where 2 people can hardly (I say with some effort) avoid each other. Geramb 1, 152.

iv   Il (escalier) est tres obscur, et ce n'est qu'à la faveur des lampes qui y brûlent continuellement qu'on y descend. *Ladoire.* Illuminated by 2 lamps, one of which burns in front of an image of Our Lady, the other in front of an image of St. Francis. Geramb. Cf. *Legrenzi* 1, 184.

v   Prokesch counted correctly as well (116). Fürer and Surius mention 22 steps. It is possible that an extra step was added later during repairs. Quite unreliable are Legrenzi with 35 steps and Ladoire with 14 or 15. According to Amico's ground plan, which I should not have followed here, the number of steps would have been bigger. S. Binos in note 6 on p. 126.

vi   Maximam partem e rupe excisi. *Fürer.* Scala tagliata nel sasso. *Legrenzi. Ladoire.* Surius sagt, that the steps are made of stone (pierres).

vii   Tucher's words (667): "Behind in the same chapel (of birth), one enters a crypt via a hidden passage," are indeed not very precise, but they are duly explained by Fabri, who says (Reyßb. 259) that "from the chapel (of the innocent children), one enters into a narrow secret passage, which has recently been hewn into the rock." According to Tschudi (278), the secret entrance was created many years ago.

pilgrims, so that it would not be immediately blocked again, and the Franciscans would lose the place if the Saracens and oriental Christians learned of it. In this way, the Minorites could go from the Chapel of St. Nicholas, which had been called the Church of St. Catherine's before and later, to the Church of the Nativity, without having to go through the large church.[i] Even in 1507 it was not obvious that the Latin brothers, when they wanted to celebrate Mass, carried the vestments, chalices, and other precious things back and forth, and this was all the more desirable because they were not allowed to do so publicly in the upper church[ii]; indeed, not yet in 1519.[iii] After the middle of the sixteenth century, the passage, deprived of its secrecy, seems to have been used, without any obstruction, by the Latin monks as well as by the pilgrims.[iv] The earlier fears of the barefoot religious order were realized in the middle of the century before last. In 1652 it was reported that the Greeks had bricked up the door at the western end of the Church of the Nativity through which one could otherwise get from it to the Chapel of St. Joseph and the Innocents and to the Church of St. Catherine.[v] This unchristian barrier still existed in 1674[vi]; how much longer I do not know. In our era, one complained that the entrance for the Roman Catholics faced westward and was underground.[vii]

---

i   Fabri 1, 452; 2, 182; also Reyßb.: "Through the secret passage I often went deep down into the holy crevice, and stood there alone for four or five hours, after the departure of the pilgrims from Jerusalem."

ii   Est etiam exinde cuniculus abditus, est usque in claustri penetralia protensus. *Georg.* 524.

iii   Tschudi.

iv   Seydlitz 474 (somewhat dark). *Fürer* (descenditur).

v   Vne porte qui estoit au bout de cette allée, et que les Grecs usurpateurs .. ont murée. *Dovbdan* 142, 144.

vi   Ignaz von Rheinfelden 128. Troilo 402. *Nau* 417. The latter said that an altar was built near the walled door to be as close as possible to the Chapel of the Nativity, because the Greeks did not allow the Franciscans to conduct mass in it.

vii   Prokesch 115.

A fourth entrance, descending eighteen steps[i] from west to east,[ii] led from the cloister[iii] of the Capuchin monastery to what was referred to as 'Jerome's cell', where he is said to have translated the Bible. The old, walled-up entrance can still be seen in the cell towards the west, where there are three steps and traces of a door. The walling up of the unusable entrance was done around 1590 on the order of the Franciscans.[iv] One should not forget that in former times Jerome's cell had no connection with the Church of the Nativity, and therefore it had a special entrance from the cloister. However, as soon as the Franciscans had driven a tunnel from their church to the Chapel of the Innocents, it must have occurred to them that a connection could easily be made between this chapel and that cell by means of a transverse tunnel about a dozen feet long, and that the whole group of tombs could be connected which would then make the special western entrance to Jerome's cell superfluous. I do not have knowledge of this transverse tunnel before the year 1556.[v] If at that time, and a few decades later,

---

i   Gumpenberg, Tucher, Tschudi. Fabri counts 19 and Albrecht v. S. even counts 24 steps.

ii   See especially the ground plans, on my copy under the letter N.

iii   And as one enters the cloister, a staircase winds down under the earth. Gumpenberg 464. Albrecht v. S. note 2109. Tucher 667. De ecclesia exivimus in ambitu et ad latus sinistrum, et in ambitu per qnoddam ostium ingressi .. descendimus. *Fabri* 1, 438.

iv   Ad occidentale ejusdem sacelli latus scala est lapidea, per quam olim ad superius delubrum (hardly) ascendebatur; ostium (ostio) tamen a Minoritis postmodum obstructo, ab aliquot hinc annis nullius usus esse coepit. *Cotov.* 236.

v   We exited the Nativity Chapel ... through another little door at the back, and came into a vault, in which some of the innocent children had been killed and buried. From there we went to the left, into a dark chapel (with the tomb of Jerome). Seydlitz 476. Tucher followed (667) the procession, first to the choir of St. Mary's Church etc., and only then into Jerome's cell. See also the history of the procession. Because the central aisle was missing at the time, the procession had to make a big detour. The apparent contradiction that Albert the Duke of Saxony was able to visit the graves of the innocent children directly from Jerome's cell, cannot be decisive here. See also what Kootwyk says about the entrance to St. Catherine's Church on p. 273. If the entrance from Jerome's cell was opened, then one could get from the cloister of the Capuchin monastery to the Church of the Nativity.

Near the Chapel of the Innocents, on the south or west side of the aisle, between the western exit of the Chapel of the Nativity and the cross aisle that leads to a pair of greetings from Jerome and Paula, there is a closed entrance that belongs to the Armenians, which, although it does not connect to their monastery, is approximately perpendicular beneath the point of contact of the first and second quarter of the line, drawn from the west corner of the northern choir wing to the west corner of the southern one, as measured from north to south. It would be easy to dig a tunnel from here to the dwelling of the southern monastery, and all the easier since one knows that there are vaults in the vicinity. I found only a few mentions in the previous centuries that refer to the entrance as one hidden under the earth.[i]

Chapel of the Crib

We now need to inquire a little more about the location of the Chapel of the Nativity[ii], which was also called the Chapel of the Crib[iii] and the Holy Grotto (ὁ ἅγιον σπήλαιον).[iv] Like the basilica above it that extends toward the south and further

---

I understood Tschudi correctly, there was also an entrance from the large church into the tomb with the altar of Eusebius (southern chamber, next to Jerome's cell).

i   On the famous ground plans. The older one from Zuallart shows nothing of the sort.

ii   Sacellum Nativitatis. *Fürer* 66. Bei Quaresmius öfter (z. B. 2, 640) Basilica Nativitatis Domini. Grotto of the Nativity. Prokesch 114. Roberts.

iii   The ground plans. However, in the strict sense of the term, the chapel of the manger must be understood only as the room containing the manger. The name was probably derived from Quaresmius's hypothesis (2, 627 sqq.) that the crib was a place (cave) separated from the chân ("cham") in the city for those qui in diversorio civitatis hospitari non poterant (628a).

iv   *Phocas* 27.

north, it stretches out from the east 15° south, towards the west, 10° north, while the eastern hill, at its rather gaping north slope,[i] beneath its peak are only a small number of steps, so far down, however, that one does not look down into the southern Wadi al-Rahib; it extends, from the east 10° south towards the west, 10° north. The chapel — dark in and of itself,[ii] but lit by many chandeliers, some of which hang down from the ceiling of the nave or aisle to other chapels,[iii] silver and gifts from Venice, France, Austria[iv] (with the double eagle), and Spain — is not very big[v] in that it measures in its length (from east to west) 37' 6",[vi] in width 11' 9"[vii] and in height about 9',[viii] and the

---

i   In declivio ad partem aquilonarem oppidi. *Fabri* 1, 465. Outside of the city, to the north and underneath. Tschudi 270. It leans against a slope where the old city walls used to stand. Schwallart 303. Dessous les murailles de la Ville, taillée dans la pierre vive du costé d'Orient. *Surius* 527. My rendition of the view from the east (attached) shows particularly clearly how steeply the ground falls from the site of the church to the north.

ii   Windowless. Ignaz v. Rh. 129. Troilo 395. Illuminated by lamplight only. *Surius* 527. Geramb 1, 156. Röser 447.

iii   The lamplight never goes out. Troilo. *Ladoire* 201. Geramb. Smoke blackens the chapel. Kootwyk (232), Ladoire, and others. In the seventeenth century 15 lamps burned here (Scheidt 70), 10 in front of the birthplace and 5 in front of the manger, in the last century there were just as many golden and silver ones (Binos 209), though another source says that there were 30 (Ladoire); in 1829, 19 lamps were kept here by the Christians: 9 by the Latins and 10 by the Armenians (Prokesch 115), in the last decade there were 32 altogether (Geramb, Röser, Schubert), namely silver ones (Röser).

iv   *Light* 167. Schubert 3, 20.

v   Not nearly as big. Tucher 667.

vi   According to *Chateaubriand* 1, 301. Prokesch 114. 40' according to Schwallart (303), Kootwyk (232), Boucher (279), Surius (526), Binos (208); 35 feet according to Gumpenberg; 30 feet according to Tschudi (276); 20' according to Anshelm (1290); 40 spans according to Troilo (395); 64 cubits according to Fürer (66); 18 cubits according to Radzivil (170); 12 steps according to Röser (447), about 15 according to Schubert (3, 20), 16 according to Scheidt (71).

vii According to Prokesch; by contrast Chateaubriand says 11'3", Schwallart, Kootwyk, Boucher, Surius, and Binos all say 12', 10 feet according to Gumpenberg and Tschudi, 24 cubits according to Fürer, between 9 and 10 according to Radzivil; Röser mentions 4, Schubert approximately 5 steps.

viii 9' according to Chateaubriand and Prokesch; the impossible height of depth from the ground to the ceiling of the chapel amounts to 9' 4"[i]. The chapel is therefore much shorter and more narrow than the church choir; for the east end of it corresponds to the beginning (west end) of the chancel arch and the west end to that of the line, but still crosses, by a few feet, into the choir, where it and the nave meet; the side walls of this chapel are even more narrow than the choir arch, so that from the south wall to the point lying vertically below the south end of the south wing would measure about 50'. The shape would basically be an elongated quadrangular, if it were not encroached upon by an additional intersection from the south by an irregularly shaped triangle.[ii] The floor of the chapel is covered with white, black, and red-veined marble slabs,[iii] which, as a Frenchman told me, the Mohammedans would want to steal.[iv] The walls consist partly of marble panels[v] behind which, to the north, a section appears exposed, where due to decay it came off. They are supposedly

---

15' can be found in Schwallart, Boucher, and Surius, 14' in Binos, at most 13 spans 11 inches in Troilo, the length of 2 bodies in Schubert.

i   10 to 12' deep underground. Joliffe 120. 7-8' plus bas que le terrain environnant. Duke of Ragusa 3, 47. Approximately 12' deep below the level of the church floor. Schubert.

ii   An oblong, with the manger a triangle. *Cotov.*

iii   The pavement is covered with marble. Breydenbach Kja. The floor below is made of all kinds of marble stones, quite beautifully inlaid and worked in the Turkish style. Helffrich 718. Ash-gray marble slabs. *Quaresm.* 2, 629b. Le pavé est couvert de grandes pierres de marbre, le plus beau qui se puisse jamais voir. *Surius* 527. White marble. Troilo 398. Beautiful marble stones. Röser. If one sees the inconspicuous marble floor today, and considers these historical notes together with Chateaubriand's statement (1, 301) – that these and other decorations come from Helena –, one does not know whether one should be more astonished about the ignorance or about the impudence of this source. Little bon sens is necessary to understand a priori that this floor, which is trodden so often, becomes gradually worn out (after all, water droplets hollow out stones), and that it has to be repaved again and again.

iv   The canon Salzbacher (2, 169), who saw several marble stones broken on the ground, learned the same thing from Father Mariano.

v   Covered de dables de marbre blanc et cipolin. *D'Estourmel* 2, 116. Schwallart 2, 493.

partially hung with silk fabrics,[i] but I found, on the north wall at least, only a very aged canvas with antique paintings which were highly esteemed by a Franciscan who happen to be present. Before 1719, however, the walls were not covered with such things but were lined completely with marble.[ii] At one point they were white with black veins,[iii] then grey, blue, long marble slabs,[iv] later with white,[v] and in 1719, with grey marble with wavy stripes.[vi] In 1646 the marble cladding was especially extolled; at a height of 6' the walls were faced with about forty of the finest white and half-black, half-grey, veined marble slabs in such a way that they shone like a mirror.[vii] Just like the chapel in general, the ceiling is unsightly[viii]; it does not impart an impression of real beauty. In the fifteenth[ix] and sixteenth centuries,[x] it was nonetheless rightly praised; a claim that I do not doubt. I do not, however, understand how it was possible to say that the chapel had a particularly good smell,[xi] or that this place was considered superior to all others

---

i   Prokesch 115.

ii *Albert.* Sax. 2110. Marmore contabulatum, *Fürer.* Villinger 93.

iii Helffrich 718.

iv Rauchwolff 644.

v   *Quaresm.* (white with black veins). Troilo 396.

vi Tables de marbre gris ondoyé. *Ladoire.*

vii *Surius* 527.

viii According to Bernardino Amico (Tav. VI), the chapel is vaulted right up to the western door. You could not tell, writes Kootwyk, what was wrong with the vault: it was in decline and covered in soot. Quaresmius says: Camera olim tota opere musaico operiebatur: sed in præsentia totum fere antiquitate corruit, et ad ejus ornatum et decorem, secundum tempus, alia superinducuntur ornamenta. Afterwards, Troilo (399) claims to have discovered that some work had been done to the vault, which, though blackened by the soot of the lamps, had been artfully decorated with gold. D'Estourmel saw the vault lined with cloth and Hailbronner (2, 301) saw the rock roof blackened by the lamp smoke.

ix In a really beautiful chapel. Tucher.

x   Beautifully built. Seydlitz 474. Beautiful. Villinger 93.

xi Redolet enim ex hoc loco, qui tamen vacuus cernitur, omni materia odorifera, adeo intensus odor, ac si esset apotheca aromatum, superat tamen omnem vim pigmentorum. This is not meant as a parable, but rather in

in Palestine,[i] the place where one believed in the incarnation of the Godhead. More than anything else, Jerusalem reminds the pilgrim of the sufferings and death of Jesus, Bethlehem, by contrast, of an event so joyful that it excites him with warmth. In such a place of worship, such varied moods were offered by the chapel, even if its architectural refinements and its alienation from its original state sometimes stirred feelings of discomfort in the modest pilgrim.[ii] Out of reverence, people took off their shoes in the choir[iii] and descended into the artificially lit room. There, deeply moved, out of sheer religious joy, one could not hold back the tears,[iv] or even a shiver intermingled with joy filled one's body at the very thought that one was unworthy to enter this earthly heaven, into which, just as into the dwelling of the blessed, nothing impure or tainted should enter.[v] When the fervent Paula entered Bethlehem and stepped into the Grotto of the Saviour and saw the Virgin's holy lodgings, she affirmed before the ears of her spiritual guide Jerome that with eyes of

---

veritate. *Fabri* 1, 442.

i   *Fabri* 1, 445.

ii   The lavishly decorated Chapel of the Nativity does not seem to be very consistent with the fact that most people prefer the place over others because it was so poor and forsaken. There you can see how one harms religion precisely when you want to serve it. *Mariti* 2, 382. Je regrettais la nudité du rocher, la rusticité de l'étable; ces tentures, qui lui donnent l'aspect d'un salon, sont-elles bonnes à autre chose qu'a recéler la peste. *D'Estourmel* 2, 118. To fully understand this passage, it is necessary to know that the Count visited the Nativity Chapel during a plague epidemic.

iii   Rauchwolff 644. Schwallart 304. *Surius* 523. Ignaz von Rheinfelden, see note 1 to p. 98. The Roman Catholics, at least the foreign ones, do not do this anymore.

iv   L'ame devote y gouste, je ne sçay quelles delices Spirituelles, si douces, et si fort attirantes qu'on y demeureroit jour et nuit sans ennuy. On a du mal assez de contenir les larmes qui coulent sans esse des yeux plus douces que les eaux d'Hesebon. *Surius.* There is truly no place in the world where the heart could feel a sweeter emotion than in this grotto...These thoughts (of Jesus, Mary, and Joseph) fill my soul with inexpressible sensations which my pen tries in vain to write down...I pray, I sigh, I raise my tear-filled eyes toward heaven. Geramb 1, 160.

v   *Ladoire* 196.

faith she saw: the child wrapped in cloth and whimpering; the adoring Wise Men; the star above the Virgin Mother; the cheerful infant; the shepherds as they arrived; the little ones, killed by Herod in his rage; Joseph and Mary fleeing to Egypt; and she said with tears of joy, I greet you, Bethlehem, House of Bread.[i]

To persuade Marcella to move her residence to Bethlehem, the eloquent letter of Paula and Eustochium was given special weight by the words: 'Here in this small hole in the earth, the builder of the Kingdom of Heaven was born; here he was wrapped in cloth; here he was seen by the shepherds; here he was shown by the star; here he was worshipped by the Wise Men'.[ii] Even many a Protestant, who usually prefer to dwell in the field of certainties of proof, did not remain cold-hearted at this place; he, too, sank into religious contemplation, and in the sixteenth century, a Protestant pilgrim, in his old, course way, implored the Godhead to comfort him ceaselessly with this blessed birth against his own damned birth, and that through it he would have a heartfelt joy and a great pleasure in love and sorrow, in happiness and misfortune, in persecution and affliction during this transient life.[iii]

Nature desires shadow along with light, tolerates vice along with virtue, godliness along with wickedness, health along with disease. Along with the precious teardrops that poured forth from eyelashes, along with the heaving breast from which sighs of devotion lofted, along with man whose desires inflamed, will set aside his old ones, the tarnished ones, now and again sites were tainted by a man beset by evil spirits. For there are

---

i *Hieronym.* in epitaphio *Paulæ*. Rauchwolff and Schwallart wrote very similarly, the latter: "Whose heart should not leap up with joy when he imagines looking at the tender little child, lying in the manger or in the arms of his chaste and immaculate mother? Etc.

ii *Paulæ* et *Eustochii* epist. ad *Marcellam*. In the opp. *Hieronymi* and probably copied from his missive to the latter woman.

iii Rauchwolff.

mortals who see no better principles by which order in human society can be maintained, much less honoured; people who live for each day, who acknowledge no limit other than that of ironclad necessity, than that of death, whose sole purpose is to pursue their own pernicious thoughts and actions. It is, in truth, not a free way of thinking that guides such people but an evil one, because this is neither liberation, nor does it liberate. What reader anticipates that I will tell of rape and fornication? In the fifteenth century, it was customary for each pilgrim to place something to be used for the construction on the altar of the Church of the Nativity. So it happened that when pilgrims offered up gold, silver, and gold rings, a knight came forward and tossed a ducat onto the stone. Behind him came a pilgrim from the Orient, who bowed toward the town clergy and in doing so took two ducats lying close by. The thief was apprehended, and the money found in his hand.[i] In 1847 the large silver star was stolen, which, as we will later investigate, was fastened above the purported site of birth[ii]; the Roman Catholic Christians in Jerusalem accused the Greeks of the theft, and the French consul worked diligently to discover the guilty party, but the Turkish governor was indifferent to the matter. From the fifteenth century, we hear the curious story that a Christian had an impure love for a Sarcenae. For a long time, she resisted his strong impositions until she finally yielded on the condition that she would only fulfil his unchaste desires in the Church of the Nativity of Jesus, namely in the Chapel of the Nativity. Arriving alone there, she managed to escape, and made a fuss among the Saracens about how bad the Christians were. This incident, in particular, spurred them on to oust the Christians from Palestine.[iii] A Spaniard publicly blamed the Greeks for fornicating in the Chapel of the Nativity

---

i   *Fabri* 1, 460 sq.

ii   Allg. Ausb. Ztg., 1848, 168a. By birthplace I mean the manger.

iii *Fabri* 1, 47 sq.

because they assumed that a child produced there was a child of light.[i] I cannot verify, based on my own research, what is accurate or inaccurate in this claim, but I must confess that the Greeks' almost infinite superstitions does not make the outrageous unbelievable. Many who realize that even Moslems approached the sacred site with reverence will be even more deeply indignant about such a desecration. What a dramatic contrast it is, when one hears about how the Mohammedan who visited the place and entered the Christian temple as if he were in a mosque, prostrated himself and prayed, with his face to the ground, which he kissed[ii]; and how he never turned his back on the altar when arriving and leaving; how he not only went on pilgrimage to Bethlehem from Jerusalem or elsewhere, but also on the hajj from Hebron or Mecca.[iii] In the lore about the night Ascension of the Prophet Muhammad, it is told that Gabriel said to him, 'Come down and perform the prayer', and after performing the prayer, he said to him, 'Do you know where you prayed? You prayed in Bethlehem'. Abdallah, the son of Amru Anlas, sent oil to light Bethlehem's lamps at Jesus' birthplace,[iv] which proves that in his time the place was held in honour by the Mohammedans. Nowadays, the love for Bethlehem's sanctuary among the Moslems seems to have cooled down considerably; at least I never saw one in the church or chapel, nor did I ever hear anything about the town's being chosen as a place of pilgrimage for them anymore. It was an auspicious confluence of Christian and Mohammedan veneration; without it the place would have been far more

i   Emanuel Garcia in his work: Derechos legales y estado de Tierra Santa. Palma, Felipe Guasp, 1814. P. 140.

ii   I have seen often and abundantly how the heathen fell down upon their faces there, and kissed it while sighing and weeping. Fabri 259. Les Turcs, je ne sçay par quelle devotion, viennent de toutes parts faire leurs prieres en ce lieu avec si grande humilité, baisans et lechans son pavé avec mille exclamations. *Surius* 584 sq. Cf. above on p. 98, note 1.

iii   Schwallart 304. *Surius* 529.

iv   *Medschired-dîn* 134 sq.

exposed to robbery, devastation, and desecration by the latter.

As far as the ownership of the chapel is concerned, I can only provide a very fragmentary history. In 1616 it was up to the Franciscans, as the owners, to be in charge of the chapel.[i] Shortly before 1656 the property was taken from them,[ii] until it was officially declared theirs once more in 1698 by the Ottoman Porte,[iii] and it is certain that the chapel belonged to the Latins in the first half of the previous century.[iv]

We will not hold it against those who do not keep such exact accounts in feet and inches in determining the birthplace, for the fact that I have not yet pointed to the exact location of this place. I can, however, imagine that others are more exact in their calculations and eagerly await more detailed information. I will give that immediately but might confess it with less enthusiasm than I feel for Bethlehem as a whole. The place where, according to tradition, Jesus Christ was born of Mary is situated at the middle of the east end of the chapel,[v] between the pair of stairs.[vi] Here is a rounded nave[vii] about 8' high, 4' wide, and slightly less encroaching towards the east,[viii] not quite in the centre, but rather slightly lower, undercut by a slab of marble blackened

---

i   Della Valle 1, 157.

ii Ignaz von Rheinfelden 131. By contrast, Monconys writes (1, 315): Les Grecs tiennent ce Sanctuaire depuis huiet années (so from 1639 until 1647) qu'ils l'ont osté aux Peres Cordeliers.

iii Hammer's Gesch. des osman. Reiches. 6, 758.

iv Korte 118. The Latins are the sole owners of the holy sites in Bethlehem, and neither the Greeks, who have a convent here, nor other sects may visit them without the Latins' permission. Hasselquist 167. See also p. 122 onwards about the ownership of St. Mary's Church.

v   *Anshelm.* 1290. Regarde l'Orient, et tient le chef à toute la grotte. *Surius.*

vi Gumpenberg. Röser (447) mentions only the staircase to the right. See the famous ground plans.

vii A hole of the size of a window. Gumpenberg. A hollow. *Anshelm.* 1290. A place hollowed out into a semicircle. Schwallart 303. Troilo 396. Prokesch 115.

viii 11 spans 6" high, 6 spans 5" wide, from east to west. 5 spans long. Troilo. About 9' high, 4' long, 5' wide. Binos 208.

below by the lamp smoke.[i] The floor of the equally sooty lower marble-lined section[ii] of the church is about ¼' above the floor of the chapel[iii] and consists of a marble slab in the centre with a gleaming stripe of silver (which, as noted, was stolen the year before last[iv]). Here in the church, beneath the altar, was where, according to legend, Jesus first encountered the world after leaving his mother's womb. This place was not always seen to be adorned in the same way, even in the last four centuries. In the fifteenth century, a star was carved into a stone,[v] and even in the first quarter of the sixteenth century a star was carved into it.[vi] It is not before 1586 that we learn that a green-speckled stone of ½' diameter was inlaid in the centre of the base and surrounded with coloured marble rays, like those of a star.[vii] This decoration was standard until more recent times, when the green stone[viii] or jasper was also introduced[ix]; only once was a hole of about 8" diameter[x] left open instead of a disk in the centre, but this did

---

i   Troilo.

ii White marble. Schwallart.

iii 2½". Troilo.

iv At the end of May 1847, one saw a sparkling sun with 14 rays, inlaid stones, and the new inscription: Hio de virgine etc. Wolff 134. See above on p. 138.

v   Gumpenberg 464. The same place where Our dear Lady God gave birth to her son has been marked by a star. Tucher 667. A white, flat stone with a star. Fabri 259.

vi Viagg. al S. Sepolcro F6b. Even Radzivil maintains (170) that the site was marked only with a marble plaque. Quaresmius also found a hewn-in star (2, 629).

vii Schwallart. You can see the star on his drawing of the chapel.

viii Circular slab of greenish marble, approximately 4" in diameter. Prokesch.

ix Un Jaspe verd d'une palme de diametre. *Surius* 527. Porphyry of 2½» (?) in circumference.Troilo. Une pierre de jaspe, un peu enfoncée, ronde, de la grandeur d'une assiette. *Ladoire* 198. Binos 208. *Chateaubriand* 1, 302. O. F. Richter 39. Jolliffe 121. Agate and jasper. Palæst. 1831, 52. (Serpentine stone. Röser.)

x   Sopra il pavimento si vede un cavo rotondo in marmo finissime, cinto con corona d'argento à modo di raggi…Questo buce é largo per diametro 8 ditta; e poco disgiunte da esso si vedone due meze Lune pure d'argento con

not last long, because it was probably finally perceived as being improper; also, the marble rays of the star were exchanged, as early as 1646, for silver ones,[i] even for gold ones[ii] or gilded ones.[iii] In the century before last, the rays even contained diamonds, garnets, rubies, and other precious gems,[iv] and in the beginning of the past century, one also saw several diamonds and other precious stones[v]; however, already in 1778 only two remained, since the rest had fallen prey to avarice or excessive devotion.[vi] The white marble base,[vii] where around the periphery the jasper disk and the silver star were inlaid, appeared to have been split in the first quarter of the seventeenth century, and, in fact, concerned that the beautiful marble might be otherwise taken by the Turks, the Minorites themselves ruined the stone.[viii]

---

picola stella nel mezo, quali dinotano il capo del bambino sostenuto nelle braccia della Vergine, ambidue figurati nel marmo. *Legrenzi* 1, 180 sq. The Greeks built the great church just before Legrenzi's visit, and it is probable that on this occasion they also repaired and changed the location of the Nativity, e.g. added the two crescent moons with the hole in the middle. Nau seems to have witnessed (403) something similar to Legrenzi. Il est pavé d'une (pierre) qui est encore plus riche, et qui est percée d'un petit rond à son milieu, où l'on a enchassé une autre de jaspe, ou de porphyre à deux pouces de profondeur. Quaresmius also spoke (2, 629) of a star, in cujus centro cavum est.

i Au tour dudit jaspe est un cercle d'argent en forme de Soleil, embelly de 14. rayons de diverses couleurs. *Surius.* L'Autel sous lequel il y a vn jaspe de serpentin entouré d'vn Soleil d'argent. *Monconys* 1, 314. The top is framed with a silver, star-like plate, which has 14 rays, it is 2 spans wide in diameter. Troilo. Une bordure d'argent, avec des rayons de même métail qui forment une belle étoile. *Ladoire*. Binos. *Chateaubriand*. Richter. Joliffe. Prokesch.

ii A hexagonal golden star. Sieber 49.

iii Röser.

iv *Surius.* Les rayons sont ornés de grosses pierreries et diamans. J'en ai compté jusqu'à six-vingt, entre lesquels il y en a de gros comme le pouce. Voyage 1699. 82.

v *Ladoire.*

vi Binos, note 208. Röser. Cf. p. 138

vii The most beautiful, polished white marble. Troilo. Binos. *Chateaubriand*. Richter.

viii *Ouaresm.* 2, 630. Troilo.

Out of veneration, the birthplace was covered with a gold cloth, which was removed only when the pilgrims were praying there.[i] The inscription often mentioned by the pilgrims: 'Hic de virgine Maria Iesus Christus natus est',[ii] which I did not see and likely overlooked, I did not find until the second or third decades of the century before last[iii]; for about thirty years prior the words appeared a little differently: 'Hic de virgine Maria Iesus Christus nasci dignatus est'.[iv] In 1821, the year MDCCXXIX was found next to the inscription; the jewel was probably given as a gift or restored in that year.[v] In the church, several lamps burn beneath the altar from which they hang down.[vi] At the very moment when I was present, an Armenian wanted to fill a lamp and broke the glass; the entire incident demonstrated a lack of devotion and cold-bloodedness that should be banned from all temples. The plate, which is placed directly above the place of birth, serves today[vii] as an altar, as it has done for a long time.[viii] Above, behind the altar, there was said to be a famous painting depicting the

---

i   *Surius.* Capellula hæc sericis tapetis et pannis ornatur. *Quaresm.* 2, 630.

ii   Here was born of the Virgin Mary Jesus Christ. See also *Bartlett* 209 and note 8 on p. 141.

iii   *Quaresm. Surius.* Troilo 395. (Jesus Dominus) *Legrenzi* 1, 180: The letters were carved in a circle and covered by a halo. *Ladoire:* Inscription engraved in a silver ring. *Chateaubriand.* Richter, Geramb 1, 157, and others.

iv   This place honored Jesus Christ, that he was born of Virgin Mary. Radzivil 170. Again, Ignaz von Rheinfelden (129) copied this source.

v   Berggren 3, 142. The gems seem to have disappeared or been stolen between 1719 and 1729.

vi   5. lampadi d'argento pendenti sotto il detto Altare. *Legrenzi* 1, 181. 6 lamps underneath the altar, et devant l'on en voit une grosse couverte de fleurs de lys, qui marquent le Monarque qui a fait un si riche present. *Ladoire* 198 sq. The same already occurs in Voyage 1699. 82. 14 lamps. Prokesch. 16 lamps. Geramb 1, 157.

vii   Supported by 2 pillars. Geramb.

viii Gumpenberg. In eodem loco illius cavaturæ est altare. *Anshelm.* 1291. Viagg. al S. Sepolcro. Schwallart. 81. A large marble tablet 4' high (?) and long, 2½' wide. *Surius* 528. White marble. Troilo. Un petit autel. *Ladoire* 197. Binos.

birth of Jesus.[i] This altarpiece appears to have come from Jacob Palma, who also completed other paintings during his time and was the most famous artist in the Orient.[ii] At one time there was a glorious angel[iii] gracing either side of the altar, which, of course, one does not see any more, and under which one recognized in the temporary marble covering the image of the Virgin, as a sort of optical illusion.[iv] Above, in the place of the angels, there seems to be bare rock; it is, however, scraped-off masonry.

Around 1620 the altar was in the possession of the Greeks.[v] In the third quarter of the last century, the Roman Catholics were not allowed to say Mass here[vi]; also in the past decades, the Sanctuary of the Nativity belonged to the Greeks,[vii] and they now share possession with the Armenians.

I now intend to delve deeper into the history of the birthplace. The oldest report of the birth of the Lord is given to us by the Gospel. I have already demonstrated above[viii] that this, according to the documents, took place in Bethlehem, without the place having been determined more closely. We do not even know for sure, according to the text of the Bible, whether the place of birth was in the city itself; but it is very likely[ix] and this opinion

---

i   An old tablet. Radzivil. Schwallart. Jesus's birth. *Quaresm.* Quite beautiful. Ignaz von Rheinfelden 129. In 1674 the Greeks had put a bad painting in there. *Nau* 403. Prokesch 115.

ii   Cf. Mariti 2, 381.

iii   See the illustrations in Zuallart and Pococke.

iv   A laquelle (Image) il manque peu de chose pour être un portrait achevé. *Ladoire* 198.

v   See the last note but five.

vi   Binos 208.

vii   Geramb 1, 159. Röser 447. Cf. above on p. 140.

viii P. 32.

ix   Matth. 2, 1. At least strictly speaking, although the phrase stays the same if a house is located near a village. In the literal sense, however, one cannot say "in" here, but rather "at". This opinion is strengthened by another biblical passage, according to which the birth took place in a chân or an inn, (Luke 2, 7) and furthermore, if we consider that nowadays in the countries of the levant, as far as I know, wherever there is a village nearby, the Chân is always

could be supported by a tradition of more than a thousand years, according to which the first bathwater of the new-born child was emptied over the city wall.[i] After the birth, the family received two visits, immediately one from the shepherds in a chân (inn), where there was also a crib with the baby Jesus that served as a cradle, because his parents found no other place or no more suitable place for their little son.[ii] In the Orient it is not unusual to find people and animals in a chân, that is, under one roof, and if there were not enough or no suitable place, nothing would seem more natural than laying the child in one of the cribs, similar to those also found in châns. I myself spent the night in a chân where cattle were kept next to me under the same roof, where the human dwelling and the cattle barn were combined without a high partition. The devout family later received another visit from Wise Men from the East and, in fact, it is no longer described as having taken place in a chân, but rather: in a house.[iii] It therefore appears as if the public chân was used only upon arrival, which fits particularly well with the concept of travel, and as if a move was made later on to occupy a private

---

located in the same spot for reasons of security. Quaresmius very extensively discusses (2, 625 sq.) the pros and cons, and decides that the Chân was outside the city of Bethlehem.

i   De illa petra extra murum posita super quam aquæ prime post nativitatem dominici allutionis corpusculi de muri summitate inclinato in quo effusa est vasculo. commemorandum estimo. quæ sacri lavacri aqua de muro effusa in petra inferius iacente. quasi quamdam natura cauatam inuenit fossam quæ eadem undula in primo dominico repleta natalicio, ex eadem die ad nostra usque tempora per multos sæculorum circuitus purissima plena monstratur limpha. sine ulla defectione uel diminutione. nostro Saluatore hoc miraculum a die natiuitatis suæ peragente. *Arculf.* 2, 3 (Cod. St. Gall. p. 267). Of course, not a drop of the then six-hundred-year-old bath water can be found today. Incidentally, one superstition gives way to another, and our age should not boast in any way. Brocardt says (869) that the Nativity rock was located near the city. Cf. Schwallart and Surius in note 3 to page 132.

ii   Luke 2, 7. Since the shepherds found the child in the manger (16) after the angel appeared to them (12), I assumed that during this visit the family was still in the Chân. Cf. *Brocard.* c. 9 (no locus alius commodior).

iii   Matth. 2, 11.

dwelling. I would like to clarify that the chân and the house,[i] where the family was visited, were in no way the same place. The text of the Bible aside, it does not seem unreasonable to us that even if it were only for a couple of weeks that the stay there could easily have occurred under more than one roof. In the middle of the second century, it was mentioned that when Joseph could not find a place to lodge in the village of Bethlehem, he chose to stay in a cave very close to the village, and when they were there Mary gave birth to Christ and laid him in a crib. I do not want to decide whether it contradicts the Bible that it suddenly says that Joseph did not find a place for himself in the village of Bethlehem before his wife delivered, whereas the Scriptures emphasized the lack of room for the child in the chân. I want to draw attention first and foremost to the fact that the place of birth is called a cave, which at that time was situated very close to the village of Bethlehem. It was nothing unusual that the burial place of a distinguished man was marked for posterity by some drawing or monument; it is, however, considered as something extraordinary that in antiquity one should know not merely the city of birth, as was commonly known, but a birth chân, verily the actual place of birth. Certainly, a cave was an excellent site at which to place the tradition,[ii] much better than a decrepit chân itself or an empty place long gone to rack and ruin,[iii] and it is therefore no surprise that the tradition adhered to that of the cave. Already about seventy years after the first mention of the Grotto of the Nativity, it was reported that a cave in Bethlehem was pointed to as the birthplace of a certain Jesus, whom the Christians worshipped and admired, for which reason Bethlehem was very famous in those places at that time. It had both a reputation and name even among those of other

---

i *Justin. Martyr.* Dialog. cum Tryphone 78. P. 175. Hag. Com. 1742. As cited by Robinson 2, note 284.

ii Herschel 155.

iii My remarks about the credibility of the tradition are above on p. 100ff.

faiths, near and far.[i] About a hundred years later, that is to say, in the first quarter of the fourth century, the cave was mentioned once again.[ii] Around the year 400, the cave was likewise noted[iii] as one with a narrow entrance,[iv] and again, around 600 as a cave with a narrow opening,[v] around 670 as a half-cave[vi] and later, more frequently,[vii] and up to the present day, as a cave; it was also suggested that the Grotto of the Nativity actually consisted of more than one cave.[viii] We must not leave undiscussed the question as to whether a rock cave is compatible with the original text in the Bible. Although it does not report anything about a cave, the chân could have nonetheless been connected to such a cave,

---

i In Bethlehem speluncam ostendi, ubi ille sit natus; quod utique et in illis locis percelebre est, ut apud eos quidem, qui a fide sunt alieni, fama et nomine circumfertur, eadem in spelunca, Jesum quendam, quem Christiani adorent et demirentur, genitum esse. Origines contra Celsum, lib. 1. Quoted in Berggren 3, note 136.

ii According to Robinson (2, 285), Eusebius mentioned the cave several years before Helena's pilgrimage. *Euseb.* demonstr. Evang. 7, 2, 343. Col. 1688. Obscurum illund antrum nativitatis. *Euseb.* de vita *Constantini* 3, 42. Cf. note 2 on p. 103. One will forgive me for returning to the temple of Adonis (p. 100), and I only note that Jerome (epist. ad Paulinum) moved the lover of Venus into the cave itself (in specu, ubi quondam Christus parvulus vagiit, Veneris amasius plangebatur).

iii Jerome in the last note. In specum Salvatoris introiens. *Hieronym.* epitaph. *Paulæ.* Socrates and Sozomenus are discussed in note 2 on p. 103.

iv Os enim speluncæ ad ingrediendum omnino angustum est. *Anonym.* vita *Hieronymi,* appended in his opera about Erasmus.

v Ibi est spelunca, ubi natus est Dominus…os vere speluncæ angustum. Antonin Plac. XXIX.

vi Quasi quædam naturalis dimidia inest spelunca…cui utique semiantro… *Arculf.* 2, 2.

vii (1099) Speluncam admirabilem vident, ubi pia Dei genitrix, salutis porta, mundi reparatorem pannis involvit et lacte pavit vagientem. *Guil. Tyr.* 9, 14. Crypta. *Sæwulf.* 35. The tomb wherein the Lord Messiah was born. *Edrisi* 346. *Phocas* 27. Cave. Thetmar in Maltens Weltkd., 1842, Febr., 192. Perdicas 77. Rudolph von Suchen 773. Rock cave. *Frescobaldi* 193 sq. *Fabri* 1, 496. Helffrich 718. Rauchwolff 644. *Cotov.* 232. *Boucher* 279. 81. Della Valle 1, 157. *Surius* 526 sq. Troilo 395. *Caccia* 24. *Ladoire* 197. Binos 208. Schubert 3, 20; 2, 493. And others.

viii Also from the one of the manger. Troilo 397. Est alia capacior (spelunca), a prima .. *Marin. Sanut* 3, 14, 11.

and I recall having seen dwellings which were built alongside or over caves.[i] However, the cave which came to light in the second century is something real,[ii] a town chân[iii] in the form of a rock cave, and thus something highly unusual; it somewhat defies the usual image, and appears, as it were, as a necessary means of survival, so that the basic principle of the birthplace would not be lost for the future. Another question that arises is as to whether there is still a cave today, as most claim, whether the natural scientist, the geognost[iv] may still speak of a vault of rock today. I paid the most careful attention to this matter, and may my words, as I hope they may be, receive more weight than those of fleeting travellers, who were more concerned with giving vent to their feelings, and who, in their religious fervour, feared, as it were, a more exact investigation, and in so doing they probably also offended the Franciscans, who had already condemned a more open examination, not to mention condemning as heresy any doubts raised about the tradition. Wherever I looked about inside the chapel, at the birthplace, behind the crib,[v] on the

---

i   In this land of numerous and large caves, as we saw especially in ancient Galilee, not only do the dwellings of people lean against rocks... they are also often connected with an adjacent grotto, in the natural vault of which, manually enlarged, a portion of the rooms continues. Schubert 3, 17.

ii   Monconys says (1, 317), that the place of the Elisabethan's visit estoit dans la terre sous le roc; ce qui est à observer, car tous les lieux que l'on voit sont tous sous le roc. So far Monconys. I cannot help but mention here an observation that must impress itself on every visitor to the Holy Land, namely, that almost all the events and narratives of the Gospel are signposted as if they had taken place in caves...and this even in cases where the circumstances and the nature of the action itself demand a locale of a different kind. Thus the place where St. Anne birthed Mary, the place of the Annunciation, the place where Elizabeth greeted Mary, the birthplace of the Baptist and the Savior, the place of his agony, the place of Peter's repentance, the place where the apostles made their profession of faith, or that of the Transfiguration, – all of these places will be inside caves. Maundrell 143 (Paulus' Samml.). Robinson 2, 286.

iii   Robinson.

iv   Schubert 3, 20.

v   On Christmas Day, it (the painting behind the manger) is taken away and the bare rock remains exposed to the worship of the faithful for some

walls, on the ceiling, on the floor, nowhere did I discover rocks,[i] but only works of art, masonry. One finds at the beginning (east end) of the great nave, where one comes from the south or from the Greek monastery, a strange wall vault southwest of the Chapel of the Nativity, further up the mountainside than the latter. The floor of this vault is 13' lower than that of the nave, which, in turn, is several steps below the level of the choir loft, so that apparently the floor of that vault is situated at a greater depth than the floor of the Chapel of the Nativity. I add to this the fact that measurements regarding the height of the Chapel of the Nativity and the perpendicular distance between its floor and the floor of the choir, leave it scarcely possible to assume a vault of rock in the form as now imagined. But I do not want to present the issue with any sort of bias; my impartiality demands drawing on all of the means possible to put one in a position to throw a clear, or at least an ever clearer, light on the object in question.

Chapel of St. Joseph

To the west of the birthplace, and somewhat more northerly than this, that is to say, to the northwest and at the same time not far away, namely on the other (n.=) side, under the nave, and corresponding to the marble vault from north to south, I saw rocks throughout, and indeed in the Chapel of St. Joseph, which lies slightly lower than the Chapel of the Nativity, and even more in the admittedly deeper hole behind the Altar of

---

time. At this time the...Father Guardian cleans it and reverently collects the small pieces that have separated from it. Geramb 1, 158. I witnessed nothing of this kind, and if one were to see a piece of rock, then it could have just been put in there. If the observer is not allowed a free and complete overview, he cannot judge for himself whether the pieces have been tampered with.

i   But just before me, Strauss's imagination (Sinai and Golgatha. Berlin 1847. P. 287) recognized here and there the natural rock, still earlier Bartlett (209 sq.), as did Marmier (2, 293) in the smoke-black vault.

the Innocents. In all probability, even if everything were to be removed, one would not find any rocks in the birth chapel now; however, I am not claiming that a rock cave was never there, since my investigations almost proved that there must have, of necessity, been rocks at the place of birth, where today there are still rocks nearby. I willingly concede the value of the historical report about there being a rock cave as part of a section of the chân, whether it was right here or a little more southwesterly, where one now encounters an abandoned vault. I imagine that the chapel's unfortunate destruction was at one time carried out by a hand hostile to the faith, and another time by the pilgrim's misguided piety in removing stones and taking them home as souvenirs. According to received wisdom, before and around the year 600, the cave had a narrow entrance, but then, about seventy years later, had become a half-cave, that is, a cave completely open on one side. It must not be forgotten that Mohammedans had destroyed much of Palestine, which had, over time, come under the command of Omar al-Khatab. In short, one does not see rocks in the Chapel of the Nativity; before one's eyes there appears no rocky cave. Were a more realistic perspective to replace what I would call an unrealistic one, of there being a very obstructed southern entrance to the choir, the birthplace so lacks the character of a rocky cave that even with the aid of one's imagination one struggles to reconstruct one.[i] This would also require one to think away the northern stairs as well as the area beneath it,[ii] where it now rests on the chapel floor, and not in the countryside, where, according to my reckoning, rocks would climb up the entrance of the cave, from east to west, and from the north.

Was the rock cave, as a birth chamber, a stable? Many maintain

---

i   A very interesting drawing of the possible original appearance of the cave is given by Doubdan.

ii   Schubert dreams (3, note 17): The actual, natural entrance leads, as one can still see now, about a foot from the surface of the hill into the high, wide rooms of the grotto.

that it was. The Bible does not mention a stable. It uses the gentler term 'chân' but also notes that there was a crib here, from which it was concluded that it was not a dwelling for people but a mere stable; such a restrictive view is, in my opinion, completely wrong. I will not continue to repeat that the oriental chân shelters travellers and their animals under one roof. If it is entirely correct that the Orientals used the caves for stables, as some pilgrims have pointed out,[i] they then used this as their main argument to justify referring to the birth cave as a stable. They nevertheless committed a great error of omission in that they only emphasized the stable section of the chân, and being human, they then skipped over in silence the section which accommodated people. I find the word 'stable' only around the year 400, not alone but next to the words: 'Inn of the Virgin',[ii] used as a kind of funeral oration, in a more spirited language that borders on the poetic. For a long time, the word stable was rarely used again in ordinary, unfettered speech, and the almost complete dominance of the term stable came about only later, a consequence of the befouled tastes from the Middle Ages[iii] and

---

i   According to local custom, a stable was built underneath a rock. Brocardt 869. Breydenbach. Kja. All over the country, there are a lot of caves, and it is customary to make them into stables. Tschudi 271. The stables in Jerusalem are built in the same way today. Joliffe 120. Nous descendîmes dans l'étable, creusé sous un rocher, comme elles le sont encore habituellement de nos jours en ces pays. *D'Estourmel* 2, 116. Schubert 3, 17. Hailbronner 2, note 300. Without dwelling on our own observation of the frequent and almost universal appropriation of caverns and recesses in the rocks wherever possible for sheltering man and beast from hot and inclement weather etc. *Lynch*, expedition to the River Jordan and the Dead Sea, Philadelphia 1849. 424.

ii   Sacrum virginis diversorium, et stabulum, in quo agnovit bos possessorem suum. *Hieronym.* epitaph. *Paulæ.*

iii   The fiery Bernhard the H. wonders: Quæ tibi civitas, si audiat, non invideat pretiosissimum illud stabulum, et illius præsepii gloriam? As cited in *Quaresm.* 2, 622. The latter himself says (2, 625a): Stabulum animalium, at qualunque aula regia dignius et illustrius. Brocardt 869. More doubtful in Marinus Sanutus (3, 14, 11: it seems). The expression 'tugurium' occurs in Pipinus 72 sq.): Item fui in bethlehem in loco illo venerando seu diversorio, ubi dominus meus Jesus Christus pro salute mundi nasci dignatus est, et vidi et tetigi venerandum presepe in ipso lapide illius tugurii sen diversorii

then continuing in the period thereafter, on into the present.[i]

The best thing would have been to leave the rocky cave, once assumed to be the birthplace of Jesus, in its natural form and simplicity, if only to avoid various doubts.[ii] What could be more sacred to the eye, the faithful pilgrim must ask, than the walls and vault of rock towards which even the eye of the venerable family had been directed? But during high Christian antiquity one thought differently, too piously, not simply enough. When the emperor Constantine the Great gave the command to raise a mighty basilica in honour of the birth of Jesus, his mother Helena thought to make even more magnificent this dark cave of birth, to glorify it with exquisite works of art, with various jewels of all kinds. Shortly thereafter the emperor himself adorned the place with royal splendour, like an imperial palace. He thereby made even more opulent that which was already glorious thanks to the efforts of the empress who had introduced works of art in gold and silver and sundry things.[iii] In 637, the Chapel of the Nativity had such a reputation among the Mohammedans that Omar al-Khatab, when he visited Bethlehem, entered the temple, and prayed at the arch where the Lord Christ was born; he also issued a charter stating that Moslems may pray there only individually and not in a formal, public assembly.[iv] Around 670 the birth site was closer to the entrance than the crib, and the inside of the cave was decorated entirely with exquisite marble to glorify the Saviour.[v] A good half century later, the underground

---

exeisum.

i   The first Christians had built a chapel in this place, which had contained the stables. Geramb 1, 149. Cf. *Nau* 405, Voyage 1699, 81 (la sainte Etable).

ii   1. Malheureusement les murs intérieurs ont été revêtus de plaques de marbre. Il est à regretter qu'une piété mal entendue ait ainsi travesti la nature première de ce lieu sacré. *Marmier.* Cf. above on p. 135, note 7.

iii   *Euseb.* de vita *Constantini* 3, 42.

iv   El-Makîn (Elmacinus) 1, 3, 28. In *Bollandi* acta sanctor., *Maji* 3, 146. *Le Quien* Or. Christ. 3, 277 sq. Cf. above on p. 139 f.

v   Alius uero surpadicto contiguus præsepio introeuntibus propior locus (the Codex at St. Gallen says irrig loco on p. 267) proprie natiuitatis

rock cave in which Christ was born was no longer to be found but rather a square house hewn out of the rock, around which the earth had been dug up and thrown away. A small altar was carried into this rock house when Mass was to be given, and out again when it was over.[i] Through this unusual piece of historical information, one learns that the original shape of the cave had been modified and that a square space had been hewn out of the rock, which resolves any doubts about whether the chapel in its outer form was a work of God or of man.[ii] Whether the original cave had also been a man-made one cannot be determined,[iii] nor whether the house or the chapel had already been enlarged to its present western end[iv]; the latter, however, seems to be true, although the removal of a smaller, portable altar could, at first glance, allow for a small room (chapel). In the beginning of the Frankish kingdom, the Nativity was located almost in the middle beneath the choir of the church, to the left and the crib a little lower to the right.[v] From the latter words, it is clear that at that time only the northern entrance existed,[vi] which still holds true today. There can be no doubt that the chapel was later quite

---

dominicæ traditur fuisse. Illa ergo bethleemitica spelunca præsepis dominici. tota intrinsecus ob ipsius saluatorem honorificentiam marmore adornata est pretioso. *Arculf.* 2, 2.

i   Ille locus, ubi Christus natus est, quondam fuit spelunca sub terra: et nunc est quadrangula domus in petra excisa, et est terra circumquaque exfossa et inde projecta.. *Willibald* (according to the nun) 20.

ii Man's Work or God's Secret: *Caccia* 24. It suited no one better than a naturalist like Schubert (2, 493) to declare that the chapel was a large, natural cave inside the mountain. More pardonable is when before him, Rudolph von Suchen (842) spoke of a natural cave.

iii The entire cave is considered artificial by Kootwyk (specus subterraneus, in rupe excisus, cujusmodi etiamnum plurima iis in locis visuntur antra. 232), Boucher (279), Surius (526), Binos (208) and others.

iv Schwallart also writes (303) that the Nativity Chapel was originally small, but that the Christians later expanded it out of devotion. Lorsque S. Helene voulut embellir cette estable, elle la fit agrandir du coste de l'Occident. *Surius* 527.

v   *Sæwulf.* 35.

vi Cf. above on p. 127.

assiduously repaired by, or at the behest of, the Crusaders, and I will now sketch a picture of the little temple from back then. The 'cave' or double cave[i] was beneath the choir or high altar[ii] on the east side,[iii] and the following verses were inscribed in gold mosaic at the birth site:

Angelicæ Lumen
Virtutis, et ejus acumen,
Hic natus vere
Deus est de Virgine Maria.[iv]

The cave was painted with gold mosaic.[v] Within a circle, the pictures depicted the mysteries that had taken place in the cave: a Virgin lying in a bed and looking at the child, a little donkey, an ox, the crib, the visit of the shepherds, and so on.[vi] In the period from 1187 to 1400, the chapel located in front,[vii] beneath the church, at the entrance, was very precious, with a marble floor[viii] and the interior was otherwise richly and beautifully decorated with mosaic,[ix] which was preserved, on the ceiling at

---

i   *Epiphan.* M. 52. However, the other writers from the time of the Latin kings speak only of one cave. See note 7 to p. 149.

ii *Epiphan.* M. In a corner of the Temple, which faces north, and under the church. *Edrisi* 346.

iii *Epiphan.* M. Phokas says (27).

iv Here God, the light and supreme majesty of angelic virtue, has truly been born of the Virgin Mary. *Johann. Wirzb.* c. 2. (490 and 534). See also later inscriptions above on p. 143.

v   *Epiphan.* M.

vi *Phocas* 27. He gives an elaborate description of the painting.

vii In capite illius ecclesiæ. Thetmar 192. Under the high altar of the church. *Frescobaldi* 139 sq.

viii *Marin. Sanut.*

ix *Marin. Sanut.* Monteuilla's words (773) "it is the place where God was born and it is of precious gold and marble," can also refer to the whole chapel. Artis ministerie marmoribus et opere Mosaico pulcherrime decoratus. *Baidensel* 119. And on the inside, the same chapel is all strewn with marble and decorated with jasper. Cod. Vienn. 4578. P. 202d. In Greek. *Anonym.* in

least, until 1719.[i] From the place of birth, towards the east,[ii] one could see a piece of the stone,[iii] and there was a superstition that if someone took a particle or even speck of dust from it, or from the crib even, he would find a cure for his afflictions.[iv] Above this site, Mass was read atop a marble tablet. [v] Ten lamps glowed.[vi] There was also shown, not far from the crib, an altar where Mary swaddled her child,[vii] and on the right side of the cave, the place where Salome hid the water with which she washed Christ, and from which an ointment like alabaster was created. This was the ointment with which the harlot anointed the Lord in the great fourth fast.[viii]

To look back on the whole thing, it follows that as soon as one acknowledges a historical Christ that more than a few steps would be required to contest the authenticity of the place of birth[ix]; that probably Helena and Constantine had already disfigured the cave; that in the seventh century it did not have a

---

Allat. 15.

i   Breydenbach. Auro florizata. *Ashelm.* 1290. Superius verò opere Musivo splendescit. *Fürer* 66. Rauchwolff 644. Ceiling or vault decorated with gilded mosaic. Schwallart 303. Pour ce qui est de sa voûte, elle est toute embellie de peintures à la mosaïque, dont la beauté ne-cede en rien à celles de la grande Eglise; mais…la fumée a tellement noirei cette belle peinture, qu'elle ne paroît presque pas. *Ladoire* 201. But already Kootwyk (232) could not recognize it.

ii   *Anonym* in *Allat.*

iii   *Marin. Sanut.*

iv   *Perdicas* 77.

v   *Marin. Sanut.* Rudolph von Suchen 842.

vi   *Anonym.* in *Allat.*

vii   Rudolph von Suchen.

viii   *Anonym.* in *Allat.*

ix   The skeptical Clarke (125) also wishes the monastery to be standing on the place where our Savior was born. Sieber, a good Roman Catholic, does not strictly assert (51) that the birthplace should be located at the customs. Buckingham (Palæst. 1831, 58) considers vulgar the belief that the chapel is actually located at the birthplace, especially since it is underground. Robinson (2, 286) disregards tradition, but does not propose anything better regarding the Nativity's location.

narrow entrance, but was, in the eighth century, hewn out into a house-like, square room; and that, for centuries, the chapel was preserved with altar and ornamentation, just as it was set up by the Crusaders and their patrons; and today has much the same form and layout.

Directly west of the southern staircase, a fathom[i] west of the Altar of the Nativity, there stands a freestanding marble column.[ii] Not very tall, the column supports the vault in the northeast corner of a special room. Situated three steps lower down,[iii] that is, over two fathoms from the south wall of the chapel, the room, which was also called the Chapel[iv] or the Grotto of

---

i   10½ d'icy vers le Ponent, il y a une colomne de Jaspe fort jolyment taschtée, qui supporte la voute de la Grotte. *Surius* 528. According to Gumpenberg (464), the distance from the altar of the Nativity to the manger is 12 feet, according to Lussy (37) 2 fathoms, according to Radzivil (170) 6 cubiti, according to Legrenzi (1, 181) 4. cubiti poco più, few according to Prokesch (115), several steps according to Röser (447). See the ground plans.

ii   At the corner, or against the altar of the Nativity. . past the south entrance ... stand 3 beautiful marble stone pillars, which support the rock that creates the vault above the stable: the one in the middle has three steps on each side that take you down to the crib. Schwallart 303. The corner pillar of green jasper. *Boucher* 281. Surius, see the last note. Vn beau Pilier de jaspe serpentin. *Monconys* 1, 314. A half-red, white-speckled marble column of 2" long, 3' 10" in circumference (to support the vault); two connected corner columns above. Troilo 397. A marble column. Hailbronner 2, 301. I did not find an adjacent corner column to the west like it is depicted in the picture of the manger room in Pococke (2, p. 25). Cf. the image in Zuallart.

iii Same in Gumpenberg, Albrecht (3 steps, 2110), Ladoire (199), Helffrich, Surius, Troilo, de Bruyn, Thompson. Rauchwolff (454), Chateaubriand (1, 302), Richter (40) falsely claim that there are 2 steps.

iv   A small chapel right next to it (of the Nativity), where there is the manger. Wormbser 409. II semble que ce ne soit qu'vne mesme Chapelle auec le lien de la naissance; mais nèanmoins s'en sont 2. coniointes, et reduites ensemble, pour la commodité du service. *Boucher* 279. *D'Estourmel* 2, 117.

the Crib[i] or was considered to be the actual stable,[ii] stretches further southward, and is slightly less long from east to west.[iii] On the west wall of this room, some 7' high,[iv] outfitted with a marble floor[v] and a plain vault,[vi] dark without artificial lighting, lies[vii] the crib (ἡ ἁγία φάτνη)[viii] or its site where, according to legend, the infant Jesus was lain. The crib you find there today is underlaid[ix] with marble,[x] its floor of white,[xi] the front (eastern) wall of grey-brown marble, and in the background an innocent

---

i   To the right of this cave, 3 to 4 steps from the birthplace of the Savior, is another small cave, which is commonly referred to as the crib or stable. Mirike, note 101. Similarly, Helffrich says: "A small cave, into which one must climb 3 steps, and which is like a small stable that fits about two donkeys. Anshelm describes (1291) similarly: Est cavatura seu præsepe cavatum, in quo bos et asinus duntaxat poterant locari.

ii   E.g. Rauchwolff. See the last note.

iii   8 feet long, 6 wide. Gumpenberg 464. 8 feet 10" long, 6 feet 9" broad. Troilo.

iv   8" *Boucher* 279. At the beginning 9 feet, 6 inches, and at the end 7 feet, 9 inches high. Troilo 397.

v   Tabulæ pavimenti .. valde pretiosæ, magnæ et omnino candidæ. *Fabri* 1, 468. Mirike 103.

vi   The manger underneath a big rock. Villinger 93. Fornix antri e viva ac nuda constat rupe lampadum ardentium fumo omnino obfuscatus. *Cotov.* 232. Same in *Quaresm.* 2, 630. The vault is comprised of bare and rough rocks, without any ornament or polish. Mirike, note 103. The small chapel (manger room) is hewn into the rock. Gumpenberg 464.

vii Southwest from the Nativity. *Anshelm.* In the southern recess, on one side. Prokesch 115. Opposite the birthplace. Hailbronner 2, 301.

viii *Epiph*. M. 52. In Greek. *Perdic.* 77.

ix   Replica of the manger. Hailbronner (Wegelin 2, 122).

x   Rimmed with quite beautiful marble. Villinger 93. Block of marble. Neret 112.

xi   For centuries, the crib was supposedly clad (Georg. 524. Helffrich 718), padded (Tucher 667. Thompson, par. 91), covered (Schwallart) or coated (Geramb 1, 158) with white, finely polished marble. This expression must be disconcerting; it presupposes that the real crib was there, but covered with marble. More appropriate is Fabri's expression (1, 446), as the crib tabulis albis expolitissimis factum in loco vero præsepis Domini, et subtili schemate ornatum, as well as Ehrenberg's (512) statement, that it was beautifully crafted of white marble stone.

child of wax. The shape resembles that of an oblong box,[i] whose long sides run from south to north.[ii] This rather beautiful[iii] object beneath it stands a good foot high,[iv] above the floor of the crib room, is about 2 ½' long inside, about 1' wide,[v] and about ½' deep.[vi] In 1829 a porphyry slab was depicted in a niche as the stone of the crib, enclosing a star of white marble.[vii] I always saw the crib uncovered; normally, though, it was covered with magnificent fabrics.[viii] In the background hung a painting depicting the Adoration of the Shepherds. Many a pilgrim has fixed his devotional gaze on the crib or on this spot and covered it with kisses.[ix] Here, a Roman Catholic receives a complete pardon for his sins.[x] In the sixteenth century the crib belonged to the Latins.[xi] In 1637 it was occupied by Christians who were

---

i   Locus quadratus, candido marmore vestitus: et hoc est præsepe Domini. *Georg.* Vas lapideum seu linter … lectulus quadrangularis. *Anshelm.* The shape of a long, square box. Schwallart 303. *Boucher* 281. En façon d'une caisse quarrée, dont les deux bouts et le derriere sont un peu plus élevez que le devant. *Ladoire* 199 sq.

ii   Troilo 397.

iii   Quite beautiful. Seydlitz.

iv   Schwallart, Ladoire. 1'. Neret, Geramb. 1½'. *Boucher.* Approximately 2'. Thompson.

v   4 spans long, 2½ spans wide according to Gumpenberg; 4 spans long, 3 spans wide according to Fabri (1, 446 sg.); 2½' long, ½' wide according to Boucher; 4' (feet) long, 2' 5" broad according to Zwinner (365); 2' (feet) 4½" long, 2' 8" wide according to Troilo; 3' long and almost 2' broad according to Ladoire; 5' long, 3' wide according to Binos (209). There must be a printing error in Troilo, since the width would be more considerable than the length. Although the measurements are varied and somewhat uncertain, it seems that from 1449 onwards, the manger did not always have the same length and width.

vi   ½' according to Schwallart and Boucher, 4" according to Zwinner.

vii   Prokesch 115. At that time there seems to have been no manger there at all.

viii The ones this week were made of white silk with golden roses, covered with golden embroidery. Geramb 1, 158.

ix   Breydenbach 131.

x   Tucher, Anshelm, Radzivil (170).

xi   Anshelm, Radzivil.

not Roman Catholic, but in 1690 it was returned once again[i]; in the present century it belongs to the Latins.[ii]

The biblical history of the crib has already been told previously. According to the legend that prevails today, the stable is imagined as located one fathom away from the place of birth, the crib itself somewhat more than two fathoms to the west, and the latter as located closer or lower, that is, lying parallel further inside the mountain slope. This recollection of the past narrative is still necessary to better appreciate the post-biblical story of the crib in its main elements. The birth of the Saviour was the main, extraordinary event. It is of lesser value to know that he saw the light of day in Bethlehem, Judah, and even less, the fact that the child was laid in a crib. Therefore, it is conceivable that the oldest reports, which were reduced to their core elements, passed over the crib in complete silence. Only from the fourth century, full of monks and imagination, does the crib surface as having existed. I cannot subscribe to the legend that Helena of Constantinople found the entire crib in rubble, within it a stone on which the head of Jesus lay, along with hay and Joseph's boots and a long shirt.[iii] I note instead that the first report of the actual crib refers to Paula, who exclaimed on her arrival in Bethlehem that she, a wretch and sinner, was deemed worthy to kiss the crib in which the Lord, as a child, had cried.[iv] This crib was adorned

---

i *Caccia* 35.

ii Geramb 1, 159. Röser 448.

iii *Fabri* 1, 468. From which source he drew, I do not know.

iv Et ego misera atque peccatrix, digna sum judicata deosculari præsepe, in quo Dominus parvulus vagiit. *Hieronym.* Epitaph. *Paulæ.* Paula and Eustochium wrote to Marcella (letter in the opp. *Hieronymi*): Et illud præsepe, in quo infantulus vagiit, silentio magis, quam infimo sermone honorandum est. The anonymous, who described the life of Jerome (in his works, which Erasmus published), expresses himself as follows: Bethlehem vero locus splendidus fuit civitas David .. ubi quondam Dominus et Salvator … in præsepio, intra speluncam, ex Virgine nasci dignatus est, et parvulus vagiit. It is striking that the Savior is supposed to have been born in the manger, and the words nasci dignatus est recall an earlier inscription of the Nativity (p. 144).

with gold and silver, and candlesticks burned without ceasing.[i] Such gold and silver ornaments and such an illumination of the crib, to which St. Theodore also went on a pilgrimage,[ii] were noted around the year 600.[iii] About seventy years later, for the first time, the site of birth was set apart as distinct from that of the crib; the inner and hindermost part of the cave was the Lord's crib.[iv] A monk of St. Sabbas by the name of John managed to denounce the Frankish monks of the Mount of Olives for their belief that the Holy Spirit emanated from the Father and the Son, so that when, on Christmas in the year 808, they were at St. Sabbas' crib, where our Lord, the Redeemer of Mankind, had been born, they were about to be expelled as they had been declared heretics with heretical books; but the Franks remained steadfast and said, 'Here we will die, for you cannot expel us'. Exposed as agitators, those laymen employed to do so, could not carry out the unchristian deed.[v] Around 865, in the centre of the church, a writing or inscription appeared under a stone, where the southern entrance and the eastern exit were located. Here, on the west side of the inscription, it noted the site of the Lord's crib, whereas on the east side it noted the place where he had cried. Mass was celebrated there on an altar.[vi] A more detailed

---

i   The unnamed biographer of Jerome whom I have just cited, partly based on the account of St. Anthony. Pourquoi cette crèche si sainte (which d'Estourmel saw) n'a-t-elle pas conservé son simple caractère? 2, 118.

ii   Pervenit ad almum præsepe. S. *Theodori* vita auctore *Eleusio* (Theodor's pupil), in *Bollandi* acta sanctor., 22. April., p. 38a.

iii   In der Höhle præsepium ex auro et argento ornatum, et jugiter ibi (there and at the birthplace) flunt luminaria. *Antonin. Plac.* XXIX.

iv   Spelunca, cujus interior ultima pars. presepe domini est (nominatur according to the Mabillon edition). *Arculf.* 2, 1 (Cod. St. Gall. 267). Cf. above on p. 155.

v   Ubi .. nasei dignatus est. Letter of complaint by the monks of the Mount of Olives to Pope Leo III. *Le Quien* Or. Christ. 3, 348.

vi   Est scriptura sub uno lapide, cujus introitus est a meridie, exitus vero ad orientem, in quo ostenditur præsepium Domini ad occidentem ipsius scripturæ. Locus autem, in quo Dominus vagiit, est ad orientem. Habet ibi altare .. *Bernard.* 16. The stone was probably the altar slab on which mass was being read, and under which, to the west side of the inscription running

report is available from the eighty-eighth year of the Frankish kingdom. When the Crusaders entered Bethlehem victoriously, they saw the crib there.[i] It was located to the right[ii] or west[iii] of or next to[iv] the Nativity, and a little lower than it,[v] and was in the form of an equilateral square, which the ancients had clad with white marble so as to leave in the centre an opening shaped like an umbilicus through which one could see part of the crib.[vi] At the beginning of the twelfth century, the stone that was supposedly in the tomb under the head of the Saviour, and which St. Jerome brought from Jerusalem, was often seen in the crib.[vii] Here, too, it is clear to our eyes that we are the heirs of something created especially by the Brothers of the Cross; from their contemporaries we become acquainted — initially, only a little bit, and then at other times, in more detail — with the lower position of the crib room, the square shape and the white marble covering of the crib. In the period from 1187 to 1400, the real crib[viii] or a part of it[ix] was mentioned as being in existence: opposite

---

from east to west, was the manger, in a chapel with the entrance from the south and the exit towards the east.

i   Gesta Francor, expugn. Hierus. 26 (573). *Guil. Tyr.* 9, 14. Around 1160, St. Raymund du Paumier also saw it. *S. Raymundi Palmarii* vita auctore *Rufino*, in *Bollandi* acta sanctor., 28. Julii, p. 647a.

ii Quasi to the right. *Sæwulf.* 35. The location on the right presupposes that there was (only) one entrance from the north.

iii (To the east of the birthplace, on the other hand) In Greek *Epiphan.* M. 52.

iv Saewulf, the monk Epiphanius. In Bethleem juxta locum nativitatis præsepe est, in quo ipse infans Jesus latitavit. *Johann. Wirzb.* cap. 2.

v   Paulo inferins. *Sæwulf.* In Greek (from the birthplace) In Greek: *Phocas* 27.

vi *Phocas.*

vii *Sæwulf.* 35 sq. Cf. the index on p. 163.

viii *Brocard.* c. 9 (Brocardt 869). See note 2 on p. 154 (Pipinus). *Frescobaldi* 140.

ix *Marin. Sanut.* 3, 14, 11; but he also says: sub qua (the cave of the crib) erat praesepe.

the site of birth,[i] about four cubits from it,[ii] four spans long,[iii] and three steps below the floor of the Chapel of the Nativity.[iv] The tradition also knew how to breathe new life into the issue by adding something new to it; suddenly iron rings embedded in lead were found near the crib, to which farmers tied their cattle when they came to the market[v]; there stood the donkey and the ox.[vi] This one crude addition disappeared again after a time; the real crib itself was, however, preserved until 1483. For in that year, a part of the crib, in which Christ was laid was left bare[vii]; but from that time on, even though Helena was credited with the creation of an opulent crib of marble and porphyry in place of the old one of wood,[viii] one could no longer justifiably claim the authenticity of the crib,[ix] especially because in 1486 Pope Sixtus V had a beautiful and very richly ornamented chapel built in the Church of Santa Maria Maggiore for the crib that was

---

i *Frescobaldi.*

ii *Frescobaldi.* The more spacious cave of the crib than the birth place is a prima quatuor tantum pedibus distans. *Marin. Sanut.* Not far from the birth altar. Rudolph von Suchen 842.

iii Petrus von Suchen r c. In Reyßb. (842) however: 4 hands' breadth.

iv Monteuilla 773. *Frescobaldi.*

v Rudolph von Suchen. By this crib one still sees an iron ring embedded in the stone. The cattle was tied to those rings when it was taken to the market. Cod. Vienn. CCCXLII, 172a.

vi Monteuilla. Appresso si è il luogo chiamato presepio, dove la Vergine Maria pose il Figliuolo … in un poco di fieno tra il bue e l'asino, involto in vilissimi pannicelli. *Sigoli* 166. Cf. note 5 to p. 160. Bonaventura and Vincentius maintained that Joseph brought an ox and a donkey to Bethlehem. See *Quaresm.* 2, 629a. Saewulf already reported about the manger where the ox and the donkey had once stood (35).

vii Breydenbach 131.

viii *Ladoire* 199. More precious to me, said Chrysostom, is the crib that had been set aside. *Fabri* 1, 446.

ix The Jesuit Neret does not advocate for authenticity at all; rather, he seems to be saying that the manger represented by a block of marble stands in the same place where, as one believes, the Savior's manger had once stood. One must wonder, however, how Thompson could have written later (par. 91), that the manger shown by the Fathers seemed only to be an imitation.

brought from Bethlehem to Rome.[i] There were, however, those who did not consider the matter completely lost. The real crib, they claimed, was made of wood and had been sent to Rome and based on the width of the one that one sees in Bethlehem; it was obvious that there must have been a wooden one.[ii] One cannot even comprehend the ineptitude that lies behind the very idea of a wooden crib. In a country like Judea, logs that can be cut into boards are a rarity, and they must be used far too sparingly to be used for cribs or, to put it better, wasted. In Palestine, I never saw a wooden crib, and no pilgrim, no traveller, will recall having ever seen one in the ancient land of the tribe of Judah.[iii] Obviously, notions from the West have been mixed into this issue without any authority, just as the refreshing of the hay[iv] found by Helena and brought over to Rome is also a reflection of occidental views, because one does not dry grass that is green, as far as I have seen and know. In Judea they do not or very seldom carry it into the crib but rather drive the cattle out to pasture, especially at Christmas when everything is green; after the hot summer sleep, when, with rain, the heavens encourage the land to flourish. However, in Bethlehem today you can still find cribs but they are for fodder other than hay. For example, several stones are placed together to form a very natural crib; and use is also made of a stone about 1 ½' high with a round, but never angular, depression.[v] Usually, one hangs on the neck of a camel, of a livestock with horns, or on a donkey, a sack with the fodder in it. It is therefore quite correct that in this

---

i *Surius* 528. Cf. Schwallart. Incidentally, Kapfman says (10): Two or three steps to the right (from the birthplace) one goes down two steps, which is where the manger is. It is entirely made of white marble.

ii "But because this manger" (carved into the rock) "is so large and wide, it can be assumed that a wooden one had once stood in it, according to the custom and tradition of this land." Radzivil 170. Cf. *Ladoire* 199.

iii Sunt enim praesepia illius terræ aut saxea aut luteæ, et non de asseribus aut truncis facta. *Fabri* 1, 446.

iv The hay was properly kept in the Church of Mary Major. *Marin. Sanut.*

v I am also referring to my drawing.

country it is customary to carve cribs out of stone,[i] but rare to carve immovable ones in rock, something noted as characteristic of the region.[ii] I do know that in lonely places the wanderer encounters man-made holes in the rocks, not to collect food but to collect rainwater for the refreshment of men and animals. Moreover, the square hollow of the crib, as it has been known for many centuries, may have been an improvisation that did not pay enough attention to the customs of the Orient, an improvisation that was not carefully considered. And that in the end one does not forget to remember in general: The post-biblical story of a real crib does not merit belief; if such a great sanctuary had been found and venerated in his time, the father of church history would hardly have concealed it.

We now leave the crib, which had been declared a crib by an interpretation of the inn based on scripture that was too clever by half,[iii] to turn to a picture of Jerome, which greatly impacted pilgrims for a long time. In 1483, opposite the crib, there was a polished, mirror-smooth marble slab, and if you looked at it properly there appeared the image of a bearded old man lying dead on his back on a mat in a monk's habit, and next to him the image of a lion. And this figure had not been made with diligence, not with artistic diligence but appeared on its own while polishing was being carried out, just as when, without the artist's intention, different drawings often appear when polishing tables of burl wood. This logical explanation, however, did not satisfy everyone, the unsatisfiable turned instead to a miracle, and believed that it was the image of Jerome.[iv] In the sixteenth

---

i *Marin. Sanut.* However, he means just like those ones that had been there before him.

ii Breydenbach. Tschudi 271. Helffrich 718. For Fabri's correct depiction, see the preantepenultimate note.

iii Praesepe esse nomen diversorii, it had been the inn adjacent to the crib. *Schultet.* Lib. 1. Exercit. Sacrar. C. 50., as cited by *J. Quistorp.* Nebo, unde tota perlustratur Terra S. S. Th. Crenii opusc. elegantior. Roterod. 1699. Fascic. IX. p. 513.

iv *Fabri* 1 447. The author leans on the side of natural explanation.

century, this image wrought from nature and miracles[i] was cited
from time to time[ii]; in the seventeenth, image and superstition[iii]
continued to haunt the tradition, even continuing into the
first half of the last century[iv]; after 1734,[v] however, no trace
of the image was found in the pilgrimage books, and needless
to say, I did not see it anywhere at the site itself. At various
points people were more or less firmly against this notion of
such a particular natural phenomenon[vi]; and whether the tablet
was removed by reason, which no longer wanted to feed the
superstition, or the decay of the marble, or opposing Christians,
is a rather unimportant mystery. This superstition was, however,
less innocuous than another, in which the Saracens indulged in
the fifteenth century. They thought that under the crib Jesus'
immense treasures were hidden. Then some young men broke

Kapfman writes: and in the manger there is on the right-hand side a portrait
of St. Jerome, a spitting image of what he looked like on this earth. Then
someone said to us God better reward him for having translated the Bible
from Hebrew into Latin.

i   This is said to be Jerome's legacy, as it was later taken to Rome. Villinger
93.

ii   An image of a monk sprouting from marble. Ehrenberg 512. In the veins
of the stone, nature clearly imitates the image of a bearded man. *Fürer* 66.
Jerome's image. Lussy 38. Zuallart and Bernardino Amico (Tav. 8) give a
depiction of the image.

iii   Sur le lieu (manger) vers le Septentrion paroist dans le marbre la figure
d'un veillard, qu'on estime estre celle de S. Hierosme, Dieu ainsi ordonnant,
que tant de temps aprés sa mort on aye encore memoire de ce s. Homme
pour le grand amour qu'il a porté à ce s. Lieu. *Surius* 528. Sedente con una
mano sotto il capo in atto di riposare. *Legrenzi* 1, 181.

iv   Dans une des tables de cette crêche à côté droit .. on diroit à voir cette
image, que c'est le portrait du grand saint Jerôme. *Ladoire* 200.

v   Thompson, par. 91.

vi   Quidquid sit, opus certe est naturæ admirandum pulchrumque. Similis
naturæ lusus e regione quoque est, forma nimirum fœminæ. *Fürer* 66. See
above on p. 145. However, those who investigate the nature and properties
of such things a little more thoroughly should regard it more as an Ideam
or Chimæram imaginarium, which man conjures up in the air or elsewhere.
The image is strange, but not necessary of Jerome. *Cotov.* 233. C'est vue des
plus curieuses choses qu'on sçauroit voir. *Monconys* 1, 314. Troilo, note 398.
Thompson.

in at night through the choir window above the Altar of the Circumcision, and lifted away the panels next to the place of birth and the crib; but according to the stroke of the monk's brush, everything that had been lifted up crumbled, and, as they dug,[i] such fear and trembling seized the wicked that rushing out in haste, they left the tools behind and disappeared from their hometown.[ii]

Close to the west by the southern staircase,[iii] very close to the crib opposite,[iv] stands an altar called the Altar of the Adoration of the Magi,[v] where, according to the legend among the Latins, the Wise Men offered their gifts of gold, frankincense, and myrrh,[vi] and worshipped him.[vii] The painting above the small altar,[viii] by the hand of Jacob Palma,[ix] depicting the adoration of the Wise Men,[x] was thought to be something of slightly higher quality.[xi] The place has been owned by the Latins[xii] for a long time.[xiii] As for history, as early as 1320 there is reference to the location in the chapel where Mary was with the Son when the Wise Men

---

i   So where are the monks' rocks?

ii   *Fabri* 1, 476. Cf. above on p. 138.

iii   To the right of the birthplace. *Georg.* 524. Hard at it. Helffrich 718.

iv   On the eastern side of the manger room. Troilo 398. About three cubits opposite the manger. Ignaz von Rheinfelden 129. 81. See especially the famous ground plans.

v   Troilo 398. (The Franken Altar) 81 sq.

vi   Tucher 667. Fabri 259. *Georg.* 524. Lussy 38. Ignaz von Rheinfelden (the kings supposedly prostrated themselves there).

vii   Seydlitz 476. Helffrich. *Fürer* 66 sq. Troilo. Della Valle (1, 157) and d'Estourmel (2, 117) merely touch upon the worship. Ladoire says (200 sq.) that the 3 kings came in there, and I was told that this was where they had stood. According to Lussy, the staircase was later built at the site.

viii *Ladoire* 200. 3 feet 10" high, 5 feet 8" long, 2 feet 7" wide. Troilo.

ix   Prokesch 115.

x   *Ladoire* 201. Binos 209.

xi   *D'Estourmel.*

xii   Geramb 1, 159.

xiii 81.

worshipped him.[i] Moreover, we know that, according to the legend, the Three Kings (shahs) presented the gifts northwest of here and about 10' higher (north in the choir),[ii] and only in 1479 was it safely moved back to the Chapel of the Nativity, beneath a rock.[iii] Because the tradition could not be attached to the locations both above and below, one later fell prey to the sophistry that the kings dismounted above and prepared themselves for the presentation of gifts[iv] before they actually presented them below. I make, as I said, a distinction between the chân and the house, between the visitation from the shepherds,] in the former and that by the Wise Men in the latter, and I cannot not remotely agree with the legend, according to which the chân and the house are merged into one, and all the less so, because the one about the location of the Wise Men comes from the later period and is obviously invented. The one-sidedness of the legend is disconcerting. Why should the legend also reveal where the shepherds were standing when curiosity drove them close to the crib? Instead of continuing to ask questions, let

---

i   Item fui in loco illo prenominato tugurio ubi erat beata virgo cum fllio quando magi ipsum adoraverunt. *Pipin* 72b. One also reads in Baldensel (119): In hoc loco (præsepii) pauperculæ virginis infantulus a magis adoratur.. stella ductore ostenditur. In quel luogo (manger) fù (Jesus) adorato da' Magi, where the Roman Catholic received a complete remission of sin. *Sigoli* 166. Earlier, St. Bernard wrote (homil. 1. in Epiphania Domini, according to *Quaresm.* 2, 633) about the three kings: A Regia civitate, ubi regem quærendum conjectabuntur, ad Bethlehem villam parvulam diriguntur, stabulum inveniunt, involutum infantem pannis etc., and a reference will be found later in Jerome's epitaph to Paula.

ii See above on p. 94. Gumpenberg, who clearly moved the scene in question to the choir, later says (464), without touching the legend again, that at the manger there is also an altar located in the same hole.

iii After that we followed the procession to the right of the chapel. Four steps away from the high altar (birthplace), there is also an altar hewn underneath a rock, where the three holy kings made their sacrifices. Tucher. Fabri. According to Georg, the altar itself was rupe excisum.

iv Like Bernardino Amico (see the depiction of his birth chapel, tav. 3), one left the choir completely, and concentrated everything in the manger room: the place of preparation to the north and the place where the wise men placed their gifts to the south.

us allow a poet to call out to the oldest of pilgrims[i] since the shepherds:

Vos quoque tergemini Reges oracula patrum
Qui legitis properate, nitens en sidus Olympo
Apparet, monstratque viam. Vos oscula plantis
Figite, et ante humiles exponite munera cunas.

Now, having seen how the legends conflict with each other, we will see how they intertwine. The legend accounted for where Mary was sitting, with Jesus in her arms,[ii] when the men from the East came in to pay their respects with the gifts,[iii] and when the Most Blessed One Among Women held up the King of Kings for adoration.[iv] Where was this place of Mary's? It was shown to others[v] and to me between the crib and the Altar of the Adoration (Magi), on the wall (south); until 1829,[vi] the same altar,[vii] which we just called the Altar of the Adoration of the Magi, was considered, with some arguments back and forth, to be the place where Mary sat. Soon the whole altar was erected as a memorial site,[viii] soon the stone that served as a seat rested under the altar,[ix] soon a white stone measuring about 1 ½ square feet was walled in the altar for it.[x] I

i *Julius Roscius Hortinus*, in *Zuallard.* 298.

ii Schwallart 304. *Ladoire* 200.

iii See Lussy 38, *Surius* 258.

iv *Chateaubriand* 1, 103. Prokesch. Röser 448. Salzbacher, 171.

v *Nau* 423. *Ladoire* 200. Röser 448. In the corner of the altar of the wise men and of the manger. Salzbacher 2, 171. The "location" of the crib is 3 steps away. Geramb 1, note 157.

vi This altar (of the adoration of the kings) rests upon the stone where the seated Virgin is said to have received the 3 kings. Prokesch 115.

vii The distances are also quite accurate: 1 fathom from the manger according to Lussy, 2 steps east according to Surius. The inaccurate Geramb's 3 steps can hardly be taken into account.

viii Schwallart. Binos 209. Chateaubriand.

ix Lussy. See the antepenultimate note.

x *Surius.*

was shown a stone that did not rise up much from the ground.[i] In cases where one assumed there was a stone that could be moved, it was still possible to avoid an intertwining of the legends; it is only when the whole altar is described as a monument from the standpoint of the Wise Men and as the seat for the Mother who blessed the world and endowed it with joy, that it cannot be avoided. Following this description, it is hardly necessary to add that the tradition, whose age as three-hundred-years old cannot even be verified,[ii] lacks all credibility.

In the northwest corner of the Chapel of the Nativity, near its western exit into the Chapel of St. Joseph, I saw on the floor a round hole, about 1' in diameter, barely 1' deep, into which refuse from the chapel is swept.[iii] Since no attention has been paid to this hole for a long time, and the legend that was attached to it has also disappeared, it now only remains for me to present its historical meaning. The Bible says that the guiding star, which the Wise Men followed from Jerusalem, stopped in Bethlehem above the place where the baby boy (Jesus) was, whereupon they entered the house and found the child with his mother Mary.[iv] Where is the house inhabited by the Holy Family, or rather its place over which the star stopped, to be found? I have repeatedly remarked that I do not consider this house, where the Wise Men went later and the chân, where the birth took place and where the shepherds came to visit, to be one and the same. And according to my interpretation of the Scriptures, I must separate and remove the scene of the star's stopping and

---

i   De cet Autel (the wise ones) jusqu'à elle (Creche), il y a un petit rebord, qui servoit de siege à la .. Vierge. *Nau* 413. Tout proche la s. Creche il y a une pierre .. sur laquelle .. la S. Vierge étoit assise tenant l'Enfant Jesus lorsque les 3. Rois vinrent l'adorer. Et tout devant il y a un petit autel, qui marque où ils étoient. Voyage 1699. 82 sq. A 1' high and somewhat chiseled stone. Röser and Salzbacher.

ii   As far as I have been able to research, the oldest source is Lussy.

iii   Towards the end there are supposed to be holes in the churches of the Nestorians. *Quaresm.* 2, 640.

iv   Math. 2, 9 and 11.

the visit of the Wise Men from the Orient from the chân or the present-day Chapel of the Nativity. However, it is far less a question here of becoming aware of my opinion on the matter than it is about that of the world of traditions. Already in the first half of the first millennium it was said that after it had performed its service, the star fell into a well near Bethlehem where all who were virgins saw it at that time, and that when three women, of whom one was a virgin and two were not, went there, only the one who was a virgin saw the star.[i] Around 825 the pilgrim attached the point of the star to Bethlehem; coming to a well, he truly saw there, moving from one edge to the other on the surface of the water what, according to the hearsay, had beforehand already filled him with admiration, the image of the star that had appeared to the Wise Men after the birth of the Lord.[ii] At the time of the Frankish kingdom, a cistern, into which the guiding star is said to have fallen,[iii] was located next to the Grotto of the Nativity,[iv] on its northern side.[v] In the later period of the Frankish rule, it was believed, among the Greeks at least, that the star was in the well water.[vi] In the subsequent centuries, according to the Greeks, on the Holy Night the star miraculously shone in a well with living water in Bethlehem.[vii] According to the Frankish description, by contrast, the star had simply fallen into it, next to the crib.[viii] It is not until the fifteenth century, and those thereafter, that there is unanimous agreement

---

i *Aymon* Serm. de Epiphania according to Gregor von Tours, as cited in *Quaresm.* 2, 639.

ii *Willibald.* 12 (after the unnamed author). Quite similar to St. Gregory (lib. 1. de gloria martyr.), in *Quaresm.* I. c.

iii Ibi est cisterna in ecclesia .. in quam stella dicitur dilapsa. *Sæwulf.* 36.

iv *Sæwulf.*

v Epiphan. M. 52.

vi Epiphan. M.

vii *Perdicas* 77.

viii Monteuilla 773.

about the location of the spot (at the present hole). The hole[i]
or large opening above a cistern without water, into which the
guiding star fell,[ii] or above which hole it had disappeared,[iii] or
into which it had crawled,[iv] was located at the back[v] or leftmost
corner of the Chapel of the Nativity,[vi] or at the entrance to the
Grotto of the Innocents,[vii] not far from the crib.[viii] After the
middle of the sixteenth century, the tradition that sought the
star's resting place at the bottom of the chapel was abandoned.[ix]
As far as I know, only from 1656 does one hear even a faint echo
that a small fountain was said to be at the bottom of the Chapel
of the Nativity, which miraculously gave water for the same
amount of time that the Blessed Virgin had lived with the dear
child in the little hut.[x] A completely different interpretation was
given to the hole around 1620, claiming that it was the place
where the Lord's cloth nappies were washed[xi] as well as another
in 1647 that stated that at the time of Jesus' birth, it was an
oil well. Anyone who knows the generally mutable nature of

---

i (In a stone) Albert. *Sax.* 2110. Kapfman 10. (In the earth) Füßli in
Mirike 224. *Jod. a Meggen* 120. Ehrenberg 512. More generally, Wormbser
(409) and Löuwenstein (359) spoke of a place in the chapel where the star
had disappeared.

ii Et in hujus memoriam derelietum fuit ibi foramen illud, *Fabri* 1, 447.
Similarly Ehrenberg.

iii *Albert. Sax. Georg.* 524. *Jod. a Meggen.* Lönwenstein.

iv Füßli.

v *Albert. Sax.* In the back of the tomb is the hole where the star shot through
the earth once it had guided the three kings to the child and would not need
to shine for them any longer. Kapfman 10.

vi *Fabri. Jod. a Meggen.*

vii *Georg.*

viii Füßli. Löuwenstein. Five steps away (from the manger), on the right side,
there is a hole. .. Ehrenberg.

ix On the Zuallartian plan the hole is correctly drawn, but not named, and
on the Quaresmius-Zwinner one it says (19): A marble harness, of which
much is said. Quaresmius briefly dismisses the tradition as contrary to scripture (2, 6355).

x Ignaz von Rheinfelden 129.

xi (the west door in the Chapel of the Nativity) 82. 11. *Monconys* 1, 315.

traditions, will not be surprised that the cistern of the star was pointed to as being both above and below,[i] not even in places that corresponded with one another, inasmuch as the cistern of the choir lie about 40' more towards the east than the hole in the Chapel of the Nativity. It would not bother them terribly that the hole was freed from the plague of this tradition. This, however, did not solve the matter, because towards the end of the sixteenth century the tradition about the star moved completely toward the choir, where it has remained until our present day. This most likely came about based on the impossibility of the star's duplication and the evident contradiction therein.[ii]

The place where Jesus was washed after the birth was also pointed out as being on the wall in the back,[iii] as was the image of our Virgin in mosaic, which supposedly wrought miracles, and even spoke with the monks.[iv]

Immediately to the right, after descending the last steps of the southern staircase, there is a double-doored sanctuary that belongs to the Greek Orthodox.

Between the western exit of the Chapel of the Nativity and the stairs of Church of St. Catherine there is a group of cells: the eastern pair of cells is more united with the corridor, and the western pair is connected to it by an elongated passage (side corridor). We come first to the remarkable features on the eastern side, then to those in the side corridor and finally to those in the western pair of cells.

First is the Chapel of St. Joseph,[v] or the Altar of Joseph.[vi] It

---

i   This is why the cistern was located below when it was shown to Georg in 1507, and above when it was shown to Anshelm in 1508. Cf. p. 95, note 5.

ii   See the note above on p. 94.

iii *Light* 167.

iv   *Monconys* 1, 314.

v   *Surius* 529. Troilo 402. Una capella con altare eretto in honore di S. Giuseppe. *Legrenzi* 1, 184.

vi   Ignaz von Rheinfelden 128. Plan von Zwinner. *Ladoire* 201. Salzbacher 2, 171.

lies between the crib and the Altar of the Innocent Children[i]; the altar actually faces east.[ii] The floor of the small chapel[iii] is paved. Five steps[iv] lead up from the altar of those children. From the door that opens towards the crib, some brickwork extends four steps to the north, and from there the rock extends to the staircase of the Church of St. Catherine. At the aforementioned door, outside the Chapel of the Nativity, there is a box situated in the southwest corner, and there seem to be traces of an earlier entrance.[v] Here is the starting point of various digressions in the legend. Before there was an altar, it was believed that fearing Herod, Mary took refuge with Jesus in the back cave.[vi] According to a later legend, Joseph took refuge here while his wife was giving birth,[vii] and according to a more recent tradition, Joseph slept here when the angel admonished him to flee to Egypt.[viii] The chapel is not old; it was established in 1621.[ix]

---

i   See also Zwinner's and my ground plans.

ii *Surius*, Zwinner.

iii 18' long, 14" wide. *Surius*.

iv 3 steps to the south. *Surius*.

v   See above on page 131.

vi Fabri 259.

vii Ignaz von Rheinfelden. Troilo. La tradition porte que ce grand Saint (Joseph) voyant que la Vierge sa s. Epouse étoit prête d'enfanter le Redempteur de tous les hommes, il se retira pour quelque tems dans cette Grotte. *Ladoire* 201 sq. According to Binos (209), this place was located about 100 steps away from the manger.

viii Sieber 48. Salzbacher.

ix Sciendum itaque, quod, gubernante loca sancta Thoma a Novaris, loci opportunitate (in the birth chapel, he says though) inventa exigui sacelli, in eo anno Dn. 1621. altare erexit, sanctoque Virginis Mariæ sponso dicavit. *Quaresm.* 2, 675. Cf. *Nau* 417.

Chapel of the Innocents

The Grotto[i] or Chapel of the Innocents is located,[ii] as can be seen from what has been said, between the Chapel of the Nativity and the stairway of Church of St. Catherine, to the east of the rocky corridor,[iii] beneath the northern wing of the large church choir. The rock vault, which starts from the man-made corridor that leads to the passage of the vaulted crib (western part of the Grotto of the Nativity) towards the north, is supported by a thick column that is exposed here.[iv] On the east side, there is an altar, in front of which 'Salvete flores martyrum' was sung during the procession,[v] and next to which, on the outside of the corridor, just towards the west, there is an unusual opening in the rock vault that is plugged with large stones. It is said that the innocent children were thrown through it. I think it is likely the mouth of an old destroyed cistern.[vi] The Roman Catholic who prays enough gets indulgences in this chapel for seven years and seven times forty days.[vii] Beneath that altar[viii] there is a low,[ix] locked, iron lattice door,[x] through which one steals a view down into a cave,[xi] and which is opened only once every year.

---

i   The authors agree that there is a rock cave here. Boucher says (283): vn antre caverneux.

ii   *Fürer* 66. Schwallart 305 and the ground plan. Troilo 401. *Ladoire* 202.

iii   *Boucher.*

iv   Schwallart says: pillar. A column is correctly drawn on his as well as Zwinner's plans.

v   Greetings, you blossoms of blood witnesses. Ignaz von Rheinfelden 128.

vi   A cave or dry cistern. *Quaresm.*

vii   Radzivil 170. Meine Lustreise 2, 101.

viii Sacellum est puerorum innocentium, in quo sub altari specus est. *Fürer.* Schwallart. *Quaresmius. Legrenzi.*

ix   Une ouverture de 2. ou 3.' de diametre. *Nau* 418.

x   Una fenestra con grado di ferro. *Legrenzi* 1, 184. *Nau.* Prokesch 117.

xi   *Legrenzi.*

On a Christmas evening, I counted myself among the lucky ones to enter. First it goes up one step and then down two high steps, as it seemed to me after careful inspection, into a natural cave,[i] which in its length from south to north measures twelve steps,[ii] and in its complete emptiness the natural simplicity is thoroughly preserved. When I was in the cave, there were no mortal remains in it other than those of mine that were still flesh-covered; for one after the other had slipped in. 'According to the sacred tradition, herein lies the final resting place of the mortal remains (of the innocent children)'.[iii]

I will now bring the sanctuary closer beneath the lamplight of history. The Bible says that Herod, enraged by the false expectation that the Wise Men from the East would bring him Jesus, had all the children up to a certain age in Bethlehem and its entire region killed.[iv] The pious Christian asked himself: 'Where was the place of this cruelty? Were the bones of the children kept?' Tradition answered these questions resolutely, and it will be seen with what good fortune it did. When that God-fearing Roman woman, Paula, entered the cave of the Saviour, influenced by her emotions and incredible passion, she imagined not only the child wrapped in swaddling clothes and other scenes to which the Book-of-Books leads us but also the little ones who had been murdered and the raging Herod.[v] These words may not be of much worth beyond that of the rapture or

---

i   Fabri (Reyßb.) 259. Est alius specus, in quem nonnisi curvato dorso ingredi poteramus, et ab intus est locus in latere speluncæ ad latus sinistrum satis profundus. *Fabri* 1, 452. According to this, it seems that originally the Chapel of the Innocent Children was closed to the south except for a narrow entrance. A deep hole according to Tschudi (278); a moderate indentation according to Quaresmius. Cf. also Schwallart and Legrenzi. Deep, says Radzivil 170.

ii   6 cubits long, not very wide. Radzivil. The cave is drawn on the Zuallart plan, but not on Zwinner's.

iii   Schubert 3, 21.

iv   Matth. 2, 16.

v   See the note above on p. 136.

poetic outpouring out of the heart. The first historical reports about the scene of the murder falls in the transition between the sixth and seventh centuries; for the report that the pious Helen built a temple to the innocent children near Bethlehem[i] may without hesitation be disregarded as a historical fairy tale. Ten minutes from Bethlehem, in the City of David, where that king was also buried, the innocent slain children had their final resting place, and one could see the holy remains.[ii] Around 728 the very site where Herod had committed infanticide was to be seen when traveling from that of the Bethlehemites to that of the Tekoaites and there stood a church and there was buried one of the prophets.[iii] The same curious opinion was held that Herod had had the children brought from the region of Bethlehem into that of Tekoa where they were first cut down, an opinion which was later abandoned some one-and-a-half centuries ago but then re-emerges again, as I will directly show. Around 865, next to the Church of St. Mary in Bethlehem, on the south side, was the Church of the Innocents.[iv] In the beginning of Frankish rule, the innocent children rested on the south side of the first church, under an altar.[v] If one did not know that I had encountered a

---

i *Nicephor. Callist.* eccles. hist. 8, 30.

ii Milliario semis de Bethleem in suburbe David jacet David: sed et infantes, quos occidit Herodes, ipso in loco habent sepulchra, et videntur eorum sanctorum ossa. *Anfonin. Plac.* XXIX. About seventy years later, Arculfus (2, 4) spoke of the church with David's mausoleum situated outside the walls of Bethlehem in an adjoining valley (most probably in Wädi er Rahi'b), which would correspond to those ten minutes. More about this later. It is remarkable, by the way, that Arculfus reports nothing about the burial place of the innocent children.

iii Venerunt in villam magnam, quæ vocatur Thecoa, ad illum locum, ubi infantes quondam occcisi fuerant ab Herode. Ibi est nunc ecclesia, et ibi requiescit unus de prophetis. *Willibald.* 20 (according to the nun).

iv Juxta hanc ecclesiam est ad meridiem ecclesia beatorum martyrum innocentium. *Bernard.* 16.

v In australi parte ecclesiæ. *Sæwulf.* 36. In the Gesta Francorum exp. Hierus. (26 or 537) is written: Ibidem (Bethlehem) in confinio passi sunt Innocentes, qui ab Herode trucidati sunt, just as if, without any actual connection to the place, one had only wanted to copy the Bible, and Theotonius (Acta

large deep vault on the south side of the temple, one could otherwise have imagined that under the floor of the southern choir wing and the nave, it was not pure rock but hollowed out areas, or at least smaller crypts, where the bodies of highly placed persons, for example, the Bethlehem bishops, could be received. This will one day be confirmed by the excavation or clearing out the area. I am now very much inclined to look for the resting place of the innocent children, which in the beginning of the Latin Kingdom was placed to the south of the church, explicitly in the aforementioned vault. It is true that in the later period of Frankish rule the resting place of the innocent children, indeed most of them, was moved away from this place. It was not, however, moved all the way to Tekoa but to a place four miles south of Bethlehem and two miles from Tekoa. It is as if the newer tradition wanted to leave a part of them in Bethlehem because upon closer inspection it must have seemed contrary to what is written in the Bible.[i] But even then the tradition did not go uncontested, which can be proved by the fact that around 1170, near the western side of the city of Bethlehem, there were two caves with the mortal remains of the murdered innocent saints.[ii] In the thirteenth century, in or near Bethlehem, many bodies of innocent babes were seen in a large cave[iii] as well as the place and the bloodstained stone where Herod's minions hurled the children.[iv] In the first quarter of the fourteenth century a

---

sanctor., 18. Febr., 112) likewise gives us nothing specific when he says: Vidit et locum (as he was walking away from the birth cave), quo saviens Herodes pro Christo parvulos interfecit, than that around the year 1112 the place of the battle was believed to be near the Chapel of the Nativity.

i *Joh. Wirzburg.* cap. 2. Same in *Eugesipp.* 112. Fetellus, however, says (14b): In bethleem ejusque finibus innocentes de collari jussit herodes. quorum pars maxima contra meridiem, tercio miliario a bethleem Secundo a thuca quiescit. Adding up the miles - 5 or 6, the distance from Bethlehem to Thekoa is given correctly.

ii *Epiphan.* M. 52.

iii Thetmar in Maltens Weltkd., 1844, Febr., 192.

iv *Perdicas* 77. Brocardus (c. 9) was also shown the locus occissionis innocentium puerorum in Bethlehem.

tradition firmly stated: A number of the children were buried in the Church of St. Mary in Bethlehem on the right side of the choir or to the south,[i] where an altar was also erected, and on the other, a larger number elsewhere, three miles south; there at the site of the church many are also said to have been killed.[ii] In the latter part of the same century, some wavering of the tradition seemed to have occurred. On the one hand, the older view was firmly held that in the wing of the southern choir wing there was an altar, where the dear children were buried.[iii] On the other hand, the cave, where the tombs of Jerome, Paula and Eustochium are now shown, seemed to be called the Tomb of the Innocent Children.[iv] The latter at least should not be doubted according to the view asserted in the fifteenth century, and up to 1479. It is certain that in 1476, from the cloister of the Latin monastery one first descended many steps to Jerome's dwelling, from which his tomb was not far away, and then went to the crypt that had many holes, into which the innocent children had once been lain. From here, one returned to the cloister and only then to the great church to visit the Chapel of the Nativity.[v] Between 1476 and 1479 a very remarkable turning point took place. Since before the last-mentioned year no underground connecting

---

i   *Marin. Sanut.* 3, 14, 11. Item fui in ipsa ecclesia sancte Marie ubi recondita sunt plura innocencium corpora ubi etiam multi ex eis dicuntur occisi fuisse. *Pipin.* 72.

ii See the last note.

iii And on the side (of St. Mary's Church) to the right is where the dear children are buried. Rechtenstain 98b. And before him, Monteuilla (773) says: "underneath the same church, eight tiers deep on the right-hand side, lie the bones of the innocent children, in a 'gerner'." Gerner means carnarium, carnajo.

iv Ivi al lato (Jerome's Chapel, which was to the left) è un altra capella, dove furono gittati molte migliaria di corpi di fanciulli innocenti. *Frescobaldi* 139. Sigoli similarly talks (167) about a complete remission of sin for Roman Catholics.

v   *Albert. Sax.* 2110. See note 5 on p. 130. According to Gumpenberg (464), the southern side chapel of Jerome's study is not determined, but very probably "the place where the three dead were tended to, and where one threw the strangled children in through holes."

passage between the Church of St. Catherine and the Chapel of the Nativity was known.[i] Not until 1479 did one hear anything about a western continuation of the Grotto of the Nativity, of a cave behind this cave. The back cave and the connecting passage were obviously something that the Franciscans had undertaken around the time of the renovation of the church. How could they have hollowed out the back cave of the Nativity Temple, of which nothing was known until 1479, if they had not already had a passage to it from the Church of St. Catherine? That the connection was not made from the Chapel of the Nativity is historically proven. Now, however, no one can imagine that apparently starting with the Latin Brotherhood, the tradition of the innocent children was moved into the innocent, newly created back cave of the Chapel of the Nativity. [ii] And yet it did happen, and to this day, tradition still clings to this place.[iii]] There are two reasons why it should not surprise us that at first the back cave and the passage in general were kept as such a secret. First, one would have greatly aroused the concerns of those pilgrims, who may have known something about the old site of the innocent children and would have been surprised by the discovery of a secret, and those who were hardly thoroughly prepared to confront the Minorites with well-founded doubts.

---

i   For the history of the passage, see above on p. 127 ff.

ii   According to Kapfman (10), the place is dark: the hole (where Jerome translated the Bible) is where in VIc or VIm (600 or 6000) the innocent children were buried. There is also Saint Jerome's tomb where he was first interred.

iii   In the same chapel (of the Nativity) one also goes into a crypt, a hidden passage, at the end of which many innocent children have been kept, and have lain hidden there for a long time. Tucher 667. From there the author went again into the Chapel of the Nativity and through the large church into the monastery. Quite naturally; if one wanted to keep the passage hidden, the procession had to return again through the great temple, because its absence could or should have been conspicuous. So Fabri also turned back with the procession into the cave of the innocent children "and did not go up into Sanct Nicolaus Capel," but rather through the little door into the Chapel of the Nativity and then into the cathedral, – "and that was the end of the procession."

Then, as already noted, were Christians or Moslems to discover this, it would have broken like a heavy storm cloud on the heads of the venturers. Perhaps enough has been said or conjectured about this already. Had the ancients left a clear and comprehensive description of these events, instead of too many dashes, it would have been possible to summarize it in short sentences. We now turn to the many-hued tradition as it has presented itself to us since 1479. It does not actually merit further historical treatment, but it is necessary to make this description less incomplete, and to show by examples how a lack of religious and historical sensitivity so easily misleads people, even the more enlightened ones, even those who set the tone, even contemporaries, upon whom one so graciously bestows the epithet of enlightenment. The new tomb was dealt with somewhat more meekly at first; it was claimed that many thousands of the holy innocents had been thrown into it without any relics being found, even in its dust, because the faithful had long since taken them away.[i] In the course of time, with the aging of the newly found crypt, the tradition grew bolder. In 1508 it was said that the many bodies of the innocent existed in the secret crypt but that for reasons that are certainly quite understandable, few had been allowed to enter.[ii] The presence of the bones[iii] or the children's crypt,[iv] where

---

i *Fabri* 1, 452. My gracious gentlemen (Franciscans) allowed the pious men to see a small cellar there in secret, where all the innocent children were buried a long time ago. Alexander 74. The place of slaughter had supposedly been "in the middle of the church."

ii Est ostium (from the birth chapel) ducens in Cryptam quan occultam, in qua multorum corpora innocentium habeantur: sed rari illuc intromittuntur. *Georg.* 524.

iii Schwallart. (Several) *Surius.* Ignaz von Rheinfelden. *Legrenzi.* (According to tradition) *Chateaubriand.* Röser. The fact that the cave contained the graves of the innocents was also professed by the less devout Fürer (in quo [specu] nonnullos illorum sepultos esse dicunt) and Prokesch (a grotto that is said to contain bones of the murdered ones). Wolff was shown the hand and tongue of a baby murdered by Herod that were being kept in a cupboard (135).

iv *Quaresmius.* He followed Bonifacius.

the bones had lain for many years,[i] was touched upon now and again. At that time, it was also assumed that not only were some of them buried here, but also killed,[ii] just as at the time of the Herodian persecution several mothers fled with their children into this tomb when they heard other great cries of murder, but that in the end they were spied out and cruelly killed in the cave,[iii] which is why a pilgrim could also tell posterity that he saw blood on a rock.[iv] One cannot help but notice that even the most learned of Greeks, from whom the Franciscans hid the tradition about this new location for so long, and who, though they were not exactly prone to superstition then at least had faithfully accepted the tradition that the corpses of the innocent children were there.[v]

Altar of Eusebius

On the north side of the passage of rock, which leads from the Chapel of the Innocents into the western chapel of rocks, lies the unprepossessing[vi] altar of Eusebius of Cremona, under which he is said to have been buried.[vii] To appreciate this tradition, one need only recall that not until 1556 was this transverse passage

---

i   Troilo.

ii   Seydlitz 476. See above note 5 to p. 130. This tradition seems less true to Quaresmius.

iii Troilo, note 401. *Ladoire* 202.

iv   Tschudi 278. He cites "small loopholes," as they were known in the fifteenth century. I saw none.

v   He probably embellished his travel description here with older information, in the absence of more precise memories.

vi   In Greek (Chapel of the Nativity) 82. What is meant here is certainly the western door, rather than the one right next to it, to the south. Nothing is known to me regarding the use of this second door, which should have also been mentioned, as an entrance into the cave or into a chapel.

vii Bon marble. *Fürer* 66.

made known.[i] At the alleged grave of Eusebius, the Franciscans sang daily in praise of him:

Hymnus. Iste confessor Domini sacratus.
Antiphona. Similabo eum viro sapienti etc.
Vers. Ora pro nobis, beate Eusebi.
Resp. Ut digni efficiamur pro missionibus Christi.
Oremus. Intercessio nos, quæsumus Domine,
beati Eusebii Abbatis commendet, ut quod nostris
meritis non valemus ejus patrocinio assequamur.
Per Christum Dominum.[ii]

Here one is granted an indulgence for seven years and two hundred and eighty days.[iii] Eusebius' body was lain naked, as he ordered, like Jerome's was, outside the church, in the tomb of the dead, where the three men who died at the same hour were also buried.[iv] Eusebius' tomb was, however, so little taken into account that I was not able to find any mention of it until 1479. Up to the middle of the sixteenth century,[v] it was then shown in the southwestern chamber,[vi] next to

---

i   The grave of St. Eusebius. Seydlitz 475. Monumentum Eusebii. *Fürer.* Radzivil 170. Une autre allée, où il y a un Autel vers [..]e Septentrion, sous lequel fut inhumé s. Eusebe de Cremone. *Surius* 530. The tomb, in the form and shape of an erected altar, in which the body of Eusebii was laid. Troilo 202. Thompson par. 91. *Chateaubriand* 1, 305. Prokesch 116. And others. For the location, consult especially the ground plans by Zuallart und Zwinner, as well as Fürer, Radzivil, Surius, Thompson. See above on p. 130.

ii   According to Pictorius Cicardus, an erstwhile guardian in the Bethlehem monastery. *Bollandi* acta sanctor., 5. Mart., 383 F.

iii   Meine Lustreise 2, 101. Cf. the Bollandists (I. c.).

iv   Eusebius commanded, se nudum instar gloriosi Magistri extra ecclesiam, in qua jacebat s. Hieronymi cadaver, sepeliri. *Cyrilli* episc. Hier. epist. ad *Augustinum.* Appended to the opp. *Hieronymi* in the Erasmus edition. According to another version, Eusebius awakened three dead. Philippus Ferrarius Alexandrinus according to *Quaresm.* 2, 677. Cf. note 5 on p. 185.

v   Almost like Tucher also Fabri, note 258. (1, 439). *Georg.* 522. The tombs of Jerome, Paul and Eusebius and the library of the translator of the Bible are supposedly all in a cave. *Jod. a Meggen* 124.

vi   After that, to the right of St. Jerome's chapel, (which is correct, because

Jerome's cell,[i] and the existence of this tomb in the southern rock
crypt coincides chronologically with the transfer of the innocent
children from the same place to its present chapel, so that these
innocent children obviously had to make room for other graves, when
the tomb of Eusebius was moved behind the corridor to the Chapel
of the Innocents in 1556[ii]; it has remained there up to the present.[iii]

Chapel of St. Jerome

We continue now through the transverse passage to the western
pair of cells and arrive first at the southern chamber; I prefer
to describe the northern one first, the staircase with which we
have already become acquainted.[iv] The Chapel of St. Jerome,[v]
which I also call his cell, and which an older pilgrim called the
place of study (studorium) of St. Jerome,[vi] is entirely hewn into
the rock,[vii] except for the northern side, which is horizontally
turned away from the mountain slope, and which consists partly

---

one descends into this chapel from the west, whereupon it turns right or
south into the adjoining chamber), one enters a crypt, there is an altar
where S. Eusebius was buried... one receives remission of sins for seven years
there. Tucher 667. He then returned to the cloister through the Chapel of
Jerome. According to Tschudi (276), if I understood him correctly, there was
a passage from the tomb of Eusebius up to the cathedral, and it is very likely
that in his time a staircase led down from the nave to the western chambers,
first to the southern one. Other construction work must have taken place in
this chamber as well, since one can no longer see the holes for interring the
innocent children.

i   Facing Jerome's tomb. *Georg.*

ii As we were walking back (from Jerome's cell) up through another corridor
(to St. Catherine's Church), we were shown the tomb of St. Eusebius on the
left-hand side. Seydlitz, note 474.

iii Wormbser mentions (409) a "burial of Joseph", behind which I put a
question mark.

iv See above on p. 130.

v   Tucher 667. A chapel also dedicated to Jerome. Geramb 1, 152.

vi *Fabri* 1, 438.

vii Villinger 94.

of masonry. The chapel is quite large,[i] vaulted[ii] from the floor of the cloister 10 ½' deep,[iii] and probably somewhat deeper than the Chapel of the Nativity, and receives some daylight from the cloister through a window on the north side.[iv] Above the altar, erected on the east side, hangs a beautiful oil painting depicting the venerable Jerome holding the Bible.[v] A chair that can still be found in the chapel has hardly any connection with an armchair shown in the fourteenth century, in which Jerome sat when he wrote books.[vi] The Roman Catholic receives indulgences here for seven years and seven times forty days.[vii] When was the cave carved into the rock? What was its original purpose? It is impossible to answer this question. I do not find reference to it before 1449, when it was believed that Jerome stayed here, devoted himself to his studies and near the stairs, found his grave.[viii] Before we continue, we must trace the burial history further backwards. Jerome's body was buried next to the Lord's

---

i   20' long and 18" wide. *Surius* 531.

ii Unam pulchram testudinatam capellam. *Fabri.*

iii Deep. Alexander 74.

iv Tantum est una fenestra desuper. *Anshelm.* 1291. Radzivil 170. *Cotov.* 237.

v   Quite good. Geramb 1, 153.

vi Monteuilla 773.

vii Tucher, Radzivil, meine Lustreise.

viii Saint Jerome had his school there and lived there for 50 years. There are also three altars there, alongside his tomb, which is underground. Gumpenberg 464. Without being completely certain, Frescobaldi (139) seems to have already indicated the presence of the same cell in the rock as follows: Dove San Girolam fece la penitenza, e dove traslatò la Bibbia d'Ebraico in Latino, ed è suppellito in medesimo luogo … E in questo luogo è una cappella sotterra dal lato manco della chiesa.

crib[i]; he had a tomb hewn out of the rock at the entrance to it.[ii] This very narrow tomb that has been identified at this location, leaves little open to interpretation. It is evident that the narrow entrance must have been entered from the north, approximately near the foot of what's now the north staircase. But now the question is: Right or left? West or east? I am in favour of the western direction, not exactly because of the later tradition, but because upon further investigation it is evident that here one is more likely to encounter a sufficient layer of rock. If the tomb could be placed at the entrance, it can be assumed that from there to the crib there was an unbroken rock wall, at least from the outside, which could still have been worked into a tomb.

Chapel of the Tomb of St. Jerome, Paula, and Eustachium

On this basis emerges a new reason that the section of the Chapel of the Nativity, west of the crib, did not belong to the original Grotto of the Nativity but is a work of art from a later period. In sum, the old, real tomb of St. Jerome, hewn out of the rock, was very close to the crib[iii]; he wanted to be close in death to that

---

i   Juxta præsepe Domini .. sacratissimum Hieronymi cadaver humatum est. *Cyrilli* episc. Hier. epist. ad S. *Augustinum*, appended in the Erasmus edition of the opp. *Hieronymi*. Further down it says: Juxta (probably a mistake for extra, which should mean except for or not in the church) ecclesiam, in que gleriosi Hieronymi cadaver sanctissimum est humatum, venerabilis Eusebii corpus honore debito nudum (embalmed?), Magistri instar, sepelivimus. Cf. note 3 on p. 190.

ii   In cujus (speluncæ of Jesus's birth) itaque ore, id est, in ipse præsepii ingressu, beatus Hieronymus saxum scalpendo, monumentum sibi fleri jussit. In the vita *Hieronymi* by Anonymous, which in the Erasmus edition is appended to the opp. *Hieronymi*.

iii   Fabri caught a whiff of the location from the Anonymous, and says that "now" the grave is outside the church, while the entrance to the cave is not (2, 335); but elsewhere he assures (1, 439) that to the study cell of Jerome adheeret alia capella haud longe a præsepio Domini, where he had chosen the tomb, "now" empty, but intact and decorated with marble tablets. Jerome's

which in his heart he was so close in life. Around 600 Jerome's tomb must still have been seen at the entrance to the Grotto of the Nativity.[i] About seventy years later, however, the tomb made a significant departure from this location. It was seen in a church built outside the town in a valley on the south side and close to the ridge of the hill of Bethlehem, which also overlooked the Church of the Tomb of David; Jerome's tomb was similar in composition to David's, and without ornamentation.[ii] The later, long silence about Jerome's resting place was interrupted by the Crusaders. In the beginning of the twelfth century, Jerome rested again in Bethlehem itself, under a northern altar of the Church of St. Mary,[iii] and later it was decided that the body rested in a cave under the basilica, not far from the crib.[iv] The northwestern cell (St. Jerome's Chapel) already falls outside the perimeter of the Church of St. Mary, while the southern cell lies just under the northeast corner of the nave, and so, in strict accordance with the wording, during the time of Frankish rule, Jerome's tomb could not have been in the northern cell, but the southern one was most likely valid. Around 1280 a pilgrim was shown Jerome's bed and tomb in the monastery ruins near the church[v]; about three decades later, a pilgrim was also shown that

---

body is said to have been buried only in the 13th century, probably between 1220 and 1290, or more precisely, brought to Rome between 1260 and 1280. *Bollandi* acta sanctor., 30. Sept., 634, 639. The Bollandists, meanwhile, could have corrected the passage from Eugesippus the Monk (113). The body of Eusebius was also interred there. *Anshelm.* 1291.

i   Hieronymus presbyter. in ipsius ore speluncæ (the birth) petram sculpsit, et ob devotionem salvatoris ibidem sibi monumentum fecit. *Antonin. Plac.* XXIX.

ii   Sepulcrum sancti ieronimi. de quo inquiritis. ego conspexi. quod in illa habetur ecclesia que extra candem ciuitaculam in ualle est fabricata. que in meridiano latere sita. supra memorati dorse monticelli est cortermina bethleem ... *Arculf.* 2, 5 (Cod. St Gall. 269)

iii   *Sæwulf.* 36.

iv   In caverna quadam. *Joh. Wirzburg.* C. 2. In bethleem infra basilicam haut longe a presepio requiescit corpus beati Hieronimi. *Fetell.* 14b. *Eugesipp.* 113.

v   Brocardt 869.

along with the place of Jerome's remorseful contrition and where
he undertook his study of the translation of the Bible in a tomb,
to which it was remarked, in the same words used by the scribes
at the time of the Latin kings, that this man was buried not far
from the crib.[i] The tomb, which was thought to be the study
cell, could be assumed, with some reason, to be in the present
Chapel of St. Jerome. In the course of the fourteenth century, it
was again said that the tomb was in the Grotto of the Nativity,
opposite the birthplace.[ii] After these historical investigations we
arrive laboriously, but surely, and, as stated, not until 1449 at
the northwestern cell (St. Jerome's Chapel), which is supposed
to contain the tomb of the much-celebrated as well. But the
tradition that places the tomb here did not last long,[iii] and in the
middle of the sixteenth century, at the same time that the tomb
of Eusebius came into the freshly hewn transverse passage, one
may well say that the resting place of Jerome was transferred
to the southern rock chamber.[iv]It has remained there up to the
present. Even before the tomb moved to the southern cell, it was
believed that here (in the northern cell) the venerable scholar was
much occupied with study,[v] especially with the translation of the

---

i *Maris. Sanut.* 3, 14, 11. Pipinus says (76a) in general: Et vidi sepulcrum
in quo diu latuit corpus ejus antequam sufferetur Romam.

ii Monteuilla 773. Rudolph von Suchen 842. After touching the place
where the star stood still, Sigoli (167) continues: Appresso si è una cappella
divotissima, nella quale S. Girolamo traslatò la Bibbia, and then after the
graves of the innocent children: Appresso si è il sepolcro di s. Girolamo.

iii 18 stairs down from the cloister, there is an underground crypt and
chapels, called St. Jerome's chapels. His grave is located there. Tucher 667.
Fabri, note 259. *Anshelm.* 129. If long afterwards, Ignaz von Rheinfelden
(128) purported the same, it is probably a copy error, of which he would
have been just as little guilty as of the highly inconsistent assertion that
"From these cells, which are not unlike a prison because of their darkness,
the saint could walk underground into the manger, the entrance to which
had been left open by the Greeks, and perform his prayers."

iv "From here (the vault of the innocent children), we went on to the left
into a dark chapel, there we saw the grave of St. Jerome, together with his
chamber where he is supposed to have translated the Bible." Seydlitz 474.

v Gumpenberg, Tucher, Fabri. From the cloister of the monastery, you enter

Bible — one owes to him the Vulgate as a living testament to his activity — yes, not only that he stayed here,[i] which already the location of the cell might prove to be a lie, but that he, which again is more probable, also read Mass here.[ii] After the removal of the tomb, the tradition could breathe even more freely, and on up to the present the pilgrims have chosen to believe with almost enviable faith that Jerome stayed here,[iii] translated the Bible here,[iv] did penance here,[v] prayed here.[vi]

South of the Chapel of St. Jerome, as I have already mentioned, Jerome's tomb has been venerated for about three centuries.[vii] The

---

into a deep hole where St. Jerome had translated the Bible from Hebrew into Latin. Kapfman 10. Bonifacius thought that he had studied here at least in the summer. The tradition of the search for the study's location is, as we have seen, older (Marinus Sanutus, Rudolph von Suchen, Frescobaldi), but does not even go back to the time of the crusaders, who otherwise liked to visit and record the bizarre.

i Tucher.

ii Tucher. Prayed and read mass. Fabri 259. At least prayed. Hence the name St. Jerome's oratory. *Ouaresm. Nau* 421.

iii Schwallart 305. *Surius* 531. Troilo 404. Prokesch 116. Geramb 1, 152. Schubert 2, 494. Röser 449.

iv Wormbser 409. Radzivil, Schwallart, Surius, Troilo, Thompson, Prokesch, Geramb.

v It was here that he thought he heard the fearful trumpet that would one day call all men to judgment; it was here that he beat his chest, bent by the weight of age and the rigors of his life, with a stone and loudly cried out for the Lord's mercy, and so on. Geramb 1, note 152. Palsgrave Alexander spoke rather simply of the penitential exercise; however, only exaggerated thoughts belong in our time, being most suitable for it.

vi The altar marks the place of translation, e non molto a lungi di qui si piegano le ginochie sopra di lui proprio oratorio. *Legrenzi* 1, 184. L'Oratoire. *Ladoire* 203.

vii Wormbser, Radzivil, Schwallart, Quaresmius, Surius, Troilo, Nau (419), Ladoire, Thompson, Chateaubriand (who also lets Jerome spend most of his life in this tomb. 1, 305), and others. See especially the ground plans. According to earlier, very imperfect historical studies, it is hardly noticeable how Jerome's biographer in *Bollandi* acta sanctor. (30. Sept., 630) could be tempted to claim that some locales related to the saint are uncertain, excepto tamen sepulcro, quod nunquam mutatum existimamus, nisi quod ex pietate fidelium plura accesserint ornamenta.

chapel carved out of the rock is very simple.[i] It also contains the tombs of Paula and her daughter Eustochium.[ii] Jerome's tomb, more like an altar, is on the west side, the altar or the so-called tombs of those women on the east side just to the left,[iii] as one enters from the altar of Eusebius. Most captivating are the accompanying oil paintings.[iv] In front of each tomb the Roman Catholic receives indulgences for seven years and seven times forty days.[v] Before I begin the story of the women's tombs, I should remind the reader that I would have approached Paula's tomb with great reverence, if only I could have convinced myself of the real one. If in our days one encounters so many nuns who merely parrot their prayers and display ignorance almost everywhere, Paula, by contrast, was a very venerable, educated, spiritually absorbed woman who not only knew her mother

---

i   Dans cette suite de chapelles sépulcrales, je voudrois qu'on supprimât les ornements maniérés qui les déparent…; le mauvais goût, qui n'est que ridicule dans un salon, me paraît monstrueux dans les tombeaux. *D'Estourmel* 2, 118.

ii   Licet verum nomen sit Eustochium, non raro tamen a recentioribus Eustochia fuit nominata. *Bollandi* acta sanctor., 28. Sept., 630b. The few following pilgrims wrote the names correctly, as the ensuing review illuminates: im Cod. Vienn. 4578 (p. 203a) and in Tucher's (667) Paulus (Cläußner) and Eustachium, in Breydenbach's Paula und Eustochia, in Wormbser (409) and Löuwenstein's (359) S. Paulus, in Helffrich's (718) Paulina, in Rauwolff's (454) Paula und Eustachia, in Della Valle's (1, 158a) Paula and Eusebia, in Legrenzi's (1, 184) Paula and Eustochia, in Bachiene's (2, 2, 37; 1, 3, 484) Paulla und Eustachia, as well as Paulla und Eustachius, in Binos's (209) Paul and Eudoria, in Mayr's (331; reviewed by pastor Appenzeller) Paula Eustochia, in Richter (40) and d'Estourmel's (2, 118) Paula und Eustachia, in Joliffe (119), Scholz (162), Prokesch (116), Röser (448), Schubert's (2, 494) Paula und Eustochia, in Berggren's (3, 143) Eudoxia (Eustochia). The older authors, including Surius, Ignaz von Rheinfelden, Zwinner, Sieber, Wolff (135), wrote correctly.

iii   See the ground plan of Quaresmius and Zwinner. Zuallart has on his plan the womens' tomb to the west and Jerome's to the east.

iv   Really touching is the depiction of the two women's expression … slumbering the death of sleep …. They rest on gold-trimmed pillows of red velvet, the mother in a black pilgrim's dress, the daughter with loosened hair braided with roses. Prokesch 116. Cf. Geramb 1, 153. Schubert 3, 21. Already Nau praised (419) a very well executed painting at Jerome's grave.

v   Meine Lustreise.

tongue, Latin, but also understood Hebrew and Greek, to be able to read the entire Bible in the original. Paula died in Bethlehem and was buried near the crib in a cave under the church,[i] as the epitaph written by Jerome attests. Above the entrance to the burial cave one reads:

> *Aspicis angustum præcisa rupe sepulchrum?*
> *Hospitium Paulæ est, cælestia regna tenentis.*
> *Fratrem, cognatos, Romam patriamque relinquens,*
> *Divitias, sobolem, Bethlemiti conditur antro.*
> *Hic præsepe tuum Christe, atque hic mystica Magi*
> *Munera portantes hominique Deoque dedere.*[ii]

On the grave itself it said:

> *Scipio quam genuit, Paulæ fudere parentes*
> *Gracchorum soboles, Agamemnonis inclyta proles,*
> *Hoc jacet in tumulo, Paulam dixere priores:*
> *Eustochii genitrix, Romani prima senatus*
> *Pauperiem Christi et Bethlemitica rura sequuta.*[iii]

But before Paula sank into the grave, her body was displayed

---

i   Subter ecclesiam (speluncæ Salvatoris) et juxta specum Domini conderetur. *Hieronym.* epitaph. *Paulæ.*

ii   Do you see the narrow grave on the steep rock? It is Paula's dwelling place, which holds the kingdom of heaven. She abandoned her brother, her relatives, Rome and her fatherland, wealth, and family, and is buried in a cave in Bethlehem.

iii   Here in the grave lies Paula, the daughter of Scipio, from the family of the Gracchi, a famous offspring of Agamemnon, mother of Eustochium, the first one who, from the higher ranks of the Roman Senate, followed Christ in poverty and withdrew to the countryside, towards Bethlehem. – One finds these inscriptions in the works by Jerome; they were also copied by some pilgrims, including Quaresmius (*Pauli* instead of Paulæ. 2, 677), Surius (530 sq.), Zwinner (380), Troilo (403 sq.), Nau (420). Abraham Buchholzer writes in his Chronologia (655), that Jerome likewise addressed an epitaph to Eustochiam, virginem, Paulæ filiam.

in the church in Bethlehem for three days.[i] In the martyrology it is said only briefly that Paula, the mother of the virgin Eustochium, passed away near Bethlehem Judah.[ii] Apart from that, I lack any information up to the time of the Frankish kingdom. At that time, according to one opinion, both women, Paula and Eustochium, rested on the south side of the Church of St. Mary,[iii] like innocent children, while according to the other (Greek) opinion, they rested in the Church of St. Nicholas.[iv] It is a real testament to gross ignorance that later, up to the end of the Middle Ages the graves of those women could have been removed from the church,[v] even a stone's throw away from it, towards the east,[vi] where the Church of Paula and Eustochium, later the Church of St. Nicholas, contained both graves.[vii] With the revival of science in the sixteenth century, Paula's burial cave was no longer allowed to be located outside the Church of St. Mary; it must, however, have been a difficult business for the monks when they suddenly broke with the last tradition and moved the tomb to under the Church of St. Mary, not to the

---

i   *Hieronym.* epitaph. *Paulæ.*

ii   Cited by Zwinner a. a. O.

iii   Duæ etiam sacratissimæ mulieres Paula et filia ejus Eustochium virgo similiter ibi (in australi parte ecclesiæ s. Mariæ) requiescunt. *Sæwulf.* 36. John of Würzburg (o. 2) is more general and Fetellus (14b) uses the same words: Paula quidem et eustochium, quibus ipse hieronimus scripsit, similiter (like Jerome underneath the church) in bethleem sepulte quiescunt.

iv   *Eugesipp.* 115.

v   Haud longe ab es ecclesia. *Brocard.* c. 9 (Reyßb. 869).

vi   About a stone's throw away quasi contra orientem est ecclesia S. Paulæ et Eustochii… ubi etiam ostenduntur earum sepulchra. *Marin. Sanut.* 3, 14, 11. Appresso (at Jerome's grave) si è la sepoltura di S. Paula e di s. Eustachio. *Sigoli* 167. The appress here is very vague. "From the church (of Our Lady) a stone's throw away towards the east is the church of St Paul and Eustachius. Their graves are located there as well." Cod. Vienn. 4578, 203a. Breydenbach 133. Tucher specifies the distance as a Welsh mile. Fabri says nothing about the women's graves.

vii   Tucher. Their funeral took place in the church of Paula and Eustochium. *Georg.* 558. St. Nicholas: Then you see their graves in an underground tomb, as you go down 12 steps. Tschudi 282.

south side of it but to the north side, a move that would have been suggested by what took place over the course of the twelfth century. The oldest report about the new tomb probably dates back to 1556,[i] that is, to the time when new arrangements were made in the underground passages and crypts, the transverse passage between the west and east caves was cut through, Eusebius' tomb was moved into it and that of Jerome from the north to the south cell. A reliable report about the marble monuments of Paula and 'Eustachium' in the southern chamber, next to the chapel of St. Jerome, comes from 1566.[ii] There has been quite an abundance of reliable reports since then. In the century before last, the inscriptions, of which I did not see anything more, were carved, one above the entrance of the grotto or above the passage westward of Eusebius's tomb in the rock and the other on the tombstone of Paula.[iii] Based on these historical investigations, the verdict that has declared as false the tomb of Paula that is shown today is probably irrevocable; although it is not far from the birthplace of the Saviour, not even her burial place escapes the most well-founded doubt.[iv]

---

i   Three steps to the left from the grotto of the innocent children lie buried St. Eusebius, St. Jerome, and St. Paul. Ehrenberg 512. Seydlitz, who was in Bethlehem in the same year, says nothing about Paula's – or "Paul's" – grave, as it is misspelled here, in Wormbser, and in Löuwenstein.

ii   Ad monumentum Eusebii descenditur, ...e cujus regione alia quoque monumenta sunt, marmorea itidem, D. Hieronymi, S. Paulæ, et Eustachii. Ante monumentum Eusebii sacellum est puerorum innocentium. *Fürer* 66.

iii   Troilo, note 403. Cf. also *Surius* 530 sq. (the actual epitaph hung on a note above the grave). *Dovbdan* 144. If one looks carefully, the inscription in the rock above the entrance can probably still be discerned today; because it was fake, one seems to have paid so little attention to it that it was left to fall into oblivion completely. Helffrich says (718) that the name Paulina was carved into the gravestone.

iv   It amounts to a licentia poética when it is said: Hoc SS. Paulæ et Eustochii sepulcrum ipsum certe vetustissimum, si sit illud ipsum, in quo primum sepultæ fuerunt, s. mater et filia: neque justa est ratio id negandi. *Bollandi* acta sanctor., 28. Sept., 631a, on which occasion *Vincent. Bellovacens.* specul. histor. 31, 65, is being quoted. Even in the present century, the graves of Paula and Eustochium in the southern cell were mentioned as if their authenticity could not be contested. See Prokesch 116. Les deux nobles romaines dont les

On the feast days of Jerome, Eusebius, Paula, and Eustochium, the Franciscans also come from Jerusalem to Bethlehem, where Mass is said over the so-called tombs.[i] The older history of the southern rock chamber I provided in the elucidation about the children's tombs and Eusebius' tomb.

We will now leave the subterranean passages and chambers, in which I otherwise did not sense anything sinister, and continue our reflections in the other churches.

Church of St. Catherine

At one time known as the Chapel of St. Nicholas,[ii] albeit only briefly, the Church of St. Catherine[iii] bears this name because while she was visiting holy sites our Lord appeared to her here and predicted the martyrdom of faith.[iv] The church is located north of the large church choir,[v] only partly a little more east,[vi] separated from the northern wing only by a wall,[vii] and in the eastern section is somewhat separated from the Franciscan monastery.[viii]

---

tombes sont sous mes yeux. *D'Estourmel* 2, 117.

i *Quaresm.* 2, 677.

ii *Fabri* 1, 452. See above on p. 128. Tschudi also follows the preacher monk.

iii Gumpenberg 464. Seydlitz 474. *Fürer* 66. Radzivil 169. Schwallart 305. La Chapelle de la bien-heureuse Vierge S. Catherine. *Boucher* 278. *Surius* 529. Troilo 400. *Ladoire* 194. Schubert 3, 21, and others.

iv *Surius* 529. Another version is given by Troilo (401) and a much earlier one by Bonifacius. More about this in Quaresmius (2, 624), who refutes the legends, and believes that the name derives, without miracles, from the worship of saints.

v To the left of the big church. Boucher. Adjacent to it. Schubert. Concerning the location, see especially the ground plans, and above on p. 125.

vi L'Eglise .. est en paralelle de la grande de Bethlehem, mais plus avancée. *Nau* 416.

vii *Quaresm.* 2, 624.

viii Troilo 400.

Not large,[i] it measures from east to west about 100' in length and 20' in width.[ii] The floor of the church is of marble.[iii] There used to be a rather large door towards the companionway, but it was bricked up and another, smaller one, was built to the north, near the northwest corner.[iv] There were three altars in 1719.[v] To satisfy people's desires, an altar had to be erected opposite the door, so that the cloister of the monastery could hold the pious,[vi] and so it was in my time there. During their daily and nightly services, the Franciscans sang in the pleasant choir; only in 1719 was there the exception that on Sundays and holidays it took place in the choir of the large church.[vii] The Franciscans usually worship in this church.[viii] It looks clean,[ix] is beautiful,[x] especially rich in ornaments and images; the picture of the birth of Christ in the sacristy, behind the high altar, was declared as especially worth seeing.[xi] In addition to the legend of St. Catherine, for whose sake Roman Catholics receive a complete indulgence of

---

i Small. Prokesch and Schubert. Helffrich (717) was able to say this earlier about the chapel as it was back then.

ii 48 steps long, 12 wide. *Quaresmius.* 103' long, 22' wide. *Surius.* 82 feet long, 12 wide. Troilo. Approximately 35 steps long, 10 to 12' wide. *Ladoire* 195.

iii Hailbronner 2, 300. Elle est pavée de pierres semblables à celles du chœur de la grande Eglise. Ladoire 194 sq. How could he find a gold mosaic on the walls?

iv Troilo 401.

v *Ladoire* 195.

vi Prokesch.

vii *Ladoire.*

viii In qua horas perfleiunt. *Fabri.* In it the monks hold the divine offices. Radzivil 169. Schwallart 303. Nos Religieux font ordinairement l'Office en cette Chapelle. *Surius.*

ix A un air de grande propreté qui fait plaisir. *Ladoire* 194.

x *Surius.*

xi Prokesch. Le maître autel .. a pour rétable un tableau qui représente le martyre de ladite Sainte (Catherine), et le transport de son s. Corps par les Anges sur ce sacré Mont (Sinai) .. *Ladoire* 195.

their sins,[i] there was another legend that said that the star from above gave a sign of the presence of Jesus and his mother to the Wise Men of the East.[ii] The Church of St. Catherine has been given the honour of attributing its foundation to the godly Paula or Helena, but this is based on mere supposition.[iii] Towards the middle of the fourteenth century, the Nubians did not yet have a place in the great church, and that is when the sultan had a special chapel built for them.[iv] We have no historical evidence for determining whether this chapel passed to the Latins a few decades later, that is, that it was the very same chapel as the Chapel of St. Nicholas near Bethlehem, where Pope Gregory XI granted the Minorites a place to live in 1375.[v] And if we knew this, we would not be sure that this Chapel of St. Nicholas and the present Church of St. Catherine are one and the same,[vi] but it is very probable. Thus, we arrive on insecure ground[vii] in

---

i In this chapel there is a full remission of sins, which all pilgrims obtain there just as much as if they were to visit Mount Sion (should be called Sinai), which not everyone reaches because of the great distance and danger associated with the place. Radzivil. Schwallart 305. En laquelle les s. Pontifes ont transferé les Indulgences du Mont Sinaï. *Ladoire* 194. I do not know if this Sinai remission is still in effect.

ii Lussy 39. Thus, another transformation of the star and the legend.

iii Antiquissima est. *Quaresm.* 2, 624 und 674. Names quite boldly (673 sq.) Paula as the donor.

iv Petrus von Suchen r c (Reyßb. 842).

v Unum locum (ecclesiæ, he says) pro usu et habitatione fratrum tui ordinis prope capellam S. Nicolai juxta Bethleem. According to a document in the Zion Archives in *Quaresm.* 1, 406. It was also stated (2, 643) that in the vestibule of the church on the Northern side, opposite the entrance to the monastery of the Armenians, there had once been a door, which had been locked in his time and had led to the chapel of St. Nicholas.

vi Not Quaresmius (2, 673); he takes this Chapel of Nicholas for the famous Chapel of Nicholas, which lay east of the large church. I will come back to this later, and only remind the reader that the church of St. Catherine is also called the Chapel of Nicholas by Fabri. See note 2 on p. 202.

vii Legrenzi (1, 183) explains the building of the church in a peculiar way. When the Greeks during his time had snatched the church and the manger from the Franciscans, they asked Constantinople for a firman to allow them to build a temple, and the request was granted, così ne eressero uno tempio) in honore di S. Catterina sopra antri, ed Eremi d'antiche [...] livote, e sante

the middle of the fifteenth century, since it is only then that we reach a more or less certain knowledge about the Church of St. Catherine. It was beautiful,[i] but so small that at that time, as later, they preferred to call the church a chapel. Between the middle and the end of the sixteenth century,[ii] it was, according to reliable accounts, extended by about a third towards the east. It was expressly reported that when in 1672 the Greeks were repairing the large church, the Franciscans also embellished the Church of St. Catherine. They covered the floor with beautiful stones and whitewashed the temple from top to bottom, moved the altar, where they also exhibited a beautiful picture frame, further to the front, with the choir behind it.[iii] In 1738 the Church of St. Catherine was newly repaired.[iv] The cistern is no longer in the church[v]; it has been moved outside the church wall.[vi]

Church of St. George

The Greek Orthodox have a chapel to the east of the choir, which can be reached by climbing up a staircase.[vii] Around 1400, on the right side of the sanctuary, one went up fifteen steps to

---

persone, che colà restrinsero la lora vita.

i   At the same place (referring to Jerome's school and the grave and the holes for the innocent children), the brothers consecrated a beautiful chapel ... in St. Catherine's honor. Gumpenberg.

ii   Zuallart and Amico's ground plan.

iii   *Nau* 416.

iv   Korte 118.

v   In this chapel is a beautiful and good well, very deeply hewn into the rock. The water must be pulled out on a wheel. Helffrich 718. Nr. 5 on Quaresmius's and Zwinner's plan. Cf. also *Quaresm.* 2, 624, Ignaz von Rheinfelden 130, *Nau* 416.

vi   See above on p. 9. By the way, when I brought it to their attention, the Franciscans did not want to acknowledge this misplacement.

vii   See the new ground plans. Cf. p. 91, note 7.

the Church of St. George, which was two stadia away from the Place of the Shepherds.[i] Around 1620 there was a church of the same name to which a staircase with a door led to the middle of the high altar,[ii] and in 1674, a church dedicated to St. George was commemorated.[iii] The Armenians also have a church in their monastery, which is new and small, and the Moslems have a small mosque.

Christmas Festival

The crucifixion, burial, and resurrection of Jesus are mainly celebrated in Jerusalem, thus in Bethlehem the main feast on which we want to dwell is Christmas (birth of the Saviour). I will first discuss the festivities of the Roman Catholics. To enhance it, the guardian or, in his absence, his delegate with several conventuals from Jerusalem, not excluding the cook, goes to Bethlehem every Christmas Eve.[iv] In 1845 the celebration was distinguished by the presence of the retinue of the French legation and forty singers, most of them French, who had rehearsed beforehand. At midnight the colourful congregation had gathered in the Church of St. Catherine, packed inside. The service began. The organ sounded like a friendly voice[v] that had not been heard for years. The magnificent singing by the association of Frenchmen and a few Germans was well-suited to filling the mind with sublime religious feelings, if only were it not for the obtuse, religiously insensitive, pithy behaviour of the native Christians. Though few in number, the Franks who were present behaved with incomparable dignity. Not until after

i *Anonymous* in *Allat.* 8.
ii 82. Cf. *Quaresm.* 2, 644 (sacrarium sacellumve).
iii Où l'on entre pour aller de la grande (church), dans leur Monastere. *Nau* 424.
iv It was already like this in 1646. *Surius* 531.
v Geramb points (1, 161) to the ravishing chords of a musical piece.

the Mass was the procession arranged, and which, as far as I could tell by looking into the crowd, was joined only briefly by the father president, and by the delegate of the guardian, who was then absent in Rome, and by the French consul, Mr. Jaurelle. Dressed in official gala, and accompanied by his wife and daughter, after reaching the cave staircase, he went straight out of the almost hot church into the monastery—despite the clausura per le donne? The other part of the congregation went in the procession down the north staircase into the caves and to the Chapel of the Nativity, on whose sanctuary the attention of the faithful was or had to be directed. I saw little or nothing of the dramatization, from which the celebration still cannot or will not detach itself, because I did not have enough air to push my way through the sweating crowd below. But I know this much: in my time there a child of night was wrapped in swaddling clothes and laid in the crib. The Jews in Jerusalem apparently believe that the actual act of birth is presented. It is, however, not presented. Only a complete lack of decency and moral feeling would motivate one to depict such a scene. It is an appalling and certainly fundamentally false opinion that the church service can reach greater heights and unction through the dramatization of the Gospel or through the factual and personal imitation of that which is presented to us in the sacred story. Such a notion can be taken so far that it inspires the educated, the religiously more deeply educated person to shake his head at such an overturning of the boundaries of what is proper and reasonable, especially during the celebration of the birth of the Saviour, whose teaching requires worshipping God in spirit and in truth. Since Christmas Eve was not always celebrated in the same way, at least in insignificant parts, I will introduce some others. On Christmas Eve in 1449, the Franciscans celebrated a magnificent vespers, and Christians speaking six languages and performing many ceremonies came there, and there was such a clamour and commotion in the church, much worse than in Jerusalem, such a clapping of hands and noise, that the

gentlemen had to stop singing for a while.[i] In 1508 Christmas
Eve was also celebrated noisily. In the large upper church there
was an incredible, discordant, and wild noise, shouting, ringing,
singing, and howling. The Greeks, Georgians, Armenians,
Indians, and other believers in Christ from the Orient all took
part. According to their customs, each nation praised God,
raised a great hue and cry with songs, blared with trumpets and
rattles, worshipped the holy sites with incense, sprinkled them
with fragrant ointments and spices, touching them, kissing
them. A chorus of women, separated from the men, danced to
the sound of the kettledrum and made winding circles through
the whole church, clapping their hands and cheering with all
their strength of body and soul. Among the women, some stood
out for their gracious behaviour and appearance. With their
fingers they beat the kettledrums rather skilfully.[ii] In 1646 the
rock was celebrated with particular solemnity and devotion.
On the 17th day of December, the Octave sermon began in
front of the monks and various compatriots who came from
all sides; after that, a solemn mass was celebrated every day.
At Christmas, the guardian, dressed as a high priest, read two
masses, one at midnight and the other during the day. While
the Te Deum laudamus was being sung, the preacher and the
servant's assistant took from the high altar a shining box of glass
crystals, a gift from the Roman princess, Camilla Peretti; in it lay
such a beautiful child that it appeared to be alive and asleep; the
priest placed the box on another altar, which was opposite the
birthplace. In front of him walked six choirboys, each carrying a
white, burning torch, six singers and other servants, all dressed in
the surplice; they were followed by a large crowd of congregants
who bore witness with tears and sighs to their devotion and

---

i   When the Vespers and the Compline were sung, we had a drunken meal
with the Guardian, who invited us to come tomorrow on Christmas Day,
and I told him I have come to ride to the court of the noble king for the
holidays. Gumpenberg 448.

ii   *Georg.* 574.

heartfelt joy.[i] In the decade before last, it was said that after the service had begun with the chanting of Gloria in excelsis Deo, exquisitely beautiful youths dressed in white cloaks sang in the gallery, whereupon the procession to the caves took place.[ii] More recently, a pilgrim observed the richness of the carpets with which the marble walls were covered, the innumerable[iii] quantity of wax candles, the splendour that surrounded the guardian during his performance, and the ornaments sparkling with gold, gifts from princes, with which those who assisted in the church service were resplendent. He continues thus: At midnight, the guardian starts the procession and walks forward with slow steps and bowed head, carrying with veneration in his arms the baby Jesus; then come the Bethlehemites, the Roman Catholic Arabs, and then the pilgrims from the various nations, each with a torch in his hand.[iv] As soon as the priest who performs the service and his entourage arrive at the place of the Nativity itself, the deacon sings the Gospel. When he reaches the words: 'And they wrapped him in swaddling clothes', he receives the child from the hands of the minister, wraps him in swaddling clothes, puts him in the crib, prostrates himself before him, and prays to it (the doll). Finally, let us listen to the report of a dispassionate wanderer: Christmas is celebrated in Bethlehem with extraordinary pomp. Introduced during the Middle Ages, the practice of presenting the mysteries in a theatre has been retained. Children play the roles of various characters from the sacred story; dressed as those whose names they bear, they evoke, one after the other, the various paintings that recall the birth of Jesus Christ. The play begins with the Annunciation by the angel to Mary; then

---

i   *Surius* 531 sq.

ii   Berggren 3, note 144.

iii   The source is Geramb (1, 161 ff.). In my day, the lamps would have been easy to count.

iv   This is probably untrue; in my time, I was glad it was not like that. Imagine a chapel packed with people, each holding a torch in their hand. Would one's hair and clothes and skin be safe?

follows Mary's pregnancy and the birth of the divine child, and the play ends with the murder of the innocent children.[i]

When the Armenians, Greeks, and Latins celebrated Christmas at the same time, the first group performed the devotions first.[ii]

The Latin Processions

For centuries, the Franciscans have held a daily procession to the holy sites. Since the modifications to the structure, the procession no longer takes the same direction as before, and it is limited to the celebrated underground places. Every evening at five o'clock, after the completion of Compline,[iii] the procession begins with each member of the monastic clergy holding a candle in his hand.[iv] It moves first to the Nativity, to the crib, to the Altar of the Adoration of the Magi, then to the Altar of the Innocents, to the tomb of Eusebius, to the tombs in the southern west chamber, after which it goes out the Catharine stairs. Then the procession, which may last a good half an hour,[v] comes to an end.[vi] At each station, printed prayers are sung, as they are in the Church of the Holy Sepulchre in Jerusalem. First one sang at the

---

i *Duc de Raguse* 3, 48 sq. The representation of the pregnancy and the like did not occur during my visit.

ii Berggren.

iii Ignaz von Rheinfelden. Voyage 1699. 83. Binos 209.

iv Troilo, note 404. With lit white wax candles, they followed in pairs. Ignaz von Rheinfelden 128.

v Lasts a whole hour. Troilo 405. Approximately. Gehlen 34.

vi So it is according to Zuallart (Italian edition) 317 sqq. As far as I remember from the year 1835, the procession at that time basically moved in this way. According to Ignaz von Rheinfelden, during his time one went from the church of St. Catherine first to the altar of the innocent children, then to the altar of Joseph, then to the tombs of Eusebius, etc., and finally to the birthplace and the manger. According to Binos, Joseph's altar was visited first, and the tomb of the innocent children last (210); according to the Voyage 1699 (48 sqq.), first the altar of Joseph, then the tomb of the innocent, of Eusebius, and so on, and last "the St. Stable"; into the latter the monks never entered other than barefoot.

birthplace: Te ergo quæsumus, famulis tuis subveni.[i] The oldest report about the 'processions' of which I am aware appeared in 1449. One visited the birthplace and the crib first through the large church, and then, from the cross aisle of Jerome's school and grave, the caves of the innocent children.[ii] According to a detailed description of the procession, thirty years more recent in origin, one went first from the cloisters up into the great church then to the Altar of the Circumcision and that of the Three Kings (shahs), then into the Chapel of the Nativity to the place of birth, to the Altar of the Adoration of the Wise Men, to the crib, and at the back to the burial place of the innocent children. Then the procession left the Chapel of the Nativity and passed through the large church into the cloister, from there it visited the Chapel of St. Jerome with his tomb and Eusebius' tomb, exiting through the former, and thus 'the procession' ended.[iii] The order of the procession was changed shortly thereafter so that the Chapel of St. Jerome and Eusebius' tomb were visited first, and in the course of the procession the cistern in the Chapel of the Nativity and the cave where Mary fled from Herod with the child (Chapel of St. Joseph) were also remembered.[iv] When in the middle of the sixteenth century the connection between the east and west caves was established by a transverse passage, the processional order became simpler: one went from the choir to the Chapel of the Nativity, from the burial place of the innocent children, directly into Jerome's burial chamber.[v]

Having described and historically illuminated the Church of the Virgin Mary, the Chapel of the Nativity, the Chapel of St. Joseph, the Chapel of the Innocents, Eusebius's tomb, St.

---

i *Zuallard.*
ii Gumpenberg 442 and 464.
iii Tucher 667. Cf. note 5 above on page 130.
iv *Fabri* 1, 438 sqq. (Reyßb. note 258). Alexander 74. See note 3 to p. 186.
v See above on p. 130, namely note 5. – See also Gehlen (32 ff.), who cites the Quotidiana processio etc. (Venetiis 1786) and the beginning of the Antiphons.

Jerome's cell, his tomb, Paula and Eustochium's tombs, the Church of St. Catherine, and so on, the celebration of Christmas and the Latin procession, I will now move onto a description of the monasteries.

The Latin Monastery

Next to the Church of St. Mary are three monasteries, to the south and southwest are the Greek and Armenian, to the north, is the Latin.[i] First, I will discuss the Latin monastery, or the one owned by the friars of the order of St. Francis de Minori Observantia.[ii] It towers above Wadi al-Kharoobeh, is quite large,[iii] has thick, strong walls,[iv] and solid terraces. To a certain extent, the monastery's solid construction brings to mind a fortress[v] and the admission by its owners and inhabitants that without such a secure dwelling they would not feel safe. The monastery is kept in good condition. The refectory facing west is very spacious.[vi]

---

i Around midnight. Breydenbach 132. To the left of the Church of St. Mary. 81. See the ground plans.

ii St. Catherine's monastery. Troilo 399.

iii A wide and funny dwelling. Rauchwolff 644. Sufficient lodgings. Ignaz von Rheinfelden 131. Large. Korte 118. Large and well-built. Hasselquist 166. An extraordinarily large building, whose walls are made of monstrous (fantastic) stones. Geramb 1, 148.

iv Very high and solidly built. *Ladoire* 203 sq. Surrounded by high and strong walls. Korte.

v Celui (Monastere) que nous y avont à present, n'a rien à la verité de magnifique, mais il est tres commode, il ressemble plûtôt à une forteresse qn'à un Convent, et bien nous en vaut. *Ladoire* 203. Les monastères de Terre-Sainte ressemblent à des foteresses lourdes et ecrasées, et rappellent en aucune façon les monastères de l'Europe. *Chateaubriand* 1, 286. And in another place he says (1, 306) that the Frankish monastery in Bethlehem was a true fortress and the thick walls would easily withstand a siege against the Turks (untrue). Cf. Röser 646, Schubert 2, 492. "It is necessary for the monasteries in Sprien to be strong castles." Hailbronner 2, 297.

vi In the same place on Amico's ground plan. See also Troilo 400. Earlier there used to be a smaller one, more to the south and a floor high. Beau. *Ladoire* 204.

Above it, on the first and top floor, part of the ground floor, in fact, are the monks' many cells.[i] The father superior lives separate from them, between the eastern and western gardens, near the sacristy, which has a door to the Church of St. Catherine on the south side. On a staircase one descends eastward to the pilgrims' inn, which has its windows facing north. Esteemed or especially well-regarded pilgrims are accommodated in the monastery.[ii] I have already noted that the monastery has a special entrance next to the Church of St. Mary.[iii] There is no lack of care for water here.[iv] The brotherhood has large gardens, one inside the cloister, another outside on the north side of the large church choir, and a third long one on the north side of the monastery. As evidence that the inventiveness of the monks has not yet ceased, it can be reported that in 1843 a pilgrim was shown a previously unknown orange tree that Jerome had planted in the garden.[v] In 1575 the Franciscans had an abundance of beautiful garden plants and good fruit in the large, walled gardens.[vi] After the mid-seventeenth century, it is reported that the monastery had only mediocre gardens, which were graced with many arbours of pomegranates and grapevines.[vii] A family of Franciscans, moderately strong in number, inhabited the pleasantly situated monastery. In 1384 it

---

i   Many cells and chambers. Troilo 400. Au dessus est un dortoir tres propre, with cells for 30 monks. *Ladoire.*

ii Several rooms for the pilgrims. *Ladoire.*

iii See above on p. 82.   See above on p. 82.

iv Cf. above on p. 9. A cistern to the east in the garden is shown on Quaresmius' and Zwinner's ground plan. The roof terraces are very well laid out with tightly laid stone slabs, so one does not need to fear dripping or losing any of the rainwater, which is collected with great care in the monastery cisterns via gutters. Berggren 3, 148.

v   Craigher 147.

vi Rauchwolff 644.

vii Troilo. More important on the ground plans are the eastern gardens, rather than the north garden.

had about six conventuals[i]; in 1483, several[ii]; in 1508, 6 to 7[iii]; in 1583, 8[iv]; in 1620, 10 to 14[v]; in 1656, 8 to 10[vi]; in 1673, 12[vii]; in 1738, about 10[viii]; in 1751, 10 to 12.[ix] It is clear from this overview that the number gradually doubled; it increased the more the pilgrims and the income of the Franciscans decreased, which is hardly compatible with a prudent administration. The monastery is provided with food,[x] or let me express in it more general terms, its needs are met, by the San Salvador monastery in Jerusalem, just as the mother monastery provides for the replacement and change of the staff. In 1583 the Franciscans were changed every six months.[xi] Income other than that which flows to them from Jerusalem is hardly worth mentioning. In 1821 it was noted that the parishioners only gave gifts to the fathers in the form of rosaries or pictures of mother-of-pearl at weddings, on Epiphany, and Green Thursday.[xii] The parish costs or expenditures are, by contrast, excessive. When inflation and shortages occur, the monastery is overburdened; it already distributed fifteen hundred loaves of bread every week,[xiii] and, in

---

i   *Frescobaldi* 150.

ii Breydenbach 132.

iii *Georg.* 550.

iv 4 priests and 4 lay brothers. Radzivil 169. Lussy, who was in Jerusalem in the same year, mentions barely 6. Incidentally, in 1581 Schweigger also heard of 8 Italian ones (122); Binos found (205) only Spanish ones who were barefoot.

v   *Quaresm.* 2, 623b.

vi Ignaz von Rheinfelden.

vii Per ordinario vi rissiedono qui dodeci frati, oltreli laici. *Legrenzi* 1, 183.

viii Pococke 2 par. 51.

ix Hasselquist 166. I can hardly believe my eyes when I read in Agapito di Palestrina (140) that there was only one Franciscan in 1684. According to Gehlen (21), there were usually 9 to 12.

x   Ignaz von Rheinfelden. So I returned to Jerusalem with a donkey driver who was fetching food for the monastery in Bethlehem.

xi Radzivil.

xii Scholz 198.

xiii Geramb 1, 196. It may have been one less.

addition, as is known, taxes. The Franciscans do not now live under such heavy political pressure, as was the case, for example, in the fifteenth century and in the last quarter of the sixteenth century.[i] In 1449 a Saracen came with sword and club just as Mass was being heard, and, after a request for wine had been refused, beat furiously on the door of the cloister.[ii] In December 1831 the Franciscans had to flee.[iii] It was said that a guardian, a Portuguese, had been caught by the rulers and threatened with death. With the rope around his neck, he said: 'You can hang me if you want, but you will not receive any money, because I have none', and these words saved him.[iv] There are many such incidents that could be told. As far as the spiritual and religious education of the Franciscans is concerned, I do not want to make a hasty judgment; elsewhere[v] I have brought up facts that can speak for themselves. If I mention here the less than favourable judgment expressed by someone else, I do not mean to suggest that everyone who has come here has been dissatisfied with how the Minorites conduct themselves. Such dissatisfaction has come mostly from those such as an Englishman whom I saw arrive in the worst of downpours and whom the Franciscans quite kindly invited to a meal but then refused him everything else. The Englishman took a quick look at the venerated places and then fled. But back to our bellowing guardian: In 1831 some Englishmen were speaking with a Greek Orthodox father superior, who revealed no small degree of arrogance and insolence against the head of the Greek monastery Mar Elias and even reviled, in a way most

---

i   Great persecution by the Turks. Radzivil.

ii   This is the wicked scum; we were not allowed to enter the churches before them...Then pagans came into the church with their wives and children, they had shaggy black beards, looked like the devil, and behaved terribly towards us... Gumpenberg 448.

iii   Troilo testifies (399) that the Franciscans are often not even sure of their lives.

iv   Geramb 1, 197. Cf. above on p. 41.

v   Abroad, 1849, June.

dishonourable, the Greeks as heretics; the Greek monks were more steadfast and friendly than the Franciscans, who were just as ill-informed as they were, but with even greater pretension, and who, moreover, also carried on in manner that was pompous, domineering, and offensive.[i]

The history of the Franciscan convent, which, as was assumed, stood at a corner of town and was the only remaining one,[ii] can be traced up to 1375,[iii] and I have already noted that the monastery was also occupied by conventuals eight years later. It is very likely that the Franciscans then occupied essentially the same site that they still occupy today; only back then they had moved in significantly closer to the church choir. Thus, as late as 1586, the eastern part of the Church of St. Catherine, which, as is known, was later extended to the east, contained living quarters for the monks.[iv] As luck would have it, after 1673, a fire broke out in the monastery that had been largely constructed from panelling; the cells were, at any rate. The fire consumed it, and thereupon the Franciscans, who already had to pay out considerable sums to the oppressive Turks merely for permission, restored it solidly or from masonry at tremendous costs.[v] During this construction such important changes took place that the older ground plans hardly correspond to the present structure. In 1829 the monastery was in complete disrepair,[vi] and in 1845 I heard that in the last four or five years it has undergone many changes.

---

i   Palæst. 1831, note 55.

ii Schwallart 303. Troilo 399. Cf. note 3 on p. 132 and note 1 on p. 146.

iii See above on p. 204. In a general chapter, held by the Order of Preachers in Lyon on June 8, it is stated that duo nova coenobia, unum construendum Hierosolymis, alterum Bethleemi, had been sanctioned. *Echard.* T. 1. Script. P. 620. Col. 2. *Le Quien* Or. Christ. 3, 1284. At least at that time, the preacher-monks were anxious to firmly settle there.

iv Bonifacio's and Zuallart's ground plan.

v   *Legrenzi* 1, 183. Nau probably saw the monastery before the fire, because he writes that many of the cells are only des cloisons de bois; the Turks did not tolerate the construction (415).

vi Prokesch 113. Cf. also above on p. 7.

Greek and Armenian Monasteries

The Greek and Armenian monasteries sit south and west of the Church of St. Mary,[i] where they form a line. The Armenian monastery forms the western part of this line, where creating a right angle with the Church of St. Mary, it advances prominently against the western hill. The eastern side of this line, where gardens can be found that refresh the senses, along with the western or entrance side, and partly the northern side, stands opposite the Franciscan monastery. Each of the two non-Frankish monasteries is larger in size than the Latin one, and in terms of their solid construction they may also surpass it. Their location higher up is also more pleasant. In 1839 three priests inhabited the Greek monastery, which had been repaired about twenty years ago, in 1845 only one priest did. Among the Orthodox, Bethlehem is the fifth bishopric in the Patriarchate of Jerusalem, and the territory of this diocese begins at the valley that lies north of Bethlehem and runs in an eastern direction to the Dead Sea; from there, the boundary extends toward the south, including all of Idumea and Judea proper, the Jabal al-Khalil; and this line then turns westward and extending northward, it encompasses the entire mountain range of Judea to the Etham brook. Towards the east, the border touches the village of Walajeh, which is thought to be the ancient Bezek, and the valley and stream of Bethlehem, where it ends.[ii] The settlement of the Greek monks does not seem to be old. At least around 1620 a Greek did not mention it, while he explicitly mentioned the Armenian and Frankish monasteries,

---

i   The Armenian one to the right of the church. 81.

ii   Description of the borders of the Jerusalem Patriarchate and the dioceses belonging to it, in A. M. Mouravieff's Journey to Jerusalem from 1830 (4th edition.), in *G. Williams*, the Holy City (Lond. 1844), p. 498, 501. Neither from this message, nor according to Bartlett (207 sq.), who was admittedly hosted in the bishop's room, does it seem to be the case that he would have lived in Bethlehem itself. In the official message, the borders are determined in a somewhat inaccurate way.

which is odd, considering that the Greeks had already had the Church of St. George much earlier, and that after the middle of the sixteenth century the building between the southern side and the choir was called the 'dwelling of the Greeks.'[i] In 1646 the Greeks, who had exercised their influence over the sacristy and other beautiful sections of it, had at the end of the church, to the east, one of their bishops and some monks.[ii] When the church was built in 1672, their influence grew, and they did not fail to make themselves even more comfortable.[iii] Western pilgrims seldom drew attention to the Greek monastery,[iv] but in recent times Protestants often visited it as an inn, and they were well cared for.[v] The Armenian monastery has three monks, and judging by the two large cooking cauldrons, which resemble the smaller cauldrons at Helen's Hospital (Tkieh) in Jerusalem, the influx of the pilgrims must be significant at times. The gardens are clearly well tended. I am not able to begin the history of the monastery before the middle of the sixteenth century. Back then, the Armenians lived on the west side.[vi] In 1674 they were quite comfortable with many rooms.[vii] In 1821 they counted in the monastery two monks and two families.[viii] More recently, Protestants have also come to live with the Armenians, and they

---

i P. Habitatione de' Greci. Bonifacio's ground plan in Zuallart. We will also learn during the visit of the milk cave that the monastery is said to have been owned by Greek monks for a long time.

ii *Surius* 524. In 1583 the Greeks also had a choir in the large church. Radzivil 170.

iii Le pouvoir qu'ils ont en de reparer l'Eglise, leur a donné la commodité de s'etendre, et de pratiquer plusieurs accommodemens. *Nau* 424.

iv To the right, next to the churches, the religious Greeks also have their dwelling, which together with the garden is surrounded by a large wall. Ignaz von Rheinfelden 131. Thompson par. 89.

v *Bartlett* 206 sqq. He describes the reception room and the hospitality.

vi Cf. the ground plans, Thompson and a few others.

vii *Nau* 425. It is supposed to be the cœnobium Syriæ in Cassian (confer. 11, 1).

viii Scholz 215.

have been most graciously received.[i]

One understands very well that already in ancient times people wanted to live near the place of birth. That is why the monasteries were founded in the fourth century. The crib (the Grotto of the Nativity) was surrounded on all sides by a large number of dwellings belonging to God's servants[ii]; many holy brothers lived together.[iii] One of the most outstanding monks was Jerome. Behind the monastery for men, on the side of the church, there were three congregations and monasteries for women. These women, noble and humble, from different regions, had only one set of clothes and went to church only on Sundays.[iv] Next to the men's monastery there was an inn (for pilgrims).[v] Most likely, the men's monastery was located on the north and east side of the church, while the women's monasteries (behind it) were located on the south side of the church or southeast of it. During Jerome's lifetime, but only a few years before his death, the monasteries met a hard fate. The Pelagians committed the most nefarious murder against the servants of God who were under the care of Jerome the priest, and a fairly fortified tower barely protected them from the assault by the wicked. Jerome himself said that his house was completely destroyed. He then left Bethlehem with his people, but halfway out, he returned [vi]; this

---

i   Wolff 134.

ii   Præsepe…plurimis servorum Dei habitaculis undique circumdatur. In the unnamed vita *Hieronymi*, appended in the opp. edition by Erasmus. Cf. above on p. 32.

iii Multitudo sanctorum fratrum in monasterio. *Epiphan.* Epist. ad *Joann.*, episcop. Hierosol., translated by Jerome, in his opp. after Erasmus's edition (epist. LX).

iv   *Hieronymi* epitaph. *Paulæ.*

v   Nos in ista provincia ædificato monasterio et diversorio propter exstructo. *Hieronymi* epist. ad *Pammachium.*

vi   *S. Augustinus* (written in 417) in libro de Gestis *Pelagii.* See *Bollandi* acta sanctor., Sept. 30, 622. The biographer himself says (623): Addo hic aliam observationem, videlicet bibliothecam S. Hieronymi direptione et incendio monasterii verisimiliter dissipatam fuisse. From this, one may see how the opinions of Ignaz von Rheinfelden (131): "From the old monastery of St.

time, however, he barely lived in an official monastery. History does not say how long it took to build again, but it is certain that around 600 there was in front of Bethlehem a walled monastery with a lot of monks.[i] At the beginning of the twelfth century, the monastery of the Virgin Mary was remembered as a great and excellent one.[ii] We do not know what changes the Crusaders made to it, and what treatment it received from the Saracens when they attacked it in 1187. What can be verified, however, is that around 1310, at the exit of the church, towards the north, stood a monastery, which one climbed up several steps to reach.[iii] I have no doubt that this building dates from the times of the Franks, or perhaps from even earlier. From the beginning of the fourteenth century,[iv] it is difficult to prove the history of the old monastery buildings. I believe that around 1330, southeast of the church, stood a tower as a part of the monastery,[v] and the existence of tower at this location was frequently noted,[vi] even though nothing of a comparable sort can be seen today. Another tower stood at some distance north of the entrance to

---

Jerome, there is still so much left that even the inferior brothers still have sufficient housing," and several others just do not hold.

i   Ante (eastern) Bethleem. *Antonin.* Plac. XXIX.

ii   *Sæwulf.* 35. According to Löuwenstein, the monastery was also named after St. Mary (539). Cf. note 2 on p. 213.

iii In exitu ecclesiæ contra aquilonem. *Marin. Sanut.* 3, 14, 11. Brocardus came across some indications (indicta quædam) of a monastery with the bed of Jerome (o. 9). The monastery which, as I have mentioned, had not improbably been built by Paula, is said to have suffered greatly from the Muslims in 1263. Berggren 1, 148.

iv   Item fui in monasterio B. hieronnimi iuxta ecclesiam B. Marie in bethleem. Ubi ipse abbas fuit et multos ibi sacre scripture libros de hebreo transtulit in latinum. *Pipin.* 76a.

v   Monteuillia 773.

vi   Beautiful church tower. Tschudi 275. The monastery had 2 small towers facing East. Scheidt 70 (in S.O.) Fortissima et magna turris sive campanile. *Quaresm.* 2, 644a. One tower facing the south. Zwinner 373. See especially the new ground plans. It is still unclear whether at the time of the crusaders, this tower served as a bell tower as well as as a kind of fortress tower. Cf. above on p. 36 and note 12 to page 111.

the Church of St. Mary[i]; even in 1734, at the northern corner of the Latin monastery towards the west, attention was drawn to a tower, which had previously suffered much in the defence of the place.[ii] In 1483 the monastery was largely destroyed, and according to its appearance at that time, it was very large, high and wide, with battlements and towers, like an imperial castle.[iii] In 1519, apart from a church tower, the monastery was found to be partly destroyed.[iv] Even two centuries later one could still encounter the alleged remains of the old St. Jerome monastery.[v]

We now want to turn to the south side and take a closer look at its historical elements. Our gaze can no longer be occupied with the old gate, the remnant of a monastery.[vi] I am wholly in agreement with the opinion that the very active Jerome gave lessons or ran a school; all that is questionable is that, as far as I

i   See Bonifacio and Zuallart's old ground plan, as well as note 12 on p. 111.

ii Thompson par. 90.

iii Fabri 260. Cf. above on p. 36.

iv Tschudi. Bonifacio's plan has (L) Appartamenti d'Antichi, northeast from the present cloister. That there is nothing strange about Jerome's old refectory in Amico, Quaresmius, and Zwinner (plan 28) apart from the name goes without saying. Fabri's words (2, 334) probably also belong to the realm of fantasy: Post comestionem ipsum S. Jeronymi monasterium undique perlustravimus et ruinas ejus (it is not said whether on the northern or southern side) mirati sumus. Bernardino Amico drew (Tav. 3, p. 8) Jerome's room west of the refectory. Ecklin (756) even made himself believe torn walls belonged to a monastery in which Jerome's sister had stayed. However, Jerome's biographer writes with prudence and solidity in the Acta sanctor. (39., Sept., 630) in 1762: At non admodum verisimile est, monasterium S. Hieronymi, sicut ipse illud habitaverat, immutatum stetisse usque ad ea tempora .. (of Kottwyk, Quaresmius and others). Hinc facile videbit studiosus lector, pleraque modo relata loca, quæ ob memoriam S. Hieronymi in veneratione a fidelibus habentur, verisimiliter non parum tractu temporis fuisse mutata, nec omnino certum esse, omnia fuisse eodum prorsus loco, eademque amplitudine, qua nunc ostenduntur. Cf. the last note but ten.

v   Ce qui reste de cet ancien Monastere fait voir qu'il étoit magnifique. Ladoire 203. Before him Surius (524) said about the Jerome Monastery: retenant encore en son entier le Pan, Refectoire, Cellules, Cisternes, Cave et autres lieux. Cf. also Quaresmius (2, 623), Ignaz von Rheinfelden.

vi Nau's opinion (397).

know, only in the sixteenth century[i] is there the first evidence of a schoolroom, which was located to the south, next to the cisterns, on the forecourt of the Church of St. Mary, that is, where the Armenian monastery now stands. In the seventeenth century this room was a beautiful, vaulted stable with red marble columns.[ii] In 1674 the Armenians used the hall to which it belonged as a stable for pilgrims' horses and mules.[iii] In 1725, on the south side of the church, in an old building, a hall thirty-to-forty paces long and fifteen-or-sixteen paces wide was designated as the school of the much-named, and the pilgrims were received in it by the Armenians.[iv] The appearance reveals that a structural change took place there. Furthermore, I must add the remark that Jerome undoubtedly lived on the south side[v] because in his writing he made it known that before him every day he saw Tekoa and because one does not see this place from the roof of the Frankish monastery, only from that of the Greek or Armenian convent.

In the history of the monasteries which surrounded the Church of the Nativity of our Saviour, we also got to know women's monasteries. Who would not suspect that the Roman Paula inhabited one of them? Who would have thought that instead of coming as close as possible to the place of birth

---

i   See the ground plan of Amico and his copyists.

ii   42 steps long, 16 wide. *Quaresm.* 2, 623. It was there before the time of St. Jerome's school. The school of St. Jerome's can be found right underneath the place of the aforementioned Armenians, facing east and west. It is 42 feet long and 16 wide, vaulted, and stands on 6 marble columns. Troilo 406. Cette cour est fermée au Midy par un ancien bastiment, qu'on nomme l'Ecole .. de S. Jerôme .. La voute de cette sale est soûtenüë de 5. ou 6. colonnes de marbre. Between 30 and 40 steps long, 15 or 16 wide. *Nau* 397. Cf. *De Bruyn* 2, 222.

iii *Nau* 398.

iv   Neret 111. Röser (448) may himself be responsible for what he understood to be a chapel belonging to the Armenians, where Jerome had taught. Cf. "that's where St. Jerome had his school" in Gumpenberg 464.

v   Ce lieu estoit aussi peut-estre une partie de l'Hôpital, et du Monastere que S. Jerôme basti-là. *Nau.*

that she had moved away from it and, at some distance from Bethlehem, abandoned herself to her pious contemplations in a monastery? If it is said that she spent three years in a modest dwelling (hospitiolum) and only later built cells and monasteries and a pilgrim hostel along the way, we know that she stayed in Bethlehem.[i] Likewise, her daughter Eustochium, the abstemious one, who had a convent of fifty virgins, carried out devout work in Bethlehem.[ii] Behind a silence of more than a millennium, the tradition which was associated with the convent of Paula arose from the grave. This late resurrection of the tradition is very well-suited to arousing the greatest distrust against it. So too is the content itself, which obviously comes into contradiction with the oldest reports. For in 1483, when I found the first trace of the tradition, one saw on the other side of the valley of Bethlehem in a charmingly situated village (most probably Beit Sahour) large ruins of walls, of which it was said that there had been the monastery of St. Paula and her virgins.[iii] In 1583 a pilgrim was shown the crumbling walls of the convent, about a good hour from Bethlehem,[iv] and on the right side a little bit away from Beit Sahour,[v] on the way up from the Place of the Shepherds, other ruins were also seen. Around 1620, a mile to the north of the Grotto of Our Lady, in a valley, but in a somewhat elevated place, one came across several ruins of the monastery of Paula, a whole cell or chapel with cisterns; a St. John's bread tree could be seen from a distance.[vi] After the middle of the seventeenth century, some ruins and foundations, located about eight minutes east and down from Bethlehem, were assumed

---

i   *Hieronymi* epitaph. *Paulæ.*

ii *Pallad.* hist. Lausiac. CXXVI.

iii *Fabri* 1, 458.

iv With 500 nuns. Destroyed and left desolate by infidels. Lussy 37. How he arrived at the 1500 monks who supposedly populated the old monastery in Bethlehem, is unclear.

v   Radzivil 170. Copy in Ignaz von Rheinfelden 132.

vi *Quaresm.* 2, 679b.

to be the convent where Paula lived as abbess for many years until her death[i]; the Mohammedans had turned the cells into a mosque.[ii] In 1719, on a hill separated from the Franciscan monastery by a ravine five-hundred paces wide, and opposite from it, were old ruins with two or three cisterns, the alleged remains of the monastery of St. Paula.[iii] Nor has the tradition vanished in the present century[iv]; in 1821 the presence of ruins northeast of Bethlehem was noted.[v] After expressing some misgivings, a Franciscan showed me the place, located about a quarter-of-an-hour northwest of Bethlehem, on the west side of the Wadi al-Kharoobeh, where some floor was still adorned with mosaic.

---

i   Zwinner, note 387. Troilo 403. About the cave where the milk of Mary had dripped on the rock, declinando per levante si vedono le rovine d'altra chiesa, e convento, a work of Paula. *Legrenzi* 1, 187.

ii   Zwinner.

iii *Ladoire* 211. Thompson wrote (par. 91), that Paula donated four convents, three for nuns, not far from St. Mary's Church, and that some traces of these buildings could still be identified in his time, and that the pilgrims' hostel was unusually constructed.

iv   Chateaubriand discovered (1, 306), in his own way, from the top of the monastery room some debris here and there, among others also the ruins of a tower, qu'on appelle la Tour de Sainte-Paule.

v   Scholz 163.

CHAPTER 10

The Milk Grotto

The Grotto of Our Lady (la Grotta della Madonna),[i] the Grotto of the Virgin Mary,[ii] the Grotto of the Our Lady's Milk[iii] or the Milk Grotto[iv] or known among the Arabs as the Grotto of Our Lady [v] (البغارة السئى) is located at the top of the eastern hill,[vi] about 200 paces from the Church of St. Mary,[vii] 80

---

i   *Boucher* 284. *Surius* 533.

ii   Grota beatæ Mariæ Virginis. *Quaresm.* 2, 678.

iii   Troilo 406.

iv   Crypta lactea. *Cotov.* 237. *Ladoire* 208.

v   Scholz 189. Mughâret-el Sidi. Berggren 3, 148. It should actually be Moghârret es-Si'deh oder es-Sitt or es-Sitti.

vi   83. In front of the mountain. Gumpenberg 464. On a bare hill. Prokesch 113.

vii   Likewise Röser (449). 60 fathoms. Monteuilla 773. A stone's throw away. *Frescobaldi* 140. About a mile from Bethlehem. Pelchinger 558. Hardly a stone's throw away. *Georg.* 558. 5 or 6 stadiums. *Anshelm.* 1291. Two miles. Lussy 38. An arrow's shot to the south. *Surius.* ½ mile. *Legrenzi* 1, 186. Between 60 and 80'. Moundrell 89. 120'. Thompson, par. 92. Boucher says (284): 200 steps from the graves of the innocent children.

paces to the east of the little town's eastern house.[i] There is not really anything of interest up there. To reach it, one walks along the flat roof of a cave, which is covered with stone slabs,[ii] and upon which one has merely to avoid the holes of air and light. The entrance opens from the north,[iii] is open,[iv] less narrow,[v] and the entrance is not too challenging.[vi] Down thirteen steps,[vii] one descends in a southerly direction into the moderately deep cave.[viii] Of irregular shape[ix] and apparently carved into the rock[x], the cave is not large.[xi] It measures about 15' in length, 9' in width,[xii] and about 8' in height. The ground is flat throughout and there is little space devoted to art. The walls are rough[xiii] and Mohammeden women had recently surrounded them with

---

i   East of the village, almost at the end of it. Scholz. If this is correct, the village has been sinking to the east since 1821.

ii Röser claims (449) that there was ("is") a beautiful mosaic floor of a small church that had collapsed.

iii Prokesch 113.

iv In the fourteenth century there were two doors here. Petrus von Suchen x c.

v   Very narrow. *Georg.* Quite narrow. *Jod. a Meggen* 118. Low. Seydlitz 477. Pour y entrer on passe par une allée, qui a de longueur 7. pas, dont la porte est large 2'. *Surius.* Low and narrow doors. *Ladoire* 210.

vi Hoggidì questo luogo è quasi abbandonato, e può dirsi alla custodia de Turchi. *Legrenzi* 1, 186.

vii 9. *Surius.* 12. Prokesch.

viii A deep and dark hole. Seydlitz 475. Troilo 406.

ix Almost round. *De Bruyn* 2, 223.

x   *De Bruyn.* Peter of Suchen, Jodocus of Meggen, Ladoire, and many others simply claim that it is a rock cave. According to George, it was originally an Armenian's cellar.

xi *Georg.* Di breve giro. *Legrenzi.* Wide. Seydlitz. Quite large. *Jod. a Meggen.* Very large. *De Bruyn* 2, 221.

xii According to Binos (211), who likewise reports the height of 5½'. Quatre pas en quarré. *Surius.*

xiii Prokesch. A view of the interior, from west to east, was drawn by d'Estourmel (116). It is, by the way, unfaithful; thus, the column on the left with the beautiful, old base embedded in the wall is missing, not to mention other errors.

numerous jugs of oil with which to collect the runoff from them.[i] One also saw some ears of corn bundled together and interwoven with flowers, which fellow Arabs probably hung up as harvest offerings in honour of Mary.[ii] The ceiling is supported by seven columns,[iii] some of which are free-standing and some of which are built into the wall. In its time, miracles were unnecessarily attributed to the fact that some of the columns sometimes sweat and almost always appeared damp.[iv] In the southeast corner a few crooked steps lead down, in a mostly easterly direction, into a low-lying side cave. Right in the very middle (to the east) we encounter an inconspicuous altar.[v] If the Franciscans want to hold services here, they always have to bring their vestments.[vi] Every Saturday they perform the offering of the Mass and then chant the Litany of Lauretania.[vii] When I visited the cave, a member of the barefoot order had just come here to pray. The cave receives some light through the holes mentioned and from the entrance. In the past, it was apparently darker.[viii]

Traditions about it have tried out different versions. According to one, Mary rested here after the birth[ix]; according to another, it was here that she nursed her child.[x] The most popular tradition claims that the family fled here; according to some accounts,

---

i   Salzbacher 2, 179.

ii Gehlen 36. Cf. *Legrenzi* 1, 188.

iii Passé au long d'un rond pillier bleu, on entre dans la Spelonque. *Surius.*

iv Je ne blasme pas pourtant la coûtume, que les personnes devotes ont d'en (Wasser) mettre sur le front. *Nau* 426.

v   In the middle there is an upright altar. *Surius. De Bruyn* 2, 222. Prokesch. Schubert 3, 22.

vi Nos Religieux celebrent sounentesfois la Messe. *Surius*, like Quaresmius (2, 678) and later Nau. Porgono il Sagraficio con ogni libertà, e quiete. *Legrenzi* 1, 187.

vii Gehlen 37.

viii Che (le Donne Turche) vi mantengono lampadi accese in honore della Vergine. *Legrenzi* 1, 186.

ix Monteuillla 773.

x   *Frescobaldi* 140. There is no further mention of superstition.

they also spent a night here on the way to Egypt[i]; according to others, they hid here for a longer or indefinite time from the persecutions of Herod,[ii] at least until Joseph had bought and packed a supply of food in the city for the journey to Egypt.[iii] For the pilgrim who believes, there is already something captivating about the place where the family stayed. However, according to the legend, something else special also took place here that attracted his attention. Some say that since Mary had a lot of milk in her tender breasts, the drops fell on the marble stone on which she used to sit[iv]; others say that only a drop[v] or a few drops,[vi] or indeed milk,[vii] fell on the rock or the ground, or even splashed.[viii] Some pilgrims specify that it did not flow immediately, but that Mary, in fear and pain, first lost the milk. Then because of her divine virtue, she got half of it back.[ix] The milk then supposedly exerted a miraculous influence on the rock

---

i   Gumpenberg. *Anshelm.*

ii   Je trouve que c'est une ancienne tradition. *Surius* 534. Petrus von Suchen (Reyßb. 842). *Georg.* (after the departure of the three kings). Viagg. al S. Sepolcro F 7a. *Jod. a Meggen.* Seydlitz 477 (until Joseph received a command from the angel to flee for Egypt). Ehrenberg 512. Löuwenstein 359. Schwallart 306. *Boucher* (according to the tradition of the oriental church) 284. In qua (crypta) fertur latuisse beatissimam semper Virginem Mariam cum puero Jesu. *Quaresm.* according to an old manuscript. 83. *Legrenzi.* Thompson. Binos. Borsum 143. Prokesch. *D'Estourmel* 2, 119. Schubert. And others.

iii   Pendant que s. Joseph accommodait à la haste leur petit bagage. *Surius. Ladoire* 209.

iv   Monteuilla.

v   Petrus von Suchen (out of fear). *Georg.*

vi   Elle répandit quelques gouttes de son lait virginal sur la terre. *Ladoire.* Prokesch. A little. *Surius.*

vii   It is also at the same place that the milk of our dear lady was spilled. Pelchinger 615. *Jod. a Meggen.* Schwallart.

viii   This is the place where MARIA spilled her virgin milk onto the hard rock. Ignaz von Rheinfelden 132. Spremute le mamelle fù tanto il latte, che spucciò fuori. *Legrenzi.*

ix   *Boucher.* Hor in questa ritirata, e somma tribulatione serivessi, che la Santissima Vergine havesse perduto il latte, e divenuta meno in se stessa triste, ed addolorata piegò le ginochia all' Eterno Padre...e ne fù tosto esaudita.. *Legrenzi.*

or the earth. Just as the versions swirled colourfully through each other, the stone on which Mary sat became stained and milk-coloured[i]; the milk-white moisture, mixed with red, did not stop flowing for longer than a millennium[ii]; the more one touched it,[iii] the whiter the milk became; the earth around it appeared a little whiter than the other earth[iv]; the earth of the cave gained, as it were, the properties of milk.[v] If the runoff from the rock was put into the water, it became white like milk.[vi] The crumbly innermost part of the limestone cave, from whose wall the bulk of the detritus has broken off, is ashen and clay-like in appearance[vii] and, according to the nomenclature of mineralogy, moon or mountain milk.[viii] The pilgrims, on the other hand, called the limestone powder woman's milk.[ix] In 1483 we come across legends that contradict each other in unusual ways. I mentioned above[x] that at the place of the later Chapel of St.

---

i   Monteuilla.

ii   Petrus von Suchen. I did not see any drizzle anywhere, although the rainy season had already arrived.

iii   *Georg.* (usque hodie).

iv   *Jod. a Meggen.*

v   *Surius.*

vi   The red earth. Pococke 2 par. 52. When you grind the earth in water. Binos 211. See also Quaresmius.

vii   Hujus antri saxum coloris subalbidi duritie cretam non superat; easy to scrape off. *Cotov.* 237. Soft and white, like tuff stone. Della Valle 1, 1585. Slick like lead. *Surius.* Che altro non è che una tenera biancha pietra della stessa grotta. *Legrenzi* 1, 186. Chalk-like, whitish gray. Schulz. Bolus. Berggren. Chalk. Prokesch. White, delicate base of the limestone that is brittle. Schubert.

viii Schubert.

ix   Ils appellent cette terre, il latte da la Madonna. *Boucher.* Della Valle 1, 158. *Quaresm.* 2, 678. *Surius* 534. Questo è il latte di nostra Dama. *Legrenzi.* Quaresmius writes about how the milk is obtained: Excavatur terra ex hoc antro, quæ potius rubra est quam alterius coloris, pila contunditur, et in minutissimum pulverem reducitur; et in vase posita, aqua abluitur et purgatur, quæ extracta et soli exposita ipsa nive albior, et lacti simillima evadit... quæ deinde in pulverem redacta.

x   P. 179.

Joseph (next to the Chapel of the Nativity) the legend moved the flight of Mary with Jesus. I will now go into it in more detail. After the visit of the shepherds and the Wise Men, Mary saw that many were coming from Jerusalem to the cave to worship the child with the mother. Afraid of Herod, she fled secretly from where she had received the Wise Men of the East in the front cave into the back cave and stayed there. In the prison, however, she left behind in the crib in the front cave, the long shirt in which she had given birth according to the custom of the childbearing women in that country. In the back cave, where Mary had taken refuge, there was a rocky outcrop where she used to sit to nurse the child. It happened by chance that a drop of milk fell from her breast onto the rock, and from that time forth, a milk-white dampness, which was somewhat reddish, dripped down from the rock. The pilgrims put glasses underneath and caught the falling drops, saying that it was Mary's milk. It was therefore shown among the relics in many churches, as in Cologne, in 'Kyrchen'. In the past, people wondered where it came from, until they learned that it was only a liquid dripping from the rock. The first time (1480) the rock could be seen, but the second time (1483) beams and blocks were brought into the cave, changing the place.[i] This tradition, which apart from the location, deviates from the others in that the sweat of the dripping rock, was thought to be women's milk, not mountain milk, soon extinguished like the flare of a rocket next to the Chapel of the Nativity. This was probably due in part to the fact that the new Catherine staircase introduced more ventilation, drying out the place — I too found it dry[ii] — and also in part because the monks were not quite pleased with the duplicity and

i   Fabri 1, 450 sq. In the German edition (Reyßb.), this tradition is missing. The contemporaneous Breydenbach was silent (132).

ii   On the other hand, Light writes about the underground grottoes of St. Mary's Church (167): These are so damp that water drops from the walls – very unsuitable for the reception of cattle, much less for a woman in child-birth.

renunciation of the historical event that had supposedly taken place above and to the east of the monastery. In short, I never again encountered this tradition, which took its place in the later Chapel of St. Joseph; for even if it was repeated in 1519, it was certainly only a copy.[i]

After this digression, we return to the Milk Cave above the monastery. If it was, as one thought, a miracle that the milk of Mary flowed away in the form of moon milk, so one must not conceal another miracle, that this mountain milk of Bethlehem promoted the secretion of milk in women,[ii] and for the same purpose even proved to be profitable with cattle.[iii] And because of this property, the moon milk was revered not only by Christians but also by Mohammedans.[iv] When it comes to accepting superstition, the latter are not the most uneducated. Some pilgrims vouch with such conviction[v] for the proven nature of the remedy that one cannot justifiably declare everything to be a fairy tale. There is still another plausible explanation that does not require

---

i   Tschudi, note 277. Incidentally, he discusses the earth there, which is supposed to help against agalactia.

ii   *Georg.* 559. *Jod. a Meggen* (is said to). Ehrenberg. Wormbser. Lussy. Schwallart (is said to). *Cotov.* 238. En memoire de ce grand miracle la terre .. a la vertu de redonner aux femmes noutrices le laict. *Boucher* 284. Della Valle. Quaresmius. Ignaz von Rheinfelden. Zwinner 385. Troilo 407. Legrenzi the doctor (successfully). *Ladoire* 209. Schulz. Binos. Unanimously (incorrectly) attributed. Geramb 1, 187. Schubert 3, 22.

iii Schwallart, Surius, Ignaz von Rheinfelden, Troilo, Ladoire.

iv   Schwallart, Surius, Ignaz von Rheinfelden, Troilo, de Bruyn (Turks and Arabs), Ladoire. Turkish women especially make a strong use of it. Binos.

v   Cujus ego vim in nostratibus feminis frequentissime certam didici, atque Orientis populi opinionem haud vanam esse comprobavi. *Cotov.* 238. Ce miracle est veritable et continuel, car j'en ay souventes-fois veu les effets. *Surius* 534. Je n'oserois pas assûrer, qu'elle serve beaucoup dans les autres maladies; mais pour ce qui est de rendre le lait aux femmes, qui l'ont perdu, et d'en faire venir à celles qui en ont peu, c'est une chose si certaine et si infailible, que les Infidelles mesmes en ont eu mille fois l'experience. *Nau* 426. The soil that I carried away with me ... has proven itself. Ignaz von Rh. I can only assure you that in a large number of people, the expected (lactic) effect has been proven. Geramb 1, 187. Lorsque j'étois à Venise, un medecin de mes amis m'en demanda un peu pour en faire prendre à und Demoiselle. *De Bruyn* 2, 221.

resorting to miracles. Or what kind of miracles does the imagination, the mental movement of man, perform? One goes to the dentist with a toothache, and in front of his house, where the painful operation was to be performed, the pain stops as if by magic. Only after a wild struggle does the warrior notice the wounds which he incurred during it. That unfortunate Queen of France turned grey one night, tormented in the night by thoughts of the bloody scaffold that her husband was to mount. An innocent white powder of sugar can cause vomiting if the person taking it is told that it is an emetic. Truly, the power of imagination, the power of faith as a medicinal power is immense.[i] 'We must', said perhaps the least biased pilgrim up to the present century, 'only consider what power prejudices have over weak minds, so we will not be surprised if we are told that this medicine (women's milk of Bethlehem) is often effective'.[ii] It is hardly necessary to add that the pharmacology of physicians does not recognize mountain milk's lactic effect but probably its acidifying one. The milk of Bethlehem once brought it fame, which certainly inspired the attempt to try another means, and the remedy was thus also praised as a curative for fevers[iii] and in our century as a medicinal substance that facilitates births.[iv] Mountain milk was used by consuming the ground stone in a little wine or water[v] or in milk.[vi] The remedy was also prescribed in powder form,[vii] a knife tip full at a time.[viii] More complicated were the boluses that are still sold today, namely round cakes ½" thick and 1 ½ to 2" long prepared from a dough of lunar milk with the imprinted Spanish

---

i   Whether the soil's power originates in the aforementioned tradition or in the imagination, or whether the actual natural effect causes such effects in man, I leave everyone to decide freely. Troilo 408.

ii   Maundrell 89.

iii Schulz.

iv   Prokesch. Shall be very salutary to the parturient. Röser 449. Ease the pain of childbirth. Salzbacher 2, 179.

v   Wormbser 409. Dabbed in wine. Ehrenberg 512. Schwallart.

vi   *Surius* 533.

vii Thompson.

viii Troilo 407. A little in water. *Ladoire* 209 sq.

cross (seal). Hence known under the name sealed earth (terra sigillata), or with the sign 'M' (Maria). To use such a bolus, it was put into a glass of water and left to stand for a while. When the water had turned whitish, the bolus was taken out and dried for further use; the coloured water was then drunk.[i]

---

i Schulz 7, 7. Borsum 143. Gehlen 37. Already de Bruyn said (2, 221) that one prints the seal of Jerusalem.

CHAPTER II

Pilgrimage

The devout pilgrim was more than a little interested in getting powder and pieces of rock from the miraculous cave, which already in the fourteenth century was being venerated with kisses[i]. Of course, the popularity was all the greater because Christians and Moslems shared the superstition fraternally. In the said century, the moon milk was carried by pilgrims everywhere.[ii] In 1507 it was said that Saracens and Christians took a lot[iii]; in 1542 the pilgrims as well.[iv] Later they also collected earth or cut out a piece of the rock as a token of their pilgrimage.[v] In the second half of the century before last, the bolus trade had already begun; a quantity of 'stones', with the Jerusalem

---

i Monteuilla.

ii Petrus von Suchen.

iii *Georg.* 559.

iv *Jodoc. a Meggen.*

v E.g. Schwallart, Kootwyk. Retournant de Hierusalem, j'en estois chargé de trois pieces estois chargé de trois pieces grandes et longues comme les pieces du savon d'Espagne. *Surius.*

seal on them, was sent to Europe and elsewhere,[i] and in 1818 the assurance was given that the trade in this sealed earth was prodigious.[ii] The industry of the Occidentals was not inactive in this matter, and abuse crept into some places, as it did in Lyon in the monastery of St. Bonaventure, where false virgin milk was presented as true.[iii] In 1616 the preparations were made more artificially than later descriptions stated that they should be. When the stone was ground, the powder was mixed with certain fragrant waters, Agnus Dei or medals formed, and various images of saints printed, which the monks then melted in the water and gave to the pilgrims to drink.[iv] There is no question that the emergence of the described side cave can be attributed to acts of piety.[v]

In 1458 it was claimed that the twelve prophets were buried here.[vi]

I have a little more history to catch up on. In 1384, one mile from Bethlehem, was the Chapel of St. Nicholas in which Mary's milk is said to have been.[vii] Around 1400 there are reports of a cave in which Mary had hidden her Christ, and from her

---

i   *De Bruyn* 2, 222.

ii   Borsum 143. According to Geramb (1, 187), the Arabs send the powder to Turkey and to the interior (why precisely the interior?) of Africa.

iii *Boucher* 284. *Surius.*

iv   Della Valle.

v   Tanta fuit ex antro ablata, et in dies aufertur, ut ex parvo et unico antro, quale erat antiquitus, ut ab oculatis testibus accepi, magnum et triplex effectum sit. *Quaresm.* 2, 678. Nau, on the other hand, shamelessly writes (426 sq.): C'est une merveille que les Chrestiens et les Infidelles ayant tant pris de cette terre depuis si longtemps, il paroisse si peu qu'on ait prit, qu'on en diroit que Dieu la fait renaistre à mesure qu'on en tire; et plusieurs le disent.

vi   Pelchinger 61b. In 1384 their graves were moved to a church 6 miles from Bethlehem. *Sigoli* 167. In 1479, according to Tucher (667), it was assumed that these prophets had their grave at the church gloria in excelsis (shepherd's place).

vii E dicesi che nella detta cappella è del latte della V. M. *Sigoli* 171. Cf. the note above on p. 199.

trickling holy milk the place had become like white cheese. Such powder gave milk to women who had none.[i] This report has the problem that it does not contain anything specific about the location of the place. About a decade later, the church of St. Paul and Eustochium was found, undoubtedly on the present site, where their tombs were shown,[ii] and under which church there was a large cave and a chapel, where, according to legend, Mary sat with her son, so that in solitude she might find more peace in which to contemplate him. Here she is said to have pressed her breasts filled with milk, whereupon the earth turned white so that it looked like curdled milk, and it was also said that just as a woman loses her milk and puts a little of that earth into a glass of water and drinks it, the milk immediately flows again.[iii] These are the oldest reports of which I am aware about the chapel and the legend of the cave; about the dripping down of the milk of Mary; about the colouring of the rock by it; about the earth as a milk-producing agent. They are communicated with a simplicity and modesty that stands out starkly against the later anarchy of superstition and abuse. There is no doubt that the main threads of the webs of legends were spun by the native Christians, as it was subsequently pointed out. But now we turn to the church above the Milk Cave and to the monastery that stood next to it. At the end of the sixteenth century, it was believed that here was the monastery of Jerome, Paula and their daughter and that here lived a Saracen who demanded a Venetian penny from anyone who wanted to enter.[iv] Towards the end of the fourteenth century,

---

i   *Perdicas* 77. Because of the similarity of the moon milk with crumbly cheese, the local name for it is mountain goat cheese. The tradition of women's milk, says Quaresmius (2, 679a), is an old Armenian one, going back to Gratianus in vita s. Joseph, and Castro in vita Deiparæ Mariæ.

ii   See above on p. 200.

iii   De subtus vero prædictæ ecclesiæ (Paulæ et Eustochii) est crypta magna: ubi est capella, in qua, ut dicitur, sedebat .. *Marin. Sanut.* 3, 14, 11. Cf. note 2 on p. 200.

iv   Rudolph von Suchen 842.

the church also bore the name of Paula and Eustochium.[i] Before the middle of the same century, the name St. Nicholas Church appeared next to it, [ii] which remained[iii] until its decline shortly before 1449.[iv] The name St. Nicholas also remained attached to the ravaged church.[v] In 1507 there was a mention of a St. Nicholas monastery that had been destroyed, of which only the women's cave remained.[vi] Around 1620 were found the foundations of a monastery with dead bodies around it.[vii] After the middle of the seventeenth century, the Christians who lived there made note of some ruins or broken masonry (west) from the Milk Cave, where the Church of St. Nicholas is said to have stood.[viii] This is the last living trace of the name, and even the

---

i   See the same note on p. 200. While Breydenbach still writes about a chapel of Paula and her daughter (133), and Georg (557 sq.) about ruinæ Ecclesiæ Paulæ et Eustochii, where the hospital built by Paula and the pilgrims' hostel used to be; the ruins seem to have been located east of the milk cave.

ii   Monteuilla 763. *Sigoli* 171. Quaresmius sets himself apart (2, 678) with the words quoted from an old manuscript: Item ecclesia s. Nicolai, in qua est crypta (Mary's concealment). Georg expresses the, probably untenable opinion (559) according to the vita patrum, that the abbot Pinufrius lived in the monastery above the cave.

iii La chiesa di San Nicolò. *Frescobaldi* 140.

iv   Newly collapsed. Once beautiful. Gumpenberg 464.

v   It is a church in ruins dedicated to St. Nicholas. Pelchinger 61b. Tucher 667.

vi   *Georg.* 558. Around the same time, the author of the Viagg. al S. Sepolcro (F 17a) wrote that from the Church of the Nativity, along the wall toward the south, one encountered a beautiful monastery with Greek canons, the St. Nicholas monastery, and a church with good foundations and masonry and an underground chapel where Mary was hiding. I will not pass judgment on this one because significant errors seem to have crept into the text. Tschudi says (282) that the place of St. Nicholas where the monastery of Paula and Eustochium supposedly stood towards the north, is desolate and wasting away.

vii It had been one of the Pauline monasteries, ut probabilis habet harum partium traditio. *Quaresm.* 2, 679b.

viii Troilo 406. Zwinner (358) probably borrowed the name St. Nicholas from Quaresmius, and said that a church or a monastery was built above the cave. The latter I could not prove to be historically credible.

rubble gradually disappeared; for today one sees none.[i] In 1673 the existing remains were interpreted as belonging to a nunnery founded by St. Paula.[ii]

The open Milk Cave is in such a condition that one would hardly want to assert formal rights of ownership. Anyone may enter there unhindered and perform his prayer and from the expansive, accessible rock break off what appears to be useful for the body and soul. In 1449 it was reported that the ravaged church belonged to the Greeks,[iii] and the monastery was supposedly held by canons of the Greek faith for a long time.[iv] This sanctuary, however, was also a subject of dispute among Christians. In the last quarter of the past century the Greeks did their utmost to take back from the Franciscans the grotto which they had seized; only arbitration by the pasha protected the Franks in their possession.[v]

Around 550 there was a monastery of Abbot John in Bethlehem.[vi]

Bethlehem is one of the most excellent sites of pilgrimage in the world.[vii] The pilgrims who come to Jerusalem also go to the nearby Bethlehem because of Jesus' birthplace, just as they had

---

i   D'Estourmel wishes to have seen above the cave des débris d'une église. To this he, like Röser, adds the alleged mosaic floors – –

ii   *Legrenzi* 1, 186. Thompson wrote even more licentiously (par. 92): Above this grotto stands one of Paula's nunneries, but adds that nothing is left but the foundations. That the grotto, as Pococke claims (2 par. 52), would be a chapel "dedicated to St. Nicholas," seems implausible. See note 2 on p. 239.

iii   Gumpenberg 448.

iv   Tschudi and the last note but six.

v   Binos 212.

vi   Procope in his (lib. 5. 41).

vii   Abulfeda (in *Schultens* index geograph. ad voc. Bethlehem, according to the vita Saladini): It was purported that in the temple there was a piece of a palm tree (?), from which Mary had eaten during birth, which was very much appreciated by the Christians and venerated by holy pilgrimages. Quaresmius says (2, 639): Alli in partibus istis dicunt, in memorato foramine (Cistern hole in the Chapel of the Nativity) fuisse palmam, cui innixa beata Virgo Maria dedit dactylos: et sapientes quidam Turcarum se in suis Codicibus legisse affirmant.

during high Christian antiquity.[i] During St. Jerome's lifetime, the crowds of monks streaming in from all over the world were so overwhelming that it was not possible either to refrain from offering accommodations nor to bear a burden that exceeded their resources.[ii] After the death of this church father, even young men from Rome came to Bethlehem to visit the body of the famous man.[iii] In the fourteenth century, on Christmas Eve in Bethlehem, it is said that all the peoples under the sun gathered, and each religious party performed the service according to its custom.[iv] In the fifteenth century the Franciscans were not so well equipped to receive the pilgrims. They had to lie on the bare ground in the cloisters,[v] and at the same time they had to provide a guard so that they would not be attacked by the Saracens.[vi] The pilgrims were usually fed with similar attention. After spreading the blankets on the ground and sitting there, they ate what they had carried in their satchels.[vii] Even with such treatment by the Franciscans, there was still no lack of reverence for the monastery.[viii] In the sixteenth century the welcome seems to have been better; it was at least, as far as I know, more ceremonial. In order to better prepare the pilgrim for the vesper procession, which the fathers always offered him, for half a crown they gave him a burning wax taper for the sake

---

i *Gregor. Nyss.* epist. de iis, qui adeunt Jerosolyma. Hinten abgedruckt in *J. Henr. Heidegger* diss. de peregr. relig. Tig. 1670.

ii Nos .. tantis de toto orbe confluentibus turbis obruimur monachorum, ut nec cœptum opus deserere, nec supra vires ferre valeamus. *Hieronymi* epist. ad *Pammach.*

iii *Cyrilli* epist. ad *Augustinum.* Appended to the Erasmus edition of opp. *Hieronymi.*

iv Rudolph von Suchen 842. Cf. above on p. 208.

v Gumpenberg 442. Tucher 667. And they divided them around the cloister, and allocated them spots on the hard, bare earth. Fabri 259.

vi Gumpenberg.

vii There was also a lot of bread and eggs there. Tucher. Fabri.

viii *Medschired-din* 135. Fabri says the same as well.

of God[i]; they led him to the Church of St. Catherine, where, according to custom, they formally received and welcomed him, blessed him sacrosanctly as a pilgrim, and swept him clean of all sins, so that he might thus be worthy to visit the holy sites. In the century before last it was customary for pilgrims on their way from Jerusalem to Bethlehem, as soon as they saw the latter, to say the Te Deum laudamus along with the words from the Bible: 'A commandment went out from the emperor Augustus', and so on.[ii] In Bethlehem itself, the monks paid no small tribute to those arriving. After a signal made with a little bell hanging in the monastery corridor, all the monks gathered, washed the pilgrims' feet, as was done in Jerusalem, sang various psalms, gave each one a lighted candle and the kiss of peace, and then led the pilgrims, always in pairs, in a procession to the Church of St. Catherine, where the ceremonies were performed with praying and singing.[iii] The somewhat burdensome reception ceremonies have, as far as I know, been completely abolished. Now the main thing, proper accommodations and good food for the pilgrims, is looked after sensibly. This is all the more possible since the Franks only rarely visit Bethlehem.[iv] Is a reproach necessary if one of these rare and lucky ones in the pilgrim's chamber tries to make himself immortal with a verse, which is written with a pencil on the whitewash of the wall? Will I be reproached if I share a copy of such a verse, admittedly nothing classical, but nevertheless the best I have come across, at least as a mirror of

---

i   The rest was given back to the monks. Helffrich 717. I also received a candle, but without being asked for anything in return, and it cannot be said at all that the Franciscans in Bethlehem try to make money off strangers. That a wealthier guest should leave a gift, which, even if not exactly a large one, would please the fathers, goes without saying. In any case, there are enough impudent parasites in the world.

ii   Ignaz von Rheinfelden 126.

iii   Troilo 387.

iv   The pilgrims can stay for 3 days free of charge. *Lynch* l. c. 426. Actually against a written proof from the board of the Salvator Monastery in Jerusalem. Cf. Gehlen 21.

the thoughts and aspirations among the more leisurely pilgrims?

The Saviour is risen.
Rejoice, O Christianity;
Rejoice with all your hearts, all Christians,
And approach the babe in the stable.
Anton Lieschke, master carpenter

And when the pilgrim has visited the different places, prayed before them, kissed them, he takes leave of Bethlehem, richly packed with traditions. Though not all Christians depart with exactly the same ones.[i] Thus, the difference is not unimportant that the Greeks distinguish between the chân as the place of birth and the house where the Wise Men visited the family with gifts, which also accords with a plausible scriptural explanation; for according to the Greek tradition this house would be under the Milk Cave.[ii]

---

i   The Greeks disagreed with the Latins about the sacred sites' authenticity. *De Bruyn* 2, 209.

ii   In Greek: (The cave, into which Mary went with Jesus during their escape to Egypt) 83. Elsewhere the author explains the same phenomenon in the Chapel of the Nativity as pertaining to the Francs. See note 5 on p. 171.

CHAPTER 12

Libraries, Schools & Cemetries

The Franciscan monastery no longer has a library. Those with introductions or who are especially esteemed may find a few pilgrim books with the monks. In 1674 the situation was better. The library was quite well stocked with books, most of which had come, along with the French coat of arms, from Paris.[i]

To Bethlehem's credit, it can hardly be said that a great deal more is done there for its traditions than for education and enlightenment through good schools. That is for the reason that something is indeed happening in this regard. There are three schools there, one for the Greeks, another for the Armenians, and a third for the Roman Catholics. The Protestant school, which existed in 1841 and 1842, admittedly with interruptions, closed,[ii] I was told, because the religion was a different one. The Moslems have no school. The Armenians have ten pupils. The Greeks' schoolroom is

---

i   *Nau* 415.
ii Cf. Whiting in Calw. Missionsbl., 1842, 26. *Bartlett* 210.

in their monastery, and the number of pupils is over fifty. Likewise, the Latin monastery instructed within the walls of its own premises. Let us linger a little longer with the Latins. The schoolroom, in the western section of the monastery building, has the form of a large Latin 'Te' (T). The long beam, surrounded on three sides by a wide stone bench, forms the main part of the schoolroom, which does not deserve praise for its light. School discipline here, as in Jaffa, belongs to barbarism. A schoolmaster from Bethlehem, armed with a whip, and a boy with the same weapon were busy making the young people feel what they should think. Shackles for the feet were also lying on the floor in readiness, to make it possible to calculate the number of lashes to the soles of the feet right away, if necessary. There is such a clamour that it takes some effort to hear a conversation. In such a school, there is a wild hustle and bustle. Whoever enters the room can hardly reproach himself for disturbing the school by his presence, for the state of confusion remains the same regardless. At the most, the presence of a European might spare a poor devil a lashing. The school is presided over by three teachers, a Franciscan priest, and two Levantines from Bethlehem.[i] The costs of teaching and the salary of the schoolmaster are paid by the monastery. And not only that, but all of the pupils also receive a daily soup from him.[ii] There is no girls' school, and the number of schoolboys has increased from 130 to 150.[iii] School is held all year round, except for Sundays and many[iv]

---

i   A school teacher who is also a guard. Prokesch 117.

ii   The Franciscans pay the teacher and feed the children. Geramb 1, 168. Similarly Craigher (Kraiger?) 124. The Franciscans pay the tuition. Gehlen 41.

iii   Over 200 local boys and girls. Craigher. 100 school children. Gehlen.

iv   The people of Bethlehem do not only spend the days for which the Church forbids servile labor, but also a great many others in the same way, in spite of all the ideas that the Holy See impresses on them in this regard. Geramb.

holidays. Children do their lessons out loud.[i] They are taught reading and writing, language, especially Italian,[ii] and religion, and singing as well.[iii] I will not return to the teaching of the Syrian Christians in the sixteenth century and to those of the Latins in the seventeenth.[iv] I add only the comment that as far as I know no word about a regular Roman and Greek Catholic school appears until 1674.[v]

The burial ground is located right at the beginning of the Wadi al-Kharoobeh on its eastern side, north of the church square, the Greek one, and below it, as below the Franciscan monastery, the Latin one. The Greek burial place is not walled, but the way the stones are laid suggests some degree of care. The Latin burial ground, by contrast, is surrounded by a wall, but the care of the tomb is negligent. This is evidenced by the fact that over the grave smaller stones are laid without mortar next to each other, forming an ellipse about the length of a man. To be able to identify such a gravestone, the Franconians would have to remember where it was. In the past, the Christians also had a lemon garden in the burial ground to the south.[vi] The present one has been known since 1674.[vii] The Mohammedans bury their dead at Rachel's tomb. Who would want to look for the tombs of those three people who were resurrected?[viii]

---

i   Gehlen (42) does not necessarily praise the acclaimed teaching method.

ii   Craigher. A schoolteacher prompts the Catholic population with the few Latin words with which they are to greet the travelers. Prokesch.

iii   Craigher. Also in mathematics, Gehlen says (14).

iv   See above on p. 68.

v   Surius (522) already said emphatically: Nos Religieux enseignent leurs enfans la Foy Catholique et les sciences. By contrast, the more sober Nau says (424): Ils (Greeks) tâchent d'imiter les Peres de l'Observance dans l'instruction des enfans; mais la difference des disciples est presque aussi grande que celle des maistres. Pococke 2 par. 51.

vi   Hammer's Gesch. des osman. Reichs. 6, 758.

vii   L'autre costé da la Cour est tout ouvert, et c'est l'endroit, où l'on ensevelit les Chrestiens. *Nau* 398.

viii In epistola Cyrilli episc. Jerosolymitani ad *Augustinum*, as cited in Fabri

History and tradition have been silent for a whole millennium about a monastery near Bethlehem, that of Marcian.[i]

(2, 183). In the latter period, the graves in the monastery garden were shown. Cf. Gumpenberg in note 5 on p. 185 and above on p. 190, as well as p. 31.

i Marcianus et Romanus: et construxit uterque monasteria, unus quidem circa sanctam Bethleem, alter vero in vico Thecorum. Kyrillos in vita *Euthymii*. *Bollandi* acta sanctor., 20. Jan., 315.

PART B

SURROUNDINGS

CHAPTER 13

Place of Jospeh's Dreams, Urging Him to Bethlehem

In the surroundings of Bethlehem, we will pay particular attention to the site of Joseph's 'Dream of Admonition' and of the shepherds.

First of all, there is the place where, according to the legend,[i] the angel of the Lord appeared to Joseph in a dream and said: 'Get up and take the boy and his mother and flee to Egypt'.[ii] The Bible does not give us a topographical placement and leaves us to speculate that Joseph had the 'Dream of Admonition' in Bethlehem or near it. Some expect there to be some alternative site, as is often the way with traditions about such things. The Bible is silent about this, though. Not until the end of the

---

i *Fabri* 1, 454. Alexander 74. *Jod. a Meggen* 118. Wormbser 409. Schwallart 306. *Surius* 534. Ignaz v. Rh. 131. *De Bruyn* 2, 280. Pococke 2 par. 52. Fabri still knew that the way via Hebron was pointed out after many odysseys. According to Tschudi (290), the angel urged that the family at least be brought to safety. Others, like Troilo (409), did not say a word about the admonition, but only said that Joseph lived in the place in question, or like Legrenzi (1, 187), that he often fled there on the way to the Holy City.

ii Matth. 2, 13.

fourteenth century do I find evidence of such a tradition. In all likelihood, it was older than that; around the year 1300 it was said that the empress Helena also built a temple for the stepfather Joseph near Bethlehem, to which at that time a tradition, if not the one in question, at least a similar one might be attached.[i] In 1320 it was reported that between Bethlehem and the Church of the Shepherds there was a church built by the ancient fathers in memory of the Blessed Virgin. After arriving there with her little son, she was tired of traveling and rested there.[ii] In 1384 there was a small church further down,[iii] about a bow shot away from the Milk Cave, where the angel admonished Joseph to flee to Egypt. Reports about the legend extended up to 1738[iv] and about the site up to 1778[v]; according to inquiries made by me, the site is still shown between Bethlehem and the Place of the Shepherds, although when I drew the attention of my young guide to it, either ignorant or at least honest, said that he was unaware of it. According to later reports, the site of Joseph's dream — or as it was assumed to be beginning the middle of the sixteenth century,[vi] Joseph's house[vii] — was situated in the place where a church or chapel was then erected.[viii] This is

---

i   *Nicephor. Call.*eccles, hist. 8, 30.

ii   Fui item in loco alio inter ecclesiam pastorum et bethleem ubi dicitur b. virgo semel fatigata ex itinere quievisse cum veniret cum filio parvo et est ibi per antiquos patres pro hoc memorali constructa ecclesia. *Pipin.* 73a.

iii   Una chiesicciuola. *Frescobaldi* 140.

iv   We have seen above (note to p. 179) that the legend about Joseph's Chapel knew how to preserve itself.

v   The only other thing that was shown was a fig tree near the milk cave, where Joseph's house had stood, without the tradition saying anything else, and the Bethlehemian Christians stopped to pray as they passed by. Binos 212.

vi   Löuwenstein 359. 10 minutes south of the Milk Cave, Gehlen (37) was shown a place marked with some large blocks of stone where Joseph is said to have lived before his marriage to Mary.

vii   Schwallart. *Cotov. Quaresm.* 2, 680. *Surius.* Ignaz v. Rh. Troilo. Pococke.

viii *Surius* 534. Anco questa casa fù anticamente trammutata in Chiesa in honore del Santo. *Legrenzi.*

because it seemed the most plausible that Joseph dwelt where he dreamed,[i] between Bethlehem and the Place of the Shepherds,[ii] halfway,[iii] or between that and Beit Sahour,[iv] not far from the latter place,[v] or a little distance below the Milk Cave.[vi] In 1483 the church was half destroyed[vii]; twelve years later it was already in a complete state of decay,[viii] even if in 1519 an altar could still be found there.[ix] Thus, from then on, only ruins were found,[x] only the traces of a church,[xi] a foundation,[xii] and finally, as a representative of the entire thing: a fig tree.[xiii]

---

i   It is more likely that Joseph had the dream inside a house, rather than in the field. Could it not be the very same one where the wise men of the East brought their gifts? Quite reasonably, the Greek legend insists on separating the chân from the house where the wise men arrived, and it seems to have merged the latter with the monument. Just the opposite is the case for the Roman Catholics.

ii Fabri, Tschudi, Jodokus von Meggen.

iii Tschudi. Almost in the middle. *Jod. a Meggen.* Troilo says: half way across the mountain when returning from Bêt Sâhü"r to Bethlehem.

iv Schwallart, Troilo, Legrenzi.

v   Wormbser.

vi *Surius.* De Bruyn says with less certainty: in the surroundings of the Shepherds' place.

vii Capellam quandam profanatam et semiruptam. *Fabri.* He then continues: Cum parum ab hoc loco descendissemus, venimus ad ruinas murorum in clivo, ubi etiam quondam capellam stetisse comprehendimus in hujus rei memoriam. According to Löuwenstein, Joseph's house was opposite the House of Our Lady, which is completely absurd.

viii Alexander 74.

ix Tschudi.

x   Sacellum dirutum. *Jod. a Meggen. Quaresm.* 2, 680. *Legrenzi. De Bruyn.* Quelques vieilles murailles d'une Eglise longue de 12. Pas, et large de 8, jadis bastie par l'Imperatrice Helene. *Surius.* If Kootwyk found only a partially ruined building, he must have been shown a different one. Quaresmius gives measurements of the house: longitudo est palm. 47. 47. latitude 26. He somewhat sloppily discusses the tradition of a house, but completely rejects that of the dream.

xi Schwallart.

xii Pococke.

xiii Binos.

CHAPTER 14

Shepherds' Field and Place

If today pilgrims go from Bethlehem toward sunrise, they will no longer be stopped part way down by a small church, like pilgrims in 1449 were, who believed that the shepherds had decided to turn back there but were admonished by the angel to continue.[i] How they heard the call from above:

> *Ite alacres ovium custodes, ite silenti*
> *Pastores sub nocte, munuscula. .. nato*
> *Ferte citi, plaudunt circumfulgentia castra*
> *Aligerûm, agnostcitque suum natura parentem*[ii];

Thus, many a believer has been drawn with a mysterious force to the Field of the Shepherds, which the Arabs call Sahil Beit Sahour,[iii] a fallow field that was barren when I was there but

---

i   Gumpenberg 448, 464.

ii *Julius Roscius Hortinus* in Zuallard. 298.

iii The shepherd's hut is in a valley, which has received the name Wâdi-el-Sawâheri from the nearby village Bejt Sahur. Berggren 3, 149. The Valley of

which others have described as a beautiful plain with fields, olive trees and fig trees,[i] and vines.[ii] Almost in the middle of this field,[iii] twenty-two minutes[iv] east of[v] and below[vi] Bethlehem (monastery), ten minutes northeast of the village of Beit Sahour, is the Place of the Shepherds,[vii] called by the Christians 'i Pastori',[viii] by the Arabs 'Deir al-Raa'wat'[ix] (دير الراءوت).[x] According to the legend shared by Christians, here is where the shepherds watched over their flocks at night in the region of Bethlehem; where the angel of the Lord hovered over them and with a glory divine exalted them; where a great fear overcame them, and then the angel spoke to them: 'Fear not, for I proclaim to you great joy, for the Saviour has been born to you'; and immediately the angels were

---

Jacob in *Surius* 532.

i   Gumpenberg 448. In vallem venimus latam arvis et agris con sitam. *Fabri* 1, 455. Where the monastery lies on the side of the mountain is where the shepherds were guarding their sheep when the angel proclaimed the birth of Jesus and the angels in the heavens sang the hymn ... This is a lovely field. Kapfman 10. *Jod. a Meggen* 117 sq. Belon 269. Oliveta camposque uberrimos continens, tam hominibus quam jumentis pastum gratum exhibens (the most beautiful area in Bethlehem.). *Quaresm.* 2, 681. (Full of olive trees) Troilo 408. *Nau* 432. *De Bruyn* 2, 719. *Ladoire* 211. (Good meadows on the plane) Binos 211. A green field shaded by trees. Schubert 2, 491. Salignac says (tom. 10. c. 2): Agro, et pascendo apto.

ii   Wormbser 409.

iii   *Fabri. Salignac.* Au milieu d'une plaine. *D'Estourmel* 2, 112. Not on a hill, like it is written in Viagg. al S. Sepolcro (F 7b).

iv   Roßlauf. Gumpenberg. Breydenbach 131. 5 arrows' shots away. Alexander 75. 1,000 steps. *Jod. a Meggen.* Approximately 1 Welsh mile. Seydlitz 475. One good hour. Lussy 37. (Almost 1 hour. Berggren) ¼ mile. *Surius.* Ignaz v. Rh. 131. ½ hour. Binos 210. Scholz 189. ½ Italian mile from Nicholas's church (milk cave). Viagg. al S. Sepolcro. ½ St.

v   E.g. the author of the Viagg. al S. Sepolcro, Troilo. Not to the north, as Tschudi says. See Maas's map.

vi   Rauchwolff (645) and others. In Greek: (of the milk cave and the house to which the wise men had brought their gifts).

vii   Locus pastorum nuncupatus. *Quaresm.* 2, 681b.

viii Boucher and Surius.

ix   Shepherds' field, Dschurun Elraawa. Scholz. A barn floor. (Râai) shepherd, Râat in the plural.

x   Robinson (3, 871): Deir er-Ra'wât.

joined by the heavenly host, praising God and saying: 'Glory to God in the highest, peace on earth, goodwill among men'.[i] This place, surrounded by olive trees,[ii] is enclosed by a double wall forming a square.[iii] At the southeast corner, one enters through a door into the first room, and from there one enters a small, walled square with an olive tree in the centre. Here, a cave[iv] descends twenty-one steps[v] into the flat field. From south to north, one first climbs eleven steps to a square, awkward door, which is easily opened. And from there onto ten other steps, down to the bottom of the cave, which is called the Grotto of the Shepherds[vi] and has been transformed into a chapel.[vii] It measures 30' in length and 20' in width.[viii] The altar is toward the east.[ix] I do not remember noticing any mosaic, rough or not, on the floor[x] or anywhere else.[xi] If one did not already know that the chapel belonged to the Greeks, the almost ridiculous paintings on wood that look as if made in school would ensure

i   Luke 2, 8 ff. See also Gumpenberg, Tucher, Fabri, the author of a host of books in Greek.

ii   The enclosure in which it is consists of a plantation of olives. *Light* 169. A fenced-in garden with olives. Scholz. The same field is walled-in. Wormbser 409. Clos d'une muraille de 3" de hauteur, et de 300. pas de quarré. *Surius.* Une enceinte en pierres sèches. *D'Estourmel* 2, 112. Cf. Schubert 8, 22.

iii   Underground vault. Troilo. *Ladoire.* Richter 41. A chapel that is halfway underground. Sieber 61.

iv   *Ladoire. Chateaubriand* 1, 309.

v   20 steps. *D'Estourmel.* A descent by steps. *Light.*

vi   *Salignac.* (But the erectum does not fit!). Schwallart 306.

vii   In Greek: *Ladoire* 211.

viii Binos. 14' long, 7 wide. *D'Estourmel.* It is not certain whether Quaresmius gives the 46 palms (= 41') length and 27 (= 24) width of the upper or lower church.

ix   Richter.

x   An altar. Binos. Containing an altar of stone, where mass is performed once during Easter. *Light.* Se termine par un hémicycle où l'autel est placé. *D'Estourmel.* Richter.

xi   On voit encore sur sa voûte mediocrement elevée quelques restes de peintures à la mosaïque. *Ladoire.* Still some remains of the mosaic cladding. Binos.

that we did. Hardly anything remarkable can be found in the whole church. It was deserted at the time of my visit; no one was there but my guide from Bethlehem and myself, and we did not ask anyone if we may unlock the door. No intruder demanded an entrance fee, as there was already reason enough to complain[i] that there was not enough 'peace on earth', not enough 'goodwill among men'. When I came out of this cellar,[ii] where no lamp had been burning,[iii] and into the boundless light of heaven, the splendour of the Lord, the gaze of the heavenly hosts, I cannot describe how pleasant it was. Safety in this region was not always such that the pilgrim could visit the Place of the Shepherds on Christmas Eve to perform devotions here; it was enough, even in broad daylight, to try to prevent any possible misfortune that may have transpired now and again.[iv] If one decided to go to the Place of the Shepherds at night, one took a Moslem escort for protection, whom one also had to pay especially.[v] The Franciscans then sang 'Glory to God' (gloria). If they did not sing during the night, they made up for what they had missed on Christmas Day after noon, when they sang vespers.[vi] Even outside the time

---

i   Thus Salzbacher (2, 182) had to pay a dirty presbyter. In 1719 four inhabitants of Bêt Sâhû'r wanted to let Franciscans and their interpreters pass only under the condition that they themselves would be the guides. *Ladoire* 207. In 1561 the Arabs could only be persuaded to allow entry in exchange for a gift. Wormbser 409. The entourage of the Count of Löuwenstein had a serious dispute with the Arabs (359). Cf. Schwallart 306. There must have been a time when this grotto was open to passers-by in order to offer some hospitality in this forlorn place. Binos 210.

ii   *D'Estourmel* 2, 113.

iii   Un Altare nella vicina grotta, di tanta devotione, che trasse ance il Cuore de gl' Infedeli, à venerarlo, e però tutto l'anno vi mantengono lampadi accese con la viva fede d'haver à conseguir abbondante raccolta di grano. *Legrenzi.* Only daylight comes in through the door. *D'Estourmel.*

iv   Troilo 409. Cf. the antepenultimate note.

v   Fabri 259. Troilo's company (409) had for protection some shepherds from the village of Bêt Sâhû'r.

vi   La cornemuse et les deux flageolets (agreable Musique de Village) servoient d'orgues, causans une joyeuse devotion aux Catholiques, aux Turcs et aux Mores qui estoient presents. *Surius* 533.

of the Feast of the Nativity, the same hymn was sung, as well as the most important passage of the Gospel.[i] Roman Catholics received indulgences here for seven years and seven times forty days.[ii] The Greeks have also been worshipping here for a long time. The recent assertation that the chapel always belonged to the Latins, and that they were only ousted from it by the Greeks about a decade and a half ago was extremely unnecessary.[iii]

In casting a glance back into the history of the distant past, what emerges foremost is the observation that the sacred records describe the site of the unusual scene with the very general words 'in the same region' (of Bethlehem), thus leaving the entire region of the town open to interpretation. It would be odd to suppose that the shepherds stayed with their flocks in an area such as the field of Beit Sahour, which in all of Bethlehem's surrounding areas is the most well-suited for cultivating fields without engendering strife of any sort, and at which time the sowing of the soil must have already been carried out. How much preferable it would have been to have met the shepherds on a road to Tekoa or Herodium (Paradise Mountain). The tradition, however, which goes back to the fourth century, sought a more convenient location. When the Roman woman Paula was in Bethlehem, she went down not far from there to the Tower of Eder or Gader, that is, the Tower of the Flocks, next to which the flocks of Jacob were grazing, and the shepherds who were watching in the night were honoured to hear: 'Glory be to God in the highest', and so on.[iv] And the Tower of Eder was about twenty minutes from Bethlehem.[v] This report is so insufficient that it is impossible to

---

i   *Ladoire* 211.

ii   Tucher 667.

iii   Salzbacher.

iv   Haud procul inde (Bethlehem) descendit (Paula) ad turrim Ader, id est, gregis, juxta quam Jacob pavit greges suos, et pasteres nocte vigilantes andire meruerunt: Gloria etc. *Hieronym.* epitaph. *Paulæ.*

v   Et mille circiter passibus procul turris Ader. *Hieronym.* (411). In the Onomastikon (ad voc. Ader) it says: Legimus quod Jacob trans turrim Ader

identify the pastoral region from then or from today without the help of tradition, for it descends from Bethlehem on more than one side. We are also missing the report about there being something more monumental, because such a thing is just as probable as a church built by the empress Helena is improbable, as one had begun to claim around 1300 and has audaciously continued to claim up to the present.[i] Because the distance is so exact, there is no doubt that the old Shepherds' Field of tradition and the one of the present are one and the same. From that time on, I was unable to find any reports about the Shepherds' Field until about 670. At that time, about twenty minutes east of Bethlehem, at the place where the heavenly host surrounded the shepherds, stood a church next to the Tower of the Flocks, which contained three tombs of three shepherds.[ii] This is not only the first report of a church but also such a precise account of the location that it stands out in its banality. Around 728 the place where the angel appeared to the shepherds was noted without mention of any temple.[iii] About a hundred and forty years later a monastery of the shepherds was noted.[iv] At the time

---

fixerit tabernaculum. I have been told by friends that the Migdal Eder is not to be found in Bethlehem, but perhaps on Mount Zion.

i *Fabri* 1, 455. Rauchwolff 645. Ignaz v. Rh., Legrenzi, Ladoire, Binos, and others. Helena had a chapel built in the grotto that was dedicated to the Blessed Virgin. Geramb 1, 189.

ii De monumentis illorum pastorum quos dominicæ natiuitatis celestis circumfulsit claritudo Arculfus notis breuem contulit relaciunculam inquiens: Trium illorum in ecclesia pastorum tria frequentaui monumenta iuxta turrim gader...quæ mille circiter passibus contra orientalem plagam distat a bethleem quos in codem loco nascente domino, hoc est prope turrim gregis angelicæ lucis claritas circumdedit. In quo eadem æcclesia est fundata eorundem pastorum continens sepulchra. *Arculf.* 2, 6 (cod. St. Gall. 269). The different readings can be consulted in Mabillon's edition. Aymon (as cited in *Quaresm.* 2, 682a) likewise remarks that the corpses of the shepherds were laid to rest here, and Fabri also mentions their burial place at the church, only, as it seems, not of his own accord, but after Arculfus, whom he was familiar with.

iii *Willibald.* 20 (according to the nun).

iv Milliario denique uno a Bethleem est monasterium sanclorum pastorum, quibus .. *Bernard.* 16.

of the Crusaders, the place gloria in excelsis[i] or the Shepherd's Place (Πόιμνιον)[ii] was not far[iii] to the east of Bethlehem,[iv] [end page between it and the monastery of Cenobiarch (Theodosius).[v] There was a monastery[vi] and a church[vii] dedicated to the angels, and where the shepherds heard the praises of the angels,[viii] there was a cave. This first mention of a cave is very insufficient, since it does not note what was undoubtedly beneath the church. Originally, it seems to have been intended only for the shepherd's graves. The tradition of angels having appeared there seems to have fled downwards over the course of time, when perhaps the destruction of the temple above it no longer permitted the quiet devotion for which one might have wished. Otherwise, it would be difficult to explain how it is that in the night shepherds came to seek refuge in a cave on a plain; for as many caves for shepherds and cattle that I have seen, and my memory preserves not a few, they were all situated on gentler or more gentle slopes. In the period from 1300 and roughly to the middle of the fourteenth century, the church[ix] called Gloria in Excelsis,[x] a

---

i   *Fetell.* 23b.

ii *Epiphan.* M. 52.

iii Eugesippus says (112): 1 mile.

iv Edrisi 346. *Epiphan.* To the left of Bethlehem. *Phocas* 22.

v   *Phocas.* Today the monastery is called Dêr Dòssi.

vi *Epiphan.* M.

vii *Edrisi.* Cf. Nikephoros Kallistos, Bonifacius in Quaresmius, who adds: Ita invenitur in vetusto manuscripto libello de Locis sanctis, et apud alios, qui de ipsis scripserunt.

viii *Phocas.*

ix *Pipin.* Monteuilla. Rudolph von Suchen.

x   Because of this angelic singing, one began also in Bethlehem with the Gloria in excelsis Deo every hour of the day, like they do in other churches: Deus in adjutorium meum etc. All masses for the souls there also commenced with Gloria in excelsis, according to a peculiar custom, as one can tell from the ordinary. Rudolph von Suchen.

mile from Bethlehem,[i] had survived; it was beautiful.[ii] In 1384 the very large church was reported to have been largely in ruins.[iii] In 1483 large ruins of walls, the remnants from old buildings, were found; the front part of the desolate and decaying church was still there, and next to it, the considerably large women's convent,[iv] Ad Gloria, (monastery Ad Gloriam in Excelsis), the rosette window and grille, the way the nuns used to keep them. Beneath the church, the crypt remained,[v] mention of which, however, I did not find since the time of the Frankish kingdom. From then on, it nonetheless played a leading role. This was all the more certainly the case, considering that the continued state of decay meant that the ruins of the great church became more and more indistinct as to their original purpose or parts of it disappeared nearly altogether. The superstition that the Saracens could not carry away any stones notwithstanding, the continued presence of the crypt thus subsumed under its mighty umbrella what remained of the church.[vi] Already in 1507 the

---

i *Marin. Sanut.* 3, 14, 11. Item fui ultra bethleem ad unum miliare et dimidium ubi angelus nativitatem Domini pastoribus annunciavit et ubi angeli cantaverunt gloria in excelsis Deo. *Pipin.* 72b. Appresso (Bethlehem) a un miglio si è la chiesa, dove gli Angioli di paradiso annunziarono ai pastori dove Gesù Cristo era nato in Belliem. *Sigoli* 167. It is very striking that Monteuilla (773) and Rudolph of Suchen (819) mention the church to be located on the way from Bethlehem to Jerusalem. Baldensel (120) is quite vague, and the anonymous Allatius (8) indicates the distance of the shepherd's place from St. George's temple to be 2 stadiums, meaning that the latter would presumably be located in Bêt Sâhû'r. Cf. above on p. 206.

ii Et ibi est ecclesia pulcra a patribus antiquis constructa. *Pipin.* Rudolph von Suchen.

iii *Frescobaldi* 140.

iv *Fabri* 1, 455. The monastery ruins were later commemorated by others, including Surius (532), Scholz (189).

v *Fabri* (and Reyßb. 260). Copied in Tschudi.

vi De lapidibus quadratis et sectis fuerunt muri ejus per circuitum, sicut videtur in cumulis lapidum ibi jacentium, quos Sarraceni nullatenus possunt auferre. *Fabri. Georg.* 558. Tschudi 282. Along with this came the superstition that, as Georg writes, cattle should not come anywhere near the place.

church was almost in complete ruins,[i] but in 1646 a fourth part of a vaulted chapel, with some traces of painting,[ii] could still be seen. Even a decade later, the length was supposedly determined to be 46 feet in length and 27 in width.[iii] Reports about there being immense ruins from a church from this time onwards[iv] deserve little credence; they belong instead to the account of the monastery situated next to it.[v] These ruins, however, still attract our attention today, even if we no longer come across three Corinthian and two Ionic knobs[vi] or column shafts[vii] as we did a long time ago. Much more interesting than the chapel below are the ruins above the cave or in its vicinity, especially the vaults facing southwest, which do not exist in such an orderly or complete form that it would be possible to draw an accurate ground plan. In any case, in terms of size and composition, their present appearance is sure evidence that something important, though admittedly not from the preliterate era, once stood here. Next to the chapel, above it, towards the southwest, one is struck by the site of a stone bench supported by two capitals and a cistern close by. These are probably the evidentiary remains from the old upper temple and from the former monastery.

I would like to return to the Tower of Gader or of the Flocks, in particular. We have seen that its location was considered to

---

i   *Georg.* Completely destroyed. Viagg. al S. Sepolcro. Traces of a temple and a magnificent building. *Jod. a Meggen.* Only a vault of a chapel, overgrown with cardamom and sideritis tragoriganum. Belon 269.

ii   *Surius.* A year later Monconys (1, 315) spoke only of ruins of a church.

iii   Troilo 408. Clearly after Quaresmius.

iv   Strong remains of a church. Pococke 2 par. 52. *D'Estourmel* 2, 112 (basilique).

v   On voit à main gauche des ruines de bastimens assez remarquables. *Nau* 435.

vi   *Chateaubriand* 1, 309 sq. He considered the discovery of the latter capitals to be a miracle; for one finds little else after the age of Helena but the eternal Corinthian.

vii   Richter 41. D'Estourmel (1, 113) seems to have seen the 6 capitals and the column shafts above (or in the books?) after all.

be the same as that of the Shepherds' Field; tradition has thus crowded the biblical-historical stage in curious ways. For several centuries, the Tower of Gader disappeared from view or at least the Shepherd's Field, the place where the devout wanderer had been content with the heavenly hosts and the shepherds, had, at any rate. I did not find it again until around 1300, when it was marked as being near the desert east of Tekoa.[i] Later, the tradition made a leap to the west of Bethlehem, near the tomb of Rachel, but this was then contradicted.[ii] By 1508 the tower had moved back into the Shepherds' Field.[iii] From that time on the Christians so greatly accepted the tradition that they no longer pushed it away,[iv] and so greatly esteemed it that they honoured it with a special name,[v] and believed in it so greatly that for the first time they discovered ruins there.[vi]

---

i Marinus Sanutus's map.

ii There it was shown by the brothers. Sed ego, said Georg (525), fidem his verbis non adhibui; In fact, he read in the life of St. Paula that before visiting Bethlehem, she descended to the tower of Ader; hæc vero turris non erat in descensu Bethlehem, imo plus est in ascensu; similarly, he read that it lay to the east, not to the west like the latter. When the monks, as it seems, were not familiar with the old tradition, they probably interpreted the passage in Genesis (35, 21), which followed the story of the tomb of Rachel, to mean that the tower of Gader (Eder) must have been located near that tomb. It may be added that the scriptural passage does not permit a narrower topographical interpretation.

iii 4 to 5 stadiums to the east of Bethlehem. *Anshelm.*

iv At the shepherds' place. Rauchwolff 645. In the Campo di Giacob. *Zuallard.* 217 sq. Cf. note 6 on p. 251. Radzivil 170. *Boucher* 285. *Surius* 532. Troilo 408. Also Adrichomius's map.

v Lemi dar gneder. *Boucher.* Ce lieu s'appelle à present Lemi Ader. *Surius.* Equally foreign to me is the name Astis, also called David's Tower, a ruin northeast of Bethlehem, in Scholz (163).

vi In our time, this tower has fallen into such a state of disrepair that it lies there as a large pile of stones. Rauchwolff. *Zuallard.* Radzivil. Anshelm noted that at the site of the herd tower b. Paula fecit sibi magnum ædificium seu claustrum virginum, cujus adhuc vestigia apparent. Cf. Pococke (2 par. 52), who also believes that Paula died at the shepherds' place. One can read about the tower of the shepherds in Quaresmius (2, 682 sqq.).

CHAPTER 15

Beit Sahour

When returning from the Place of the Shepherds to Bethlehem, one encounters to the left of Beit Sahour,[i] also called Beit Sahour al-Nasara,[ii] that is, the Beit Sahour of the Christians, called by the latter the Village of the Shepherds.[iii] It lies twelve

---

i   Beit-sahùr. Della Valle 1, 158b. Beit Sahur. Berggren 3, 149. Bethzaour. *D'Estourmel* 2, 112. I heard the natives say Bêt Sâchû'r. There are also the following corruptions: Beth sabor (*Fürer* 67), Schora (Schweigger 311), Bethahour (*Boucher* 285, *Surius* 534), Dia el natour (*Roger* 204), Dael Natour (*Bremond* 2, 13). Boucher says about Bethahour: c'est à dire maison de trafic, on the contrary, Surius says of Bathahour: qui veut dire maison des Bergers. Roger and Bremond also say that it means shepherd village. In Arabic, by the way, a shepherd is not Sâhû'r, but Sâûh. The latter is as far away from Sâhû'r as the Bethsaon mentioned by Robinson (2, 394) which is what is used on Berghaus' map in Pococke.

ii   Robinson 3, 871.

iii   Bethsabor.., ubi villa est pastorum. *Fürer.* Villagio de' Pastori. *Zuallard.* 218. Pagi (cui a pastoribus nomen est). *Cotov.* 226. Villa pastorum. *Quaresm.* 2, 681. Della Valle. According to the inhabitants of the country Pastour. *Roger.* Ad Pastores. Troilo 408. *Light* 109. Geramb 1, 187.

minutes east of Bethlehem,[i] on a hill running from west to east,[ii] where it joins the Wadi al-Rujum to the east, and the Sahil Beit Sahour to the north, south under the village stretches a valley, the Wadi Beit Sahour, towards the east. The site is lovely but offers a rather limited vista. There is no lack of cisterns.[iii] Those versed in history will note one of very ancient appearance. In previous centuries, it was an incredible thing that a venerated woman once wanted to drink water here. The inhabitants, in their unwillingness to help, refused to draw it from the cistern, which was located almost in the very centre of the village. Then, by the grace of God, to the great astonishment of the cruel barbarians, the water rose up to the edge of the cistern, from which she then immediately quenched her thirst.[iv] The area is not barren. The village of about fifty houses[v] stretches quite a distance from west to east. At the top (west), a tall house stands out because of its arched form. One can still see large stones at several dwellings, which probably date back to the time of the old Christian Greek emperors. The village is inhabited by a few Moslems, mostly Orthodox (Schismatic) Greeks. The population of Beit Sahour and Beit Jala together is estimated to be equal to that of Bethlehem.[vi] In the century before last, there

---

i   500 steps from the grotto where Mary's milk had dripped. *Boucher.* ½ mile east of Christ's manger. *Quaresm.* ¼ hour from Bethlehem. *Surius.* See the location on the maps of Berghaus (too north) and Robinson (too south). Surius and Troilo say: east of Bethlehem.. Cf. above on p. 262.

ii   Pagus hic situs est in colle non multum eminente, sed saxoso, cryptis et cavernis plurimis pertuso et fere concavo. *Cotov.*

iii   With a good well. Berggren 3, 149.

iv   Löuwenstein 359. Wormbser 409. *Zuallard. Quaresm. Surius. Nau* 431. Reservoir. *De Bruyn* 2, 220. Steiner (8) describes it somewhat differently: "Here there was the well, where the Mother of God wanted to drink. The people would not let her. Since then, there has been a great scarcity of water; the well disappeared around the same time. Pococke says (2 par. 52) that it is probably David's well. Geramb (1, 188) was shown a well in which Mary washed the swaddles of Jesus.

v   A small village. *Light.* Each house was a pile of stones without any order. Geramb.

vi   Whiting in Calw. Missionsbl., 1842, 26.

was a superstition that if more than thirty householders lived in the village,[i] those beyond that number would die in two or three days.[ii] The inhabitants have a somewhat unfriendly appearance and when I wanted to take a closer look at individual things in the village my guide showed fear and insisted that I leave. They are not held in high esteem by the Bethlehemites, and if one hears little or nothing of open feuds, it is explained by the fact that the superior strength of the Bethlehemites is too great. The Sahouris are still engaged in cattle-breeding and in beekeeping.[iii] To the east or northeast of the village, towards Al-Raa'wat (Place of the Shepherds), the inhabitants have their burial place over which stones have been laid without care, and no wall.

According to my research, the history of the village goes back no further than 1561.[iv] In 1598 there was a miserable village of rock caves and low, narrow, flat-roofed houses made of rough stones and dung and clay-covered tree branches. The inhabitants, all Moors, were very poor, extremely needy, sunburnt, very skinny, without shoes or trousers, and had nothing to cover themselves with except for a cotton shirt and a simple waistcoat of camel and goat hair called 'haba' or 'gaba'.[v] Even in the seventeenth century, the small, poor village[vi] with a few houses[vii] was inhabited by Moors,[viii] a poor and lowly class of people.[ix] I am not able to

---

i   *Boucher.* Surius says: over 40 paterfamilias.

ii   Chose experimentée de temps immemoriel. *Boucher.* In 4 days according to Surius.

iii Nowadays, the inhabitants of the village are still called Pastori. *Zuallard.* 218.

iv   Later (after visiting the place Gloria in excelsis) we wandered about again and came to a village, where there was a well, where our dear Lady got a drink of water from a farmer .. Wormbser. Cf. note six.

v   *Cotov.* Pococke also found (2 par. 52) different grottoes that served as stables and dwellings.

vi   *Boucher, Quaresmius* (2, 681a), *Surius, Bremond.*

vii *Boucher, Surius.*

viii *Quaresm.*

ix   *Quaresm.* Ceux qui l'habitent, et qui sont en petit nombre, sont gueux et

determine when the Christians mixed with the Moslems. The statement that Greeks and Roman Catholics made up half of the population in 1832 is to be distrusted.[i]

---

miserables, et on ne souvient pas de les avoir jamais veu autrement. *Nau* 432.

i   Geramb. Cf. Robinson 3, 871.

ADDENDUM

After this had already been printed, I came upon this travel book, *Orientalische Reise Deß Edlen und Besten, Hanß Jacob Breüning, von und zu Buochenbach, so er...so wohl in Europa als Asia und Afrika, ohne einig Euchium oder FreyGleit, benantlich in Griechenland, Egypten, Arabien, Palestina, das Heilige Gelobte Land und Syrien* (1579) *verrichtet.* Straßb., J. Carolo, 1612. Gr. 4. Because such a text is so rare these days, I will add a little from it at least.

It (the Church of St. Mary in Bethlehem) is built from ashlars of a very great height, covered with lead, and has above, in the middle, a column, also covered with lead, which can be seen from far away (p. 257).

Here I would like to introduce what I have recently discovered about this crib around the year 1580, *in mense Aprili*, in Rome in the Church of Santa Maria Maggiore. While pointing out to my travel partner Jean Carlier de Pinon and myself various shrines and *Sanctorum reliquiis*, a monk pointed to a crib, without saying that this was indeed the place in which our

Lord and Saviour Christ was laid in a stable. I was not thinking about where I was and simply spoke out, saying: 'I do not know how I am supposed to understand this? We were *in Octobris* in Bethlehem in the 79th year, where the true crib was pointed out to us'. Perhaps confounded by my words, filled with rage, he made a hostile, ugly expression. My companion, however, redirected such contrariness. Interrupting my speech, he said: 'It would not have been so strange had we not been in Bethlehem in person and seen the place where the holy *Praesipium* stood. This, however, as the right and true one had been transferred from there to across the sea, all the way to Rome'. With that, the monk was again satisfied (p. 258, et seq.).

And it is to the chapel (of St. Catharina) that the Knights of Jerusalem used to take the half wheel (only to this point and not to Mt. Sinai in Arabia), p. 259. See also p. 203, note 9.

APPENDIX

MAPS

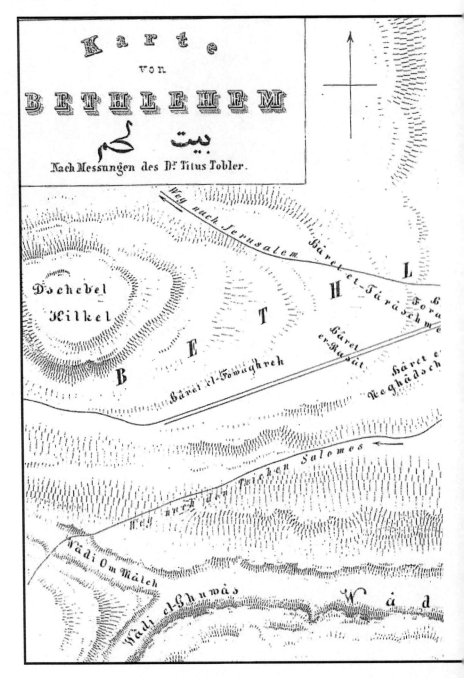

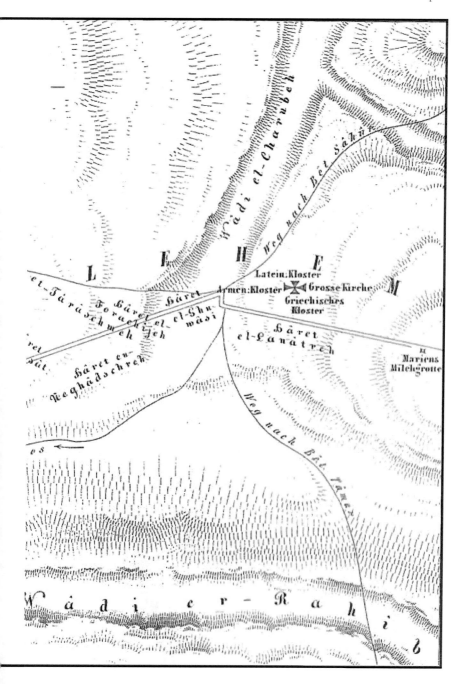

Appendix

Mountains of Moab.	1	Moabiterberge.
Wâdi Zerqa-Ma'în.	2	Wadi Serka-Maïn.
The Snowhill.	3	Schneehügel. Wüste Juda.
Callirrhoë.	4	Kallirrhoë.
Dead-Sea, east-shore.		Ostufer des Toten Meeres.
Tower of Jacob.	5	Migdal-Ader.
Shepherds' fields.		Jakobsturm & Hirtenfeld.
Road Jerus.-Hebron.	6	Strasse Jerusalem-Hebron.
Machaerus (martyrdom	7	Machärus (Enthauptung
of S. John B.).		Johannes des Täufers).
Christian Brothers' College.	8	Institut der Schulbrüder.
S. Vincent's Hospital.	9	St-Vincenz-Hospital.
Swedish Hospital.	10	Schwedisches Hospital.
Sisters of S. Joseph.	11	Schwestern vom hl. Joseph.
Salesian Orphanage.	12	Waisenhaus der Salesianer.
Franciscan-Convent.	13	Franziskaner Konvent.
Basilica of the Nativity.	14	Geburts-Basilika.
Greek and Armenian Conv.	15	Griechisches Kloster.
German Church.	16	Deutsche evang. Kirche.
Valley of Arnon.	17	Wadi Modschib. Arnontal.
Jebel Shihân.	18	Berg Sehon.
Fathers of the S. Heart.	19	Väter von Betharrâm.
Carmelite Sisters' Convent.	20	Karmelitinnen-Kloster.
Bêt Ta'amir.	21	Beduinendorf Bêt-Ta'amir.
Mount of the Francs, Mausol.	22	Frankenberg. Mausoleum
of King Herod the Great.		Herodes des Grossen.
Ruins of Herodium.	23	Ruinen von Herodium.
Vineyards of Bethlehem.	24	Weingärten von Bethlehem.
Descent to S. Chariton.	25	Abstieg zur Laura v. Suka.

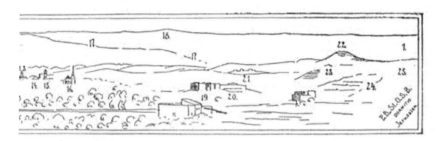

Montagnes de Moab.	1	Montagne di Moab.
Wâdi Zerka-Ma'în.	2	Wâdi Zerqa-Ma'în.
Colline de Neige.	3	Collina di Neve.
Callirrhoë.	4	Callirrhoë.
Est Mer Morte.		P. orientale del Mar Morto.
Tour de Jacob.	5	Torre di Giacobbe.
Champ des Pasteurs.		Campo dei pastori.
Route Jérusalem - Hébron.	6	Strada Gerusalem. - Hebron.
Machéronte (Martyr	7	Macheronte (Martirio
de St. Jean Baptiste).		di S. Giovanni B.).
Frères des Ecoles Chr.	8	Fratelli delle Scuole Crist.
Hôpital Français.	9	Ospedale di S. Vincenzo.
Hôpital Suédois.	10	Ospedale Svedese.
Sœurs de St. Joseph.	11	Suore di S. Giuseppe.
Orphélinat Salésien.	12	Orfanotrofio Salesiano.
Couvent Franciscain.	13	Casa Nova. Conv. Frances.
Basilique de la Nativité.	14	Basilica della Natività.
Conv. Grec et Arménien.	15	Conv. Greco ed Armeno.
Temple protestant.	16	Chiesa evangelica.
Vallée de l'Arnon.	17	Valle dell'Arnon.
Jebal Schihan.	18	Gebel Scihân (Mons Sehon).
P. P. du S.C. de Bétharram.	19	P. P. del S. Cuore.
Couvent des Carmelites.	20	Convento delle Carmelitane.
Village bédouin.	21	Bêt-Ta'amir.
Mont des Francs. Mausolée	22	Monte dei Franchi, Mausoleo
d'Herod le Grand.		di Erode il Grande.
Ruines des l'Hérodium.	23	Ruine della città Herodium.
Vignes de Bethléem.	24	Vigne di Betlemme.
Descente à St. Chariton.	25	Discesa a S. Charitone.

Appendix

Grundriss der MARIENKIRCHE in Bethlehem.

Nach Bernardino Amico und verbessert von Dr Titus Tobler.

Eine Krippe in Bethlehem.

Die Marienkirche in Bethlehem.
(von Ost)

Ein Haus in Bethlehem.

Lith.Anstalt von J.Wurster & Comp. in Winterthur.

264

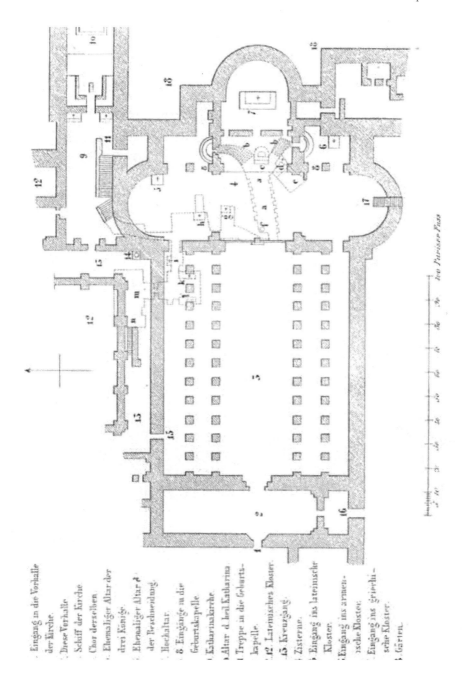

1. Eingang in die Vorhalle der Kirche.
2. Diese Vorhalle.
3. Schiff der Kirche.
4. Chor derselben.
5. Ehemaliger Altar der drei Könige.
6. Ehemaliger Altar der Beschneidung.
7. Hochaltar.
8. Eingänge in die Geburtskapelle.
9. Katharinakirche.
10. Altar d. heil Katharina.
11. Treppe in die Geburtskapelle.
12. Lateinisches Kloster.
13. Kreuzgang.
14. Zisterne.
15. Eingang ins lateinische Kloster.
16. Eingang ins armenische Kloster.
17. Eingang ins griechische Kloster.
18. Garten.